Herodotus

Twayne's World Authors Series

Ruth Scodel, Editor of Greek Literature

Harvard University

TWAS 645

Herodotus

By J.A.S. Evans

University of British Columbia

Twayne Publishers · Boston

Herodotus

J.A.S. Evans

Copyright © 1982 by G.K. Hall & Company
Published by Twayne Publishers
A Division of G.K. Hall & Company
70 Lincoln Street
Boston, Massachusetts 02111

Book production by Marne Sultz

Book design by Barbara Anderson

Printed on permanent / durable acid-free
paper and bound in The United States of
America.

Library of Congress Cataloging in Publication Data

Evans, J.A.S. (James Allen Stewart), 1931–
    Herodotus.

    (Twayne's world authors series; TWAS 645)
    Bibliography: p. 186
    Includes index.
    1. Herodotus.   2. Herodotus.   Historiae.   3. History,
Ancient.   4. Greece—History.   I. Title.   II. Series.
D56.52H45E9   938'.0072024 [B]   81-6395
ISBN 0-8057-6488-7   AACR2

Contents

About the Author

J. A. S. (Allan) Evans is professor of classics at the University of British Columbia, Vancouver, Canada. He received the B.A. in honors classics at the University of Toronto, and the Ph.D. at Yale University under the direction of the late Professor C. B. Welles, and prior to his appointment as professor at the University of British Columbia, he taught at McMaster University, Hamilton, Canada, and at the University of Texas in Austin. He is the author of *Procopius* (Twayne World Authors Series), 1972, and *A Social and Economic History of an Egyptian Temple in Greco-Roman Egypt,* published in *Yale Classical Studies,* vol. 17 (1961), as well as numerous articles and reviews.

Professor Evans has served as vice-chairman of the American Society of Papyrologists, chairman of the Gennadeion Library Committee of the American School of Classical Studies in Athens, Greece, first vice-president of the Classical Association of Canada, and secretary-treasurer of the Association of Ancient Historians.

He has received fellowships from the Nuffield Foundation, the Killam Foundation, and the Social Sciences and Humanities Research Council of Canada. He has served as editor of the periodical *Vergilius,* and is currently editor of *Studies in Medieval and Renaissance History.* He is at the moment on leave from the University of British Columbia, doing research on the social and economic aspects of the reign of Justinian, emperor, A.D. 527–565.

Preface

"Quite possibly, the lack of a mythic element may make my history seem less pleasant to listen to. But it will be enough if those judge it useful who want clearly to examine what happened in the past, and what will happen very like it some time again in the future, human nature being what it is. For my work is a possession for all time, rather than a prize lecture for immediate applause."

Famous words. When Thucydides wrote them, he may not have been thinking only of Herodotus, but his great predecessor was somewhere in the forefront of his mind. For Thucydides and men of his ilk, history was a serious matter, intended to instruct rather than entertain. Herodotus may have instructed, to be sure, for he had one foot in the epic tradition, and most of his contemporaries would have been surprised had anyone told them that epic poets failed to educate. But Herodotus, who gave lectures and received payment for them, did not forget that epic poets also entertained.

Thucydides, however, set the style, and after him, real history was a serious business. Herodotus's reputation suffered as a result. In the early decades of this century, it was still standard procedure for historians of the Persian Wars to emend or alter the evidence he gave to fit their own theories, with the simple excuse of "Herodotus has misunderstood. . . ." The pendulum has swung in the opposite direction in the last generation, partly as a result of topographical research in Greece, partly because archaeology has opened up the ancient Near East, and much of the *History* has been vindicated. Herodotus has acquired the reputation that the ancient world denied him, of an historian who told the truth. In fact, some *aficionados* may have gone too far; Herodotus was not entirely above bias or naiveté.

But he was more than a reporter; he had a genuine concern to discover why things happened as they did. What sparked the Persian attack on Greece? He noted that the ships sent by Athens and Eretria in response to Aristagoras's appeal for help in the Ionian Revolt were the beginning of evil, for he saw them as the start of a chain of wrong, followed by revenge, that led to Xerxes' invasion. But history was not made only by vengeance and countervengeance. When Xerxes announced his expedition to his assembled nobles, he told him he was following the time-honored Persian custom to expand, and when he changed his mind, he was warned in a dream that the invasion was not quite a matter of free choice. Persia was imperialist; expansionism was a Persian custom (*nomos*), and like all men, the Persians were governed by their customs. So were the Greeks; as the Spartan Demaratus told Xerxes, they feared *nomos* more than Xerxes' men feared him.

His own attitudes were ambiguous. He would not denigrate the Persians or sing hosannas for the Greeks, but there cannot be much doubt that he agreed with Pausanias, the victor at Plataea, who pointed out graphically how foolish Xerxes was to covet the poor possessions of Greece when he was already surrounded by fabulous wealth. Toward Athens he had some of the ambivalence that a colonial feels for his metropolis, for he came from a tribute-paying city, Halicarnassus. He praised her courage and resolution; by standing firm, she saved Greece, and by so saying, Herodotus lent his authority to a charter myth of the Athenian Empire. But he also noted her ambition; she accepted Spartan leadership in the war, but as soon as the immediate danger from Persia was past, she grasped eagerly at empire. He was no devoted democrat; he noted that Aristagoras failed to inveigle Sparta, where he had to deal with a single man, into the Ionian Revolt, whereas the thirty thousand Athenians were more easily deceived. Yet he thought democracy was good for Athens, for he dates the growth of her power from the establishment of the Cleisthenic constitution. But for that matter, Sparta's power greatly increased too after the reforms of Lycurgus. The cities and nations that grew powerful, it seems, were those that discovered the *nomoi* that suited them. But greatness came and went; cities that were once powerful became insignificant. Herodotus was a gentle pessimist, and like Hesiod, he saw his own period as a time of travail. Greece had seen more troubles in the last three generations than in the twenty that preceded them.

This book follows the general format of the Twayne series: first a chapter on Herodotus's life, followed by an analysis of the content of the *History,* and a chapter on the *nachleben.* As for the two chapters that intervene, one on the sources was a necessity, and instead of devoting it entirely to the well-trodden paths of Herodotean *quellen-forschung,* I have tried to show that he lived in a period of transition, when Greece was moving from oral to written tradition, and that Herodotus's persona of an oral historian should be taken seriously. The chapter on characterization is included to demonstrate some of Herodotus's value judgments, and a chapter on the great battles of the war had to be omitted for lack of space.

It remains for me to thank those who have assisted me: the late Mary White of Trinity College, Toronto, and Henry Immerwahr, director of the American School of Classical Studies in Greece, both of whom taught me Herodotus in their seminar rooms and must take some responsibility for my enthusiasm. Malcolm McGregor read the manuscript through and made many helpful suggestions, though I claim the errors as my own. I owe thanks to the University of British Columbia for a sabbatical leave, to the Killam Foundation for the means to enjoy it, and to the American School of Classical Studies for providing me with hospitality as well as the communion of like-minded souls. Finally, and not least, I owe a debt to my wife for much patience, and not a little help over the past three years.

J. A. S. Evans

University of British Columbia

Chronology

Chapter One
The Career of Herodotus

The fifth century before Christ opened with the Persian Wars. It had barely begun when the Greeks of Asia Minor and the off-shore islands under Persian domination revolted, and appealed to the chief cities of the Greek mainland for help. Sparta declined, but Athens and Eretria on the island of Euboea heeded the call, and thus attracted the malevolent attention of Persia. So began the Persian Wars, which were to close with great victories at Salamis, Plataea, and Mycale, and the destruction of the greatest army and navy that the Greeks had known.

By the end of the century, the wheel came, if not full circle, at least part way around. The years 431 to 404 B.C. were taken up with the Peloponnesian War between Athens and her empire, and Sparta and her allies. Persia's intervention on Sparta's side ensured Athens's defeat, and as her reward, Persia regained the Greek cities in Asia that she had lost after her debacle of 480–79 B.C.

It was in the early years of the Peloponnesian War that Herodotus drew up the final draft of his *History* and published it. They were something new: neither a chronicle, nor local history nor geography, but *historia:* researches into a major event of the past. It was a life's work, and Herodotus had mulled over it, revised it, and given public readings of parts of it long before it appeared in the bookstalls. We do not know the exact year he died, but probably he did not long outlive the final publication.

"If Herodotus was the first to write history, Thucydides was the first to research it,"[1] wrote one scholar, expressing the difference that the modern reader feels instinctively between the two great historians of the fifth century B.C. Thucydides was intensely serious about historiography, which he separated sharply from mythology, and he aimed at producing an analysis of the past that might serve as a guide for the future. His earlier contemporary was entertaining and anecdotal; he states openly that whether or not he believed a story true, he should record it[2] although at one point (7.96) he indicates that excessive detail is unnecessary. He has been treated as biased, and, worse, superficial. Modern historians who reconstruct the Persian Wars have rarely had great compunction about discarding his testimony if it cannot be reconciled with their views. Yet he has survived his critics. The *History* was flawed, but it was also a remarkable, innovative achievement.

Life

The fullest biography of Herodotus comes from a tenth-century Byzantine lexicon called the *Souda* and it is notably brief. "Herodotus, the son of Lyxes and Dryo, a man of Halicarnassus, belonged to a prominent family and had a brother, Theodoros. He emigrated to Samos because of Lygdamis, the tyrant of Halicarnassus, the third in line after Artemisia. For the son of Artemisia was Pisindelis, and Lygdamis was Pisindelis's son. While in Samos, he mastered the Ionic dialect, and wrote a history in nine books, starting with Cyrus the Persian, and Candaules, the king of the Lydians. He returned to Halicarnassus and drove out the tyrant, but afterward, when he saw that he was hated by the citizens, he went as a volunteer to Thurii when it was being colonized by Athens, and there he died and was buried in the marketplace. But some authorities state that he died in Pella. . . ."

Halicarnassus, Herodotus's birthplace, is modern Bodrum, on the Aegean coast of Turkey, a city founded by settlers from Troezen in the Peloponnesos, and Dorian by origin, although the Dorian dialect had given way to Ionic by Herodotus's day. He did not have to learn Ionic in Samos. Cheek by jowl with the Greek community was the Carian settlement of Salmakis; an inscription from Halicarnassus dating from the mid-fifth century B.C. records a decree passed by a "joint meeting of citizens from Halicarnassus and Salmakis, together with Lygdamis."[3] The language is Ionic Greek, but the names of the city officials indicate a mixed Carian-Greek population. There is even a Persian name: Megabates, son of Aphyasis. Halicarnassus was on the fringe of the Hellenic world, where Greeks and non-Greeks rubbed shoulders in civic life. Things were ordered differently in the Athens of Pericles.

Herodotus was born shortly before the expedition of Xerxes.[4] He was possibly himself of mixed Carian-Greek origin, for his father's name was Carian, and in his *History,* he treats the Carians with a sympathy that he withholds from the Ionian cities that were Halicarnassus's neighbors.[5] One of his family, an uncle, or a first cousin, was the epic poet Panyassis, one of whose works, the *Ionika,* was an historical poem on the foundation of the Ionian cities.[6] Herodotus may have been introduced early to historical traditions within his own family. Such traditions existed locally, for there has survived an inscription from Halicarnassus that lists the priests of the temple of Isthmian Poseidon there through fifteen generations, from the time of the original settlers.[7]

Halicarnassus brought some advantages to the future historian: among them a balanced perspective of the barbarians. He was sharply aware of the differences between Greeks and barbarians, as the Persians, and non-Greek speakers generally, were named by all the Greeks but the Spartans, who simply called them *xenoi* or "foreigners."[8] But there is no hint that barbarians are inferior. He notes the courage of the Persians (9.102), and their physical strength, equal to that of the Spartans, who were the best soldiers Greece produced (9.6.2.3). Yet to be born in Halicarnassus was probably to be something of an outsider. The city was a Dorian foundation, but not a member of the Dorian Pentapolis. It once had been. Herodotus relates the story of Halicarnassus's expulsion from this league, with undertones of sarcasm directed at the exclusiveness not only of the other Dorian cities but also the more numerous Ionian settlements (1.143–44). The Dorian cities held games in honor of Apollo at their common sanctuary at Triopium. The prizes were bronze tripods, and it was the custom for victors to dedicate their tripods to the god. However, a Halicarnassian took his prize home, whereupon the other five cities expelled Halicarnassus, and thereafter, she remained outside the Dorian Pentapolis. The Ionian League was equally unwelcoming, but the exclusiveness of the Ionian Twelve Cities was matched by the unwillingness of outsiders to join them. "The other Ionians and the

Athenians too, avoid the name and do not want to be called Ionians; even at the present time the majority of them seem to be ashamed of the label" (1.143.3).

When Xerxes led his expedition against Greece, the Halicarnassian naval contingent was commanded by its tyrant, a redoubtable lady named Artemisia, whom Herodotus treats with respect and a touch of pride. The dynasty was Carian, and it remained in power after Xerxes' defeat. By 454 B.C. (the first year for which we have evidence), Halicarnassus was a tribute-paying member of the Athenian Empire, but the tyranny may have still survived, for though Athens preferred democracies as a matter of principle, she was not prepared to be rigid about it.[9] At some point, however, probably before the midpoint of the century, Herodotus and Panyassis took part in an abortive *putsch* against Artemisia's grandson. It cost Panyassis his life, and Herodotus went into exile on Samos.

If he had not already begun his researches, he started them there, for he is well-informed about Samos. In the great, unfinished temple of Hera, he saw a picture of the floating bridge over the Bosphorus that had been dedicated by Mandrocles of Samos, who built it for King Darius's expedition against Scythia, and he noted down the inscription (4.88). In the market, he saw the memorial raised to the eleven Samian ship captains who did not desert the Greek fleet at the crucial battle of the Ionian Revolt, that was fought at Lade off Miletus in 494 B.C. (6.14.3). Samos could claim the three greatest engineering works in all Greece: the Heraion, an aqueduct designed by Eupalinus of Megara, and a mole built to protect the harbor (3.60). There was no need for Herodotus to learn Ionic there, but he did note that Samos used an Ionic dialect peculiar to itself (1.142.4).

The tradition goes on to say that Herodotus returned to Halicarnassus and expelled the tyrant, Lygdamis. Presumably, since this second attempt was successful, he had effective backing, and it may have come from Athens. The dynasty must have enjoyed some support, particularly among the Carians, and if Herodotus acted as an Athenian agent, his subsequent unpopularity is understandable. In any case, finding he was disliked in Halicarnassus, he left the city.

He was now a Greek without a state, and when the colony of Thurii was founded in south Italy, he went there, and became a citizen.[10]

The initiative for the foundation came from the Sybarites, whose city had been destroyed in 510 B.C. by its neighbor, Croton, and they failed to reestablish it, although they had tried twice. Their second attempt had been in 453 B.C., but once again, Croton had forced them out. Shortly before 443, they appealed to Athens and Sparta for help in refounding their city. Sparta declined, but Athens dispatched a contingent of ten ships, and an oracle from Apollo indicated where the site should be. However, in the new city, the Sybarite descendants tried to act as a ruling class, and the other citizens rebelled, slew them, and issued an invitation for Greek volunteers to join them in their colony.

Such is the tradition. Modern historians have treated Thurii as an Athenian colony, and have regarded Herodotus's participation as proof of his enthusiasm for Athens.[11] But if Athens intended Thurii as an outpost of empire, it was a failure. Shortly before the Peloponnesian War, the Athenian colonists quarreled with the Peloponnesian group over Athens's claim to be the mother city of Thurii, and Delphi settled the matter by announcing that Apollo should be regarded as the founder.[12] During the Archidamian War, Thurii's attitude to Athens was one of chilly neutrality, and after the Athenian disaster in Sicily, she became a Spartan ally. The colonists included many who were no friends of Athens, and if Herodotus was among them, it proves nothing about his sympathies.

But the new colony did promise citizenship and a land grant, and that must have been attractive. Herodotus might have preferred to become an Athenian, but there was no hope of that. Athenian citizens had to be born of Athenian fathers *and mothers,* according to a law put forward by Pericles in 451–450 B.C. Thurii also attracted the sophist Protagoras of Abdera, who wrote laws for the colony,[13] and the town planner, Hippodamus of Miletus. There may have been a utopian atmosphere surrounding the foundation. In any case, sometime after 443, Herodotus took up the invitation to join the venture, and he lived in Thurii for a period.

He may have died there, though we cannot say so with complete confidence. A late Byzantine lexicographer[14] quoted the epigram on what purported to be his tomb there, for it gave Thurii the odd spelling of "Thourion." But, as time went on and relations between

Athenian and Peloponnesian settlers grew worse, Herodotus may have found Thurii increasingly uncomfortable. The Peloponnesian War was perhaps in its second or third year when Herodotus wrote the famous passage in his *History* where he gave his considered opinion that Athens, by remaining true to the cause of freedom, saved Greece from Persia in 480 B.C. "If the Athenians had panicked before the oncoming danger and abandoned their land, or even if they had not abandoned it, but stayed and surrendered to Xerxes, no one would have tried to resist the king by sea" (7.139.2). He prefaced this statement with the remark that he had to make it because it was true; yet, he knew most men would hate it. The apologia was aimed at non-Athenians, for the Athenians themselves would have considered the judgment only just. But at Thurii, which like Athens, had tribes, Herodotus would have belonged to the tribe of the Dorians, and few of his fellow tribesmen could have liked praise of Athens. This may be a clue as to his whereabouts as the Peloponnesian War began, for his verdict on Athens seems aimed at Sparta's partisans.

Herodotus's Travels

The *History* leaves no doubt that Herodotus traveled widely.[15] He visited Egypt and Cyrene, Babylon, the Black Sea and the Ukraine, the north Aegean area, and ultimately Italy. He seems to have made his journeys with ease: while in Egypt, curiosity inspired him, he wrote, to compare the Egyptian Heracles with the god of Tyre, Melkart-Ba'al, whom the Greeks identified with Heracles, and "since I wanted to get some clear information about this from those who could give it, I sailed to Tyre" (2.44.1). The implication is that the motive for his rovings was thirst for knowledge, and he gathered information as he went, though how systematically we cannot say. He cannot have traveled with an immense file of notes. But when did he make his journeys? And how did he support himself?

The latter question might have an adequate answer if Herodotus were a man of private means. But we cannot prove that. His family was prominent in Halicarnassus, but for a good portion of his life, Herodotus was in exile, and though family connections may have opened doors, he cannot have relied on inherited wealth. He may have engaged in trade:[16] he remarks on the contempt in which Greeks held men who worked with their hands in a manner that suggests he did not share the prejudice (2.167). Moreover, he followed the trade routes and knew people engaged in trade. At Olbia, at the mouth of the Bug River, he spoke to the agent of the Scythian king, Tymnes, a Carian from his name (4.76.6), who no doubt handled trade between the Scythians and the Greeks. Quite as revealing is the fact that Herodotus calculates distances by the number of days it took a sailing ship to travel between two points. "A ship travels about seventy thousand fathoms in a long day, and at night, sixty thousand. . . . In this way, I have measured the Pontus, the Bosporus, and the Hellespont, and they are as I have described them . . ." (4.86). It is possible that Herodotus took his information from some sailors' manual, but if we take his words at face value, then his familiarity with the Black Sea and the Sea of Marmora came from the fact that he criss-crossed them himself in merchantmen, for warships preferred not to travel at night on the open sea.

But if Herodotus turned his hand to trade, it could have been only for a brief period. Facts are lacking, but we can conjecture that he soon acquired a reputation for his lectures and public readings. A satirical essayist of the second century A.D., Lucian of Samosata[17] tells how Herodotus determined to become known as an historian quickly by going to the Olympic Games and reading his *History* there to the assembled notables. Lucian's accuracy is not beyond reproach, but Thucydides (1.22.4), who was in a position to know better, makes a backhanded reference to Herodotus's search for acclaim. He is supposed to have received a generous honorarium from Athens (the sum, ten talents, is too large to be credible)[18] and to have been refused one by Thebes; indeed the Thebans refused to let Herodotus converse with their young men.[19] He lived at a time when lecturers could command good fees, before the label "sophist" acquired a pejorative connotation. One sophist who was a commercial success, Hippias of Elis (the story may be fictitious but the circumstances are not), told Socrates that he made more than 150 minas from a lecture tour in Sicily, even though he was competing against the great Protagoras. Even Sparta was on his circuit, though the Spartans were no intellectuals, and considered thinking bad for the physique. What did the Spartans like to hear, Socrates wanted to know. Not geometry, or harmony, or anything of the sort. "Socrates," said Hippias, "they like hearing about the genealogies of heroes and men, and the founding of cities, about how they were originally established, and, to put it in a nutshell, the whole study of the past."[20] There was an appetite for history, and we may well believe that Herodotus found public recitation profitable.

The question of when he made his journeys has no precise answer. All the evidence comes from the *History* itself, and the *History* we have was written from notes, or memories that may never have been jotted down, after the travels were over: in some instances, long after. It may be true that the voyage to the Black Sea and Scythia antedated the trip to Egypt,[21] but the best we can hope to show is that Herodotus *composed* his description of Egypt after he had visited Scythia. It might also be logical to suppose that some of his longer and more arduous journeys were taken before he was past his prime, and that his home base was Samos, or even Halicarnassus, before he was forced into his first exile. Babylon might have been easier to visit while Halicarnassus was still part of the Persian Empire. But the argument is hazardous, for we do not know when Halicarnassus ceased to be subject to Persia. Greeks could move with some freedom within the Persian Empire, whether they were Persian subjects or not, particularly if they had contacts with the Persian nobility.

One snippet of evidence gives an upper limit for the journey to Egypt. As Herodotus describes the battle of Pelusium (525 B.C.) where the Persian invaders routed the Egyptians after a stubborn fight, he digresses to describe a phenomenon that he had learned from the local inhabitants. The skulls of the Persians were so thin that a pebble thrown at one would break it, whereas the Egyptian skulls were tough and strong. The reason was, Herodotus explained, that the Egyptians shaved their heads and exposed them to the sun, thereby thickening the skulls. "And I learned of another example of this same thing at Papremis, where the Persians were wiped out by Inaros the Libyan, along with Achaemenes, son of Darius"(3.12.1–4).

The battle at Papremis took place in 459 B.C. It was the major success of a revolt led by Inaros, whose base was Mareia, south of Alexandria. A brief notice in Thucydides is our best source for it;[22] yet Herodotus's audiences should have known it well, for Athens sent help to the rebels, and suffered heavily when the revolt failed. The Athenian fleet sent to Egypt at first swept everything before it, and briefly controlled the Nile; some Samians served in the fleet[23] and it is not impossible that Herodotus accompanied them. But the rebel position soon deteriorated, and travel must have become impossible until after the Persians regained control. Inaros was liquidated about 455 B.C. but in the northern Delta, one Amyrtaeus still held out as late as 449 B.C. Herodotus describes the island that was his base (2.140), and notes that the Persians appointed the sons of both Inaros and Amyrtaeus to their fathers' positions (3.15.3), and elsewhere he speaks of Persian troops guarding the Nile embankment south of Memphis "even now" (2.99.3), implying that he saw them there. On the whole, it is likely that Herodotus saw Egypt after the revolt, though we cannot show that he made only one trip.[24]

On his way back from Egypt, he visited Tyre; at least he tells us that his curiosity about the Egyptian Heracles took him there (2.44.1). As his ship sailed along the coast, he may have seen the city of Cadytis (Gaza?) and judged it to be not much smaller than Sardis (3.5.2). His route may have taken him from Tyre inland, down the Euphrates to Babylon, for he includes in his description of Babylon a number of comparisons with Egypt, as if memories of it were still fresh. But hypotheses such as these rest on fragile bases, for Herodotus revised before he published, and some of the snippets on which we base our theories may belong only to the final revision.

But we can be sure that Herodotus saw the Nile in flood; that is to say, he was there in the summer, between June and the end of September,[25] and he may have left before the waters receded. The Aswan dam has now ended the Nile floods, but for the nineteenth-century traveler, Herodotus's description of the Delta under water was still accurate. "When the Nile floods the country, only the cities appear above it, looking like the islands in the Aegean Sea. . . . When this happens, travelers are no longer taken by boat along the river courses, but right over the level ground" (2.97.1). Further south, Herodotus must have visited the Faiyûm and seen "Lake Moeris" when the Nile was in flood; his measurements of the lake are exaggerated,[26] but the lake itself was not a figment of his imagination as was once thought. Herodotus's journey upriver from Memphis to

Elephantine (Aswan) was made by river boat, constructed of acacia and caulked with papyrus, and what he saw was determined by the number and length of the stops that the boat made. Unless we are to convict Herodotus of outright lying, we must believe that he did make this voyage as he claimed, using his own eyes to gather information, and asking questions about the regions south of Aswan (2.29).

When Herodotus came to write down the accounts of his travels, he worked not only with notes, which cannot have been voluminous, for the ancient world had no microfilm, but also with recollections. When he describes the Great Pyramid at Gizeh, he notes: "There is an inscription in Egyptian letters on the pyramid, indicating how much was spent on radishes, onions, and garlic for the workers. *If I remember rightly what the interpreter said,* they cost one thousand, six hundred silver talents" (2.125.6). The words conjure up a picture of a dragoman giving Herodotus a fanciful translation of an inscription, and of Herodotus, some years later, trying to recall just what was said. He had taken no notes at the time.

Similarly Babylon. Herodotus implies that he visited the city. He says that he did *not* see the gold statue of Marduk-Ba'al, which was stolen by Xerxes, and we may infer that he *did* see the other temple treasures he describes (1.183). He claims to know how high the millet and sesame grew in the fertile fields around Babylon, but he will not tell his readers, for those who had not visited Babylon would disbelieve it (1.193.4). Yet, it is likely that he reconstructed his descriptions of Babylon from memories of a short visit to the city that may have taken place long before. The Babylon he describes has a touch of literary evocation about it.[27]

On the other hand, the descriptions of the Scythians are a *tour de force* of anthropological research that is remarkably accurate as far as it can be checked, including the story of the ritual intoxication of the Scythian shamans by inhaling smoke from burning hemp seeds.[28] Herodotus spent much of his time in the Greek trading settlements along the Black Sea coast, but he went up the river Bug, as far as Exampaeus, where he implies he saw a bronze vessel of incredible size, six times greater than the one that Pausanias had had dedicated at the entrance to the Black Sea (4.81.2). He may have gone up the Borysthenes (Dniepr) on a forty-day voyage to the land of the Gerrhi, where were the Royal Scythian graves, for his information about the Scythian burial customs is abundant and well-founded.[29] But we cannot trace his journeys with any exactitude. One passage is revealing. Speaking of the Argippaioi up the Dniepr River, he writes, "Some of the Scythians make trips to them, and it is not difficult to get information from them and from the Greeks in the trading stations on the Borysthenes and the other posts on the Black Sea" (4.24). Greek and Scythian traders, who commanded several languages, must have been the source of much of Herodotus's information. Metal goods from Olbia, particularly mirrors, have been found as far afield as Hungary, Kiev in the Ukraine, and the Urals, and the trade routes which took the goods there were the channels along which information seeped back to Black Sea settlements.

As far as we can judge, Herodotus was fluent only in Greek, though he may have had some competence in Carian too.[30] Not that he was without interest in foreign languages. In Egypt, he noted correctly that the word for an upright man was *piromis*,[31] and the Egyptian word that he gives for "crocodiles," *khampsai*, probably represents his effort to transliterate into Greek what his interpreter told him.[32] Among the Scythians, he made queries about the one-eyed men on the edge of the known world called the Arimaspoi, already known to him and some of his audience from the lost poem of Aristeas of Proconnesus, the *Arimaspea*. "Arimaspoi" was a Scythian word, he says, for *arima* is Scythian for "one," and *spou* for "eye." He may not have been entirely wrong; "Arismaspoi" may derive from the Mongolian words meaning "one-eyed," but here too he was at the mercy of his interpreter.[33]

We might have expected Herodotus to acquire a smattering of Persian, but his competence does not seem to have extended beyond a few words.[34] One passage in particular betrays ignorance. He observed that all Persian names ended with the *s* sound: the letter called *san* by the Dorians and *sigma* by the Ionians (1.139). But this is true only of the Greek transliterations of Persian names; Herodotus did not know the Persian originals, and the transliterations are not his own.[35] Foreign words were among the curiosities of alien lands, like crocodiles and griffons, but Herodotus's competence did not extend beyond a few phrases.

Herodotus's great journeys had probably ceased some few years before he left to settle in Thurii. He visited Thurii's neighbor, Metapontum, and made queries there about Aristeas of Proconnesus (4.15.1–3). It was a short trip, and tied up a loose end. But his wandering was over. The reason was not so much advancing middle age, perhaps, as a change of interest. The researches which Herodotus had made on his voyages had been primarily geographical and anthropological. He was examining the deeds and achievements of men, to steal a phrase from his own introduction, and the lands and customs of foreign people. His great theme, the rise of Persian imperialism and its collision with Greece, was not yet his dominant interest.[36] Once it was, the nature of his researches changed. The Greek mainland became his major source of information, particularly Athens and Sparta, with additional comments from Delphi, to which Herodotus lent a respectful ear.

About the historian's final years, all is conjecture. I cannot think that he lived serenely in Thurii, polishing his *History* and traveling a little in Italy and Sicily. Life there could not have been entirely quiet, for shortly after the colony was founded it was at war with its neighbor, Taras, modern Taranto, for control of Siris.[37] Before the battle of Salamis in 480 B.C., Themistocles had held over his reluctant allies the threat that the Athenians would depart with their ships for Siris, to which Athens had an ancient claim (8.62.2). The story may have acquired new relevance for Herodotus once he became a Thurian himself. But his Italian experiences, whatever they were, leave little trace in his *History*.

Probably he continued to make lecture tours. The *History* had not yet reached its final revision, and was not to do so until the first years of the Peloponnesian War. Herodotus seems to have found his great theme: Greece, united—with some exceptions—in the cause of freedom against the barbarian, at a time when Greece was splitting into two warring camps fighting for supremacy. That fact may not be without significance.

The Athenian Period

Nowhere in his *History* does Herodotus state that he visited Athens. Nor does he name any informant in Athens, as he does in Sparta (3.55.2). Yet his knowledge of the city, and his familiarity with the history of some of the great Athenian families, argues for a visit of some duration. Whether or not he admired Athens unreservedly is another question, though he notes early in his *History* that she rose above the unremarkable level of the other Ionian cities. "The Ionian is much the weakest of the [Greek] races, and least noteworthy. Except for Athens, there is no city worth talking about" (1.143.2). Backhanded praise, indeed; later, Herodotus was to do better. But there is some external evidence for his visit.

He was a friend of the tragic poet Sophocles, though the evidence for his friendship is not invulnerable to skepticism. Plutarch[38] quotes a little epigram that Sophocles wrote for Herodotus; it is, however, only a fragment, and Plutarch neglects to identify the Herodotus of the epigram. Besides this morsel of evidence, however, we have a number of instances in Sophocles' surviving plays where Sophocles shows that he is familiar with Herodotus's researches long before the *History* reached its present form. The most striking of these comes from the *Antigone*. When Antigone is taken offstage to her death, she defends her defiance of Creon by saying that she would never have done for a husband or children what she did for a brother. "For if one husband died, I might have another, and a son from another man, if I had lost the one I had. But my mother and my father have gone to Hades, and I shall never have another brother." The reasoning is foreign to modern readers. But in Herodotus (3.119), there is an almost exact parallel. King Darius arrested his old comrade-in-arms, Intaphrenes, and all his kinsmen, but Intaphrenes' wife stood weeping at the palace gates until the king took pity and offered her the freedom of one man. She chose her brother. The king expressed surprise, but she replied, "Oh King, I may have another husband, if Heaven wills, and other children, if I let these go. But no way might I get another brother, for my father and mother are no longer alive." Darius was sufficiently impressed to release her eldest son as well as her brother; the rest of the family he slew.

The closest parallels we can find to the story of Intaphrenes' wife come from India, and the folktale motif is probably Oriental.[39] Herodotus has picked up a Persian variant. Did Sophocles in turn pick up the motif from Herodotus?

It is likely he did, and for no other reason than that it appealed to him. It is a justification that sits awkwardly in the *Antigone*. Why should Antigone think that a brother's claim to burial is better than a husband's or a child's? Intaphrenes's wife saved her brother so that he could beget children and maintain her family line, but Antigone had no such motive. It seems that Sophocles has borrowed the motif simply to emphasize Antigone's hardness. Her priorities are her own. She is magnificently courageous and marvellously stubborn.

Other parallels are less close: distant echoes or similar sentiments expressed by both, and we can find parallels of the same sort between Herodotus and both Aeschylus and Euripides. Athens was a great marketplace of ideas in the fifth century, and Herodotus was affected by it. The burden of evidence indicates that Herodotus's researches were known in Athens long before the *History* reached its present form, and that he belonged to a circle of friends there that included Sophocles.[40] But he remained an outsider; he could never be an Athenian citizen.

One reference suggests that, after his departure for Thurii, he did not see Athens again. On the left, he tells us (5.77), as one entered the gateway to the Acropolis, stood a bronze quadriga made from a tithe of the booty taken from the defeated Boeotians and Chalcidians, who had combined with Sparta in 506 B.C. in an abortive effort to restore tyranny in Athens. This was the "Old Propylaia," built after the Persian sack of the Acropolis in 480 B.C.,[41] and swept aside to make room for the Propylaia designed by Mnesikles, that Athens began in 437 B.C. as part of the Periclean building program. The quadriga was probably moved at that time to the vicinity of the Athena Promachos statue, where Pausanias saw it in the second century of our era, and mentioned it briefly in his *Description of Greece* (1.28.2). The Old Propylaia had been demolished for about ten years when the *History* was published, and yet Herodotus seems unaware of it.

The other scrap of evidence for Herodotus's whereabouts at the outbreak of the Peloponnesian War has already been cited. It is his tribute to the steadfastness of Athens in the face of Xerxes' onslaught (7.139), which he prefaces with the opinion that most people would find it hateful. The defensive attitude is understandable if Herodotus was living where Athens was unpopular. That could hardly be Athens itself, but it might have been Thurii.

Conclusion

The evidence that we have reviewed for Herodotus's life has been meager, and we cannot flesh out a full biography. But we have an outline, based on a mixture of accepted fact and probability, with some conjecture added. He was born in Halicarnassus of a Greco-Carian family of good standing. Along with his kinsman, Panyassis, he took part in an unsuccessful *putsch* against the ruling house of Halicarnassus, and had to retire to Samos: luckier than Panyassis, who lost his life. He began his travels early, before his exile, and continued them from Samos, perhaps as a trader, perhaps even as a diplomatic functionary, for in Sparta, he tells us that he interviewed the Samian *proxenos,* the Spartan who kept an eye on Samian interests in his own country (3.55.2). He saw Athens before the Periclean building program got under way, and he probably lived there for a period before he left for Thurii. He may have travelled to Egypt more than once, but one trip at least we must date after Persia crushed the rebellion of Inaros, and had the country firmly under control again.

He returned to Halicarnassus to drive out the tyrant Lygdamis, but then, finding himself heartily disliked, he left his native city for good, and devoted himself to his researches, supporting himself by giving public lectures in the major centers of Greece. When the invitation came from Thurii for new settlers, Herodotus was one of those who accepted. He had no chance of citizenship in Athens nor, it seems, did he want to live there as a resident alien, which may suggest that his feelings toward the great imperial city were ambivalent. Thurii remained his base for the rest of his life; the evidence is largely negative, but the burden of proof falls on those who would prove the opposite. It is not likely that he moved back to Athens in time to suffer privation and plague in the Peloponnesian War.

There remain two problems. When was the *History* published? And when did Herodotus die?

The Date of Publication

To speak of a publication date is to introduce a concept that needs explanation. Our unvoiced assumption is that, at some point, Herodotus laid down his pen and a first edition of the *History* appeared in the book stalls, not yet divided into nine books named after the Muses (that was to be done later, in Alexandria) but otherwise more or less as we have it. In the latter half of the fifth century, there was a growing book trade in Greece,[42] and when Socrates defended himself before an Athenian jury at the beginning of the next century, he remarked that papyrus rolls of Anaxagoras's works were for sale for a drachma each in the orchestra, located in the northwest corner of the Athenian marketplace.[43] But Herodotus had one foot in the oral tradition. He gave public readings of his work in progress, possibly even before he knew in what direction it was progressing. In that there was nothing odd, for as we have seen, the practice was beginning for authors to give public readings from a script, sometimes speaking for themselves, sometimes, like the sophist Protagoras on one occasion that is documented, borrowing someone else's voice. Hence Herodotus's work was known before it reached final form. We must even reckon with the possibility of pirated copies of the *History* appearing before the "publication date," which marked only the final act of the publication process.

The canonical view puts the date of publication between 430 and 424 B.C., and the proof rests on two passages.[44] At 7.137, Herodotus mentions the death of the Corinthian Aristeus, whom the Athenians executed in late summer, 430 B.C. Hence publication must be later than 430. However, at 6.91.1, he notes the expulsion of the Aeginetans from their island in 431 B.C., but fails to mention their destruction seven years later. This is a significant silence, for Herodotus was relating a story of divine vengeance: the well-to-do Aeginetans had suppressed an uprising of the lower classes supported by Athens, and had torn a fugitive away from the sanctuary of Demeter's temple, thus incurring the goddess' anger. In 431, Athens expelled the Aeginetans, but Sparta gave them the land of Thyrea to settle. There the Athenians attacked them again in 424 B.C. and extirpated them.[45] Herodotus points to the first atrocity as evidence of Demeter's wrath, but fails to mention the second, even though it would have served as a more striking demonstration of it. Thus the argument goes that by 424, the work must have been already published.

However, there has always been a strong minority opinion in favor of a later date, perhaps as late as the Peace of Nikias of 421, that ended the first phase of the Peloponnesian War, the so-called "Archidamian War." Most of the evidence is ambiguous, but one morsel deserves notice: near the end of the *History* (9.73.3) Herodotus states that, because of an ancient claim which Decelea had to Spartan gratitude, the Spartans did not plunder it in the "war that took place later. . .," using the aorist participle *genomenon* to refer to the war. Spartan strategy in the early years of the Peloponnesian War was to make annual raids into Attica (the last was in 425 B.C.), and since the aorist denotes completed action in the past, we can be reasonably sure that the passage was written after Herodotus knew the annual raids had ceased. Can we go further and claim that the passage was written after 421 B.C.? That is less certain. However, this must be one of the latest passages in the *History*.

That need not occasion surprise. When Herodotus made his final redaction, he probably started at the beginning and worked to the end,[46] ordering what he had written, and rewriting to fit the requirements of his theme: the rise and consolidation of Asia under Persia, and the clash with Greece. Papyrus rolls with some of the early sections may have appeared in the bookstalls shortly after the Peloponnesian War began. In his *Acharnians* (ll.63–92) produced in 425 B.C., Aristophanes parodies Herodotus, and it is not likely that he would parody an author with whom his audience was unfamiliar. But publication was probably not complete until after 424 B.C. There was no single year of publication; rather it was a process that stretched over a period of time, and even before it began, Greeks had already gained a degree of familiarity with parts of the *History* from public readings.

This was a method of publication that did not allow for last minute changes. If Herodotus decided to omit a section to which he had already referred in an earlier part of the *History* that was already for sale, there was nothing that could be done about the cross-reference. This may account for one famous lapse: Herodotus promises to tell his readers about the murder of Ephialtes, the traitor at the battle of Thermopylae (7.213), but the story never appears. Or again, he twice promises a section on Assyria (1.106.2; 184), where he would tell how Nineveh fell, and what kings ruled in Babylon, but the promise is never fulfilled. Either a section has been lost, or Herodotus himself found no place for Assyrian *logoi* as his work progressed, and omitted them. But the promise had already been published and remained in the text.[47]

Chapter Two
The Consolidation of Asia
The Proem

"This is the publication of the research of Herodotus of Halicarnassus,[1] written to save from time's oblivion the deeds mankind has done, and to give due glory to the great and marvellous works performed, some by the Greeks, some by the barbarians. Especially does he wish to show for what cause they warred with one another." The opening of the *History* states its purpose. The publication of Herodotus's research, which is what *historia* means, will keep great deeds alive in the minds of men, and give renown to the achievements of mankind. The concern that the works of men should get their due portion of fame would strike a responsive chord in Greek hearts, for the same concern is expressed in epigrams on gravestones and commemorative monuments of the sixth and fifth centuries B.C.[2] The epic poets brought renown to the Trojan War, and Herodotus would do the same for the Persian Wars. But the last words strike a different note. Herodotus will also search for the cause of the conflict.

"Cause" (*aitia*) he could not dissociate from "fault," for the primary meaning of the Greek word is "blame" or "accusation." He sought for who, or what was to blame (we should remember that the word *histor*, found in the *Iliad*, meant a "judge" who knew right and wrong), and he set about unraveling the long skein of grievances and countergrievances. He imagines Persian memorialists arguing the case with their Greek counterparts. The Persian story was that the Phoenicians began the strife when they stole Io from Greece; the Greeks in turn stole Europa from Tyre, and then, rather overdoing it, Medea as well, from Colchis. In the next generation, an Asiatic prince, Paris of Troy, evened the scale by taking Helen from Sparta. Then the Greeks escalated hostilities by sacking Troy, which, as the Persians pointed out, was more offensive than kidnapping women. Herodotus's

Persians make a clear distinction between a *casus belli* and war itself, and it is those who make war who are to blame for it, not those who furnish the incident that provokes it. So the Trojan War started the hostilities, for the Persians thought of Asia as theirs.

That was the Persian account, though the Persians who gave it are mere literary creations. By the time Herodotus wrote, the Persian Wars had become, in Greek minds, part of a long struggle between Greek and barbarian that went back at least to the Trojan War. The Persians became the barbarians *par excellence,* and it was the struggle against the imperialism of Persia that made Greeks conscious of their common blood, language and religion.[3] Homer's world had had no barbarians, and only a glimmering of the concept of foreignness, but from the fifth century B.C. onward, the opposition of Greek to barbarian was to inform the myth of Troy. But Herodotus wastes no further time with these ancient grievances. He will start with the man who he knows was the first to wrong the Greeks without provocation: Croesus of Lydia, and so proceed, dealing fairly with states great and small, for he recognized that human fortune was mutable, and that some states that were great in his own day were once small, and vice versa.

Thus Herodotus launches into his first story, or to use his own term, *logos,* a word that, for most of his coevals, meant a narrative which might be true, partially true or wholly mythical.[4] The present division of the *History* into nine books named after the Muses was made long after Herodotus's death.[5] As Herodotus wrote it, the *History* proceeded from *logos* to *logos:* twenty-eight of them, according to the count of a recent scholar,[6] though we may quibble about the exact number, and just where the seams come. The first of them is the story of the fall of Croesus.

The Croesus-*logos*

Turning his back on the grievances that belonged to the mythical past, Herodotus started with Croesus. It was not that he made a sharp distinction between history and myth, although admittedly, with Croesus, he does move on to firm historical ground. He could have talked at Halicarnassus with men whose grandfathers had known Croesus, and at Delphi he did talk to witnesses who could point to concrete evidence of Croesus's greatness: the rich dedications that he had made there. But Herodotus's treatment of myth and history in his work as a whole does not encourage us to believe that he made a sharp distinction between the two.[7] Nor, for that matter, was Croesus the first of his dynasty to attack the Greeks, as Herodotus knew well. But he did believe that Croesus was the first to subdue Greek cities and impose tribute on them,[8] and tribute was the distinguishing feature of empire. Croesus was the first Asiatic imperialist to conquer Greeks.

For chronological considerations as well, the fall of Croesus made a good starting point. It was not that the Greeks had a calendar date for his fall, but rather that it was one of those events, like "The War" in the American South, which existed in the Greek mind as a fixed point in the past. "How old were you when the Mede came?" was a question one might ask a guest, according to Xenophanes of Colophon[9] who had lived through the period. The end of Croesus had become a legend. Bacchylides (3.23–62) introduced it into an ode that he composed for the tyrant of Syracuse, Hiero, who won an Olympic victory in 468 B.C. As he told the story, when the Persians took Sardis, Croesus with his wife and family mounted the pyre to immolate themselves, but before the flames could overcome the king, Zeus wrapped him in a cloud and Apollo snatched him away to live with the Hyperboreans. Herodotus has Croesus saved by the Persian king, who makes him his advisor. The Akkadian chronicle of Nabonidus from Bablylon informs us that in the ninth year of Nabonidus, Cyrus of Persia annihilated the king of *Lu——*;[10] an unfortunate rasure leaves us uncertain of the reading, but the best guess is Lydia. Croesus left a good reputation behind him, for though he conquered the Greeks in Asia, he cultivated Sparta's friendship, and his gifts to Delphi were munificent. In the *History* he is an attractive, generous character who learned, through suffering, the truth about human life. He did not deserve to die, and Greek legend saved him.

The Mermnad dynasty, to which Croesus belonged, descended from Gyges, the favorite bodyguard of king Candaules, a monarch who was "fated to come to a bad end." Candaules was intoxicated by his wife's beauty, and felt compelled to show her off to Gyges. He hid Gyges in the royal bedroom while his wife undressed, and Gyges slipped out after he had viewed the queen naked, not, however, unseen. Next morning, the queen summoned him, and gave him a hard choice: either to slay Candaules and take the kingdom, and herself, or to die.

Gyges chose to live. He killed Candaules, and when civil war resulted between the legitimists who supported Candaules and Gyges' party (the novella of Gyges, it seems, is a myth that transformed an actual rebellion by Gyges against the previous dynasty which claimed descent from Heracles and hence may have been at least partly Greek),[11] the combatants asked Delphi to arbitrate. The oracle favored Gyges. But, Herodotus notes, it added that Gyges' fifth descendant would pay for the murder of Candaules.

So Gyges became king. Herodotus inventories his dedications at Delphi, which he himself had seen. "This gold and the silver that Gyges dedicated is called *Gygadian* by the Delphians," he states (1.14.3); the term was a tribute to the purity of the metal, for Lydian wealth derived from gold washed down by the Pactolus River, and to their skill at refining it. Gyges' line continued for five generations, through Ardys, Sadyattes, and Croesus's father, Alyattes, who fought a long war with the Greek city of Miletus until its tyrant, Thrasybulus, inveigled a favorable peace, using a trick wherein he had the help of his friend Periander, tyrant of Corinth. The mention of Corinth and Periander gives Herodotus a neat transition to a story about a famous resident of Periander's court, Arion, famed for his lyre and the invention of the dithyramb. As Arion was sailing between Italy and Corinth, the sailors robbed him and tossed him overboard, whereupon a dolphin took him on his back and brought him safely home. Periander, skeptical of Arion's story, asked the sailors when they reached Corinth, for news of Arion, and when they claimed they had left him alive and well in Italy, he confronted them with the poet in the flesh. Periander was included among the seven wise men of Greece, and the interlude on Arion was meant to illustrate his wisdom.

Croesus succeeded Alyattes when he was thirty-five, and quickly reduced, first the Greek cities of Asia (but not the islanders), and then almost all the tribes west of the Halys River. Among the visitors to his capital, Sardis, was Solon, the Athenian lawgiver who was archon in 594–593 B.C.; the name appeared on a list of archons set up about 425 B.C. in the Athenian *agora* where four small fragments of it have turned up, and the position of Solon's name can be inferred.[12] Solon's travels belonged to the decade after he made his reforms, and thus he was too early for Croesus. The traditions about him have shaken loose from their chronological framework, but the story Herodotus had to relate was too good for a mere date to spoil it. Croesus, at the height of his power, asked Solon who was the most enviable man he had met. Solon gave him two examples of men who had died in high honor. Croesus, who had expected to hear his own name, was indignant. "Is our prosperity so worthless in your eyes that you do not think us the equal of private men?" Solon replied that one cannot pronounce a man happy until he is dead, for such is the mutability of human fortune. Contemptuous, Croesus dismissed Solon.

The rest of the Croesus-*logos* describes the enlightenment of Croesus, until, on his funeral pyre, he acknowledges the wisdom of Solon. First, he loses his son, Atys. The tale of Atys's death uses the motif of the old Phrygian myth of the death of the god Attis;[13] retold by Herodotus, it illustrates the futility of man's attempt to avoid his fate. The same theme dominates the final act of Croesus's reign. After mourning Atys for two years, Croesus roused himself, for he was alarmed at the rise of Cyrus of Persia, who overthrew Astyages, king of the Medes, in 550 B.C. But before he attacked Cyrus, he consulted the oracles, testing them first, and concluding that those of Amphiaraus at Oropos and Apollo at Delphi were the most truthful. To them Croesus's envoys addressed his questions: should he lead his army against the Persians and should he seek allies? The oracles replied that if Croesus fought Persia, he would destroy a great empire, and that he should find the most powerful people among the Greeks and make them his allies.

Delighted, Croesus prepared for the campaign. First, he sought out the most powerful Greeks, and discovered that they were the Athenians and Spartans. Now Herodotus gives us the first of many digressions that are to appear in the *History* like pendants attached to the general theme of the growth of empire in the east. This one allows him to fit gobbets of Athenian and Spartan traditions into the chronological pattern of Asiatic history. Croesus found Athens under the tyranny of Pisistratus, who had been twice exiled, but now was back, firmly in control of the city and with a client, Lygdamis, ruling the island of Naxos. Sparta, once the worst-governed state of nearly all

Greece, had been reformed by Lycurgus, and grown powerful in the Peloponnesus. Croesus made an alliance with Sparta (Athens he seems to have disregarded) and prepared to cross the Halys River into Cappadocia, part of Cyrus's empire.

But before he started, one Sandanis, a Lydian, advised him against the invasion. Sandanis is a figure from tragedy, though the type is borrowed ultimately from the clever counselors of folktale. He is a type of wise advisor that appears frequently in the *History,* usually when catastrophe is at hand, and usually to give advice that disagrees with the consensus.[14] Should the Lydians attack a poor people, with neither good food nor wine? Their conquest would bring Croesus no wealth, whereas he had much to lose if he were defeated. But Croesus paid no heed. Wise advisors like Sandanis generally have their advice ignored in the *History.* Their function is like that of the blind seer Teiresias in Sophocles' *Oedipus the King;* they introduce dramatic irony and remind us that, if Croesus's actions were limited by fate, his own obtuseness was fate's ally.

So Croesus invaded Cappadocia. Herodotus gives his motives: desire for more territory, confidence in the oracles, and determination to avenge Astyages, who was his brother-in-law. Herodotus explains the connection: during the reign of Croesus's father, the Medes and Lydians had fought an inconclusive war for six years, until an eclipse of the sun (May 28, 585 B.C.) interrupted a battle between them, after which they were willing to accept mediation and make peace. Astyages married Croesus's sister to seal the peace, and thus, when Astyages fell, Croesus had a personal motive for revenge.

He crossed the Halys by bridges, Herodotus thought, though he records a Greek tale that Thales of Miletus diverted the stream for him. He took Pteria, the chief stronghold of Cappadocia and ravaged the land, while Cyrus collected an army that was numerically superior. The battle, when it came, was indecisive, and Croesus, realizing he needed more men, decided to retire to Sardis, summon help from his allies and face Cyrus the next year with a larger force. It was late in the season, and Croesus never imagined that Cyrus would campaign in the winter months. He disbanded the non-Lydian part of his army with orders to muster in the spring. But he mistook his enemy.

Cyrus marched on Sardis, and Croesus was caught by surprise. But he still had with him his formidable cavalry, and they might have saved the day, had not Cyrus adopted a stratagem suggested by Harpagus the Mede. He took the camels from his pack train and posted them in his front line, facing the Lydian horse, for he knew that untrained horses would not face camels. In the battle that followed, the Lydian horses fled as soon as they saw the camels, but their riders dismounted and put up a tough fight before the Persians drove them back to Sardis.

The city fell in the winter of 547–546 B.C.,[15] after a fourteen-day siege. Herodotus says that Cyrus put Croesus, and fourteen Lydians on a great pyre, intending to burn them alive, but as Croesus sat on the pyre, facing death, he remembered the advice of Solon and cried out his name. Cyrus heard the cry, and sent interpreters to discover the reason. When he learned it, he had a change of heart, for he realized that the man whom he was about to burn alive was one like himself, and, moreover, he remembered how uncertain human affairs were, and feared retribution. He ordered the fire extinguished. But his men could not put it out, until Croesus called upon Apollo, who sent a downpour of rain and quenched the flames.

The Croesus who descended from the pyre was a new man. His sufferings had transformed him; when Cyrus asked why he made war on him, he replied, "The god of the Greeks is to blame for this, for he incited me to war. For no one is so foolish as to prefer war to peace; in peace sons bury their fathers, in war, fathers their sons."[16] One request he made: he asked permission to send envoys to Delphi to reproach Apollo for the deceitful prophecy he had given. The oracle's reply brings the story full circle. "Even for a god, it is not possible to escape allotted fate. Croesus in the fifth generation paid for the sin of his ancestor who was spearbearer for the Heraklids and was led by a woman's guile to slay his lord and take his throne, to which he had no right." Apollo had not willed Croesus's fall; he had delayed it for three years and could do no more. Croesus had only himself to blame, for he had misunderstood the prophecy. His doom was inescapable, but his failure to foresee it was his own fault.

Such, then was the story of Croesus, the first Asiatic to subjugate Greek cities, though the Greeks remembered him as a monarch whose "grace and goodness did not fade."[17] Herodotus did not let him die;

instead, he made him into a literary figure. He became a wise advisor at the Persian court and ceased to belong to history. Cyrus was now his heir as the instrument of imperialism, and was to prove as blind to the mutability of human fortune as Croesus, in spite of the momentary enlightenment at the funeral pyre. Herodotus moves on to him.

The Cyrus-*logos*

With Cyrus, Herodotus reaches the main line of imperial consolidation in Asia. But the story started before Cyrus, with the Medes, who were the first to revolt against the Assyrians and win freedom, but then they rapidly fell under the tyranny of Deioces. How they did so is told in a model study of how to win absolute power. Deioces is the Hellenized name of a Median chieftain who appears in the annals of Sargon II (722–705 B.C.); he allied himself with the king of Urartu against Sargon but was defeated, captured and exiled to Hama in Syria.[18] The task of uniting the Medes fell to his successor and close relative, Kashtaritu, whose Greek name, Phraortes, comes from his cognomen, Fravartish (Protector). But for Herodotus, Deioces was the founder of the Median Empire, and he used one of the classic weapons of a would-be Greek tyrant: trickery. He coveted absolute power, and therefore cultivated a reputation for uprightness and justice, until all the Medes came to him to have disputes judged, for there was no rule of law in Media at the time. Then, when the Medes had come to depend on him, he chose to retire, for it did not pay him, he said, to spend time looking after the affairs of others while neglecting his own. Violence promptly increased, and the Medes turned to Deioces, and offered him the the kingship. Deioces accepted, provided that he was given a palace and a royal bodyguard. Once he received them, he built a great city with seven circuits of walls, the innermost of which surrounded his palace and treasuries, established court ceremonial and a secret service, and made himself absolute. Yet he did enforce justice. Sly methods were not incompatible with good rule, and even the lawgivers Solon and Lycurgus were willing to employ trickery to establish their laws.

After Deioces came Phraortes, probably a relative of Deioces, if not his son, as Herodotus has it. It may have been he rather than Deioces who founded Ecbatana,[19] and either he or his son Cyaxares made vassals of the Persians. Herodotus says that he lost his life in an attack on Nineveh, the Assyrian capital, and that under his son, the kingdom was overrun by the Scyths, who defeated the Medes, conquered Syria, and would have attacked Egypt, had not the pharoah, Psammetichus I, bought them off. They dominated Asia for twenty-eight years until Cyaxares expelled them. Herodotus's story is generally sound; the Scythian interlude belongs to the period 675–625 B.C., and the Scythian king, Partatua, Herodotus's "Protothyes," felt himself important enough to ask for an Assyrian princess as wife.[20]

Cyaxares was followed by his son Astyages, the last king of the Medes.

The birth of Cyrus

The story of the rise of Cyrus had come down in several versions. Herodotus knew four, and the one he chose was that least given to hagiography (1.95.1). The sparest version of all comes from the Chronicle of Nabonidus, which states simply that Astyages marched out against Cyrus, king of Anshan, but his army rebelled and handed him over to Cyrus. Herodotus's story is a folktale, with elements in common with the myths of Oedipus and the House of Atreus. Astyages' daughter, who was married to Cambyses I, the vassal prince of Parsumash, and the adjacent lands of Persia and Anshan, gave birth to Cyrus. Astyages, warned in a dream that his daughter's boy would become king and supplant him, took the infant and gave him to a kinsman, Harpagus, to destroy. Harpagus handed Cyrus over to his cowherd with orders to expose him, but when the cowherd got home his wife begged him to save the boy. She had, by coincidence, just lost a boy herself in childbirth; consequently, the cowherd could convince Harpagus that Cyrus was dead by showing his own son's corpse.

But in folktales, royal blood will out. Cyrus's playmates as a game chose him as king, and he organized them into a miniature court. Word of this came to Astyages, who summoned Cyrus, was struck by the family resemblance, and got the truth out of the herdsman. But he did the herdsman no harm, nor Cyrus, whom he returned to his real mother, for the *magi* told him that the prophecy had been fulfilled. The boy had been made a play king and he would not become a king a second time. But from Harpagus, Astyages exacted dreadful retribution. He invited him to a banquet and fed him his own son, nicely dressed and roasted, and when the banquet was over showed him his son's head, feet, and hands. Harpagus said nothing. But when Cyrus grew up, he incited him to rebel, and when Astyages, forgetting the wrong he had done him, put him in command of the force sent against Cyrus, he betrayed his king. Astyages mustered a second army, fought again, was defeated and taken captive. But Cyrus did him no further harm.

Now, with two brief sentences, Herodotus sums up the story thus far and looks ahead to what will follow. "In this way, Cyrus was born, reared, and became king, and afterward he subdued Croesus, who started the fight, as I have already related. He overcame Croesus and thus became ruler of all Asia."[21]

The imperial expansion of Persia

From this point on, Persian imperialism is to run like a thread through the *History*, and when it touches on a nation, there follows an ethnographic section. It is usually at the point where the Persian lust for empire involves an intended victim, that Herodotus digresses to describe the victim's *nomoi* or way of life, that makes a people act as it does. Herodotus's criteria for relevance were formal; the mere mention of a name, for instance, was enough to generate a digression, but his digressions were tied to the theme of Persian expansionism, and he himself notes that his manner of composition required them (4.30.1). When Cyrus takes over Croesus's role as imperialist, Herodotus describes the Persian *nomoi*.[22] What were these men like who conquered Asia and tried to extend their empire to Europe?

There is nothing pejorative in Herodotus's description. On the contrary, there are elements of utopian thought: the Persians, for instance, educated their sons from the age of five to twenty in only three things: to ride a horse, shoot the bow, and tell the truth. Herodotus approved (1.137.1). He noted especially those customs which would strike a Greek as different: the Persians built no altars or temples, and when they sacrificed they made no libations nor did they use music, fillets, or barley meal; on the other hand, he fails to mention the adoration of fire that was central to Zoroastrianism, perhaps because the Greeks had their own cult of the hearth, and thus he did not find the Persian custom particularly curious. There is even a hint of Samuel Butler's *Erewhon*: the Persians deliberated when drunk and reexamined their decisions when sober, and if they deliberated sober, they made their reexamination when drunk. "Lack of humor in historians has erected into a system what was merely due to excess," notes the standard commentary on Herodotus, with a hint of Victorian rectitude.[23] The digression ends abruptly. "And now I return to my earlier *logos*" (1.140.3).

The second subjugation of Ionia

We left the Ionian and Aeolian Greeks as subjects of Croesus. At the start of his war with Lydia, Cyrus invited them to revolt, but they declined. Now they were anxious to establish the same relationship with the new conqueror as they had had with Croesus. Cyrus replied with a fable: fitting enough, for fables were popular in the Orient since the days of Sumer and Akkad. A piper piped to the fish in the sea to entice them to shore, but they would not come. So he caught them in a net, and when he saw them leaping about helplessly, he said that since they had not danced before, they might as well stop now. Whereupon the Greeks prepared to defend themselves.

It is here, on the eve of the Persian attack, that Herodotus digresses to describe the Ionian *nomoi*. There were twelve Ionian cities, ten on the mainland: Miletus, Myus, Priene, Ephesus, Colophon, Lebedos, Teos, Clazomenae, Phocaea, and Erythrae, and two on the Dodecanese Islands, Samos and Chios, and they belonged to a loose federation that centered on the precinct of Poseidon Heliconius at the foot of Mt. Mycale, modern Samsun Dagi, where excavations have uncovered an altar dating to the end of the sixth century, and a meeting house for delegates. It was an exclusive club, but only one city ever applied to join, and that was Smyrna, an insignificant place in Herodotus's day, for it was sacked by the Lydians about 600 B.C. and did not recover. The five Dorian cities were equally exclusive and had once expelled Herodotus's own native city. Old wounds, perhaps? In any case, the description of Ionia is seasoned with contempt. The Ionians were the weakest of the Greeks: their only city of importance was Athens and she did not like to be called Ionian. Only the members of the federation were proud of the name. The tone is sour, and at variance with contemporary Athenian propaganda that made Athens the mother city of Ionia.[24] Herodotus acknowledges this theory, but he chooses to stress instead the mixed ancestry of the Ionians (1.146).

The Aeolian cities receive less attention, but neither does Herodotus show the latent disdain for them that he does for the Ionians. The Aeolians resolved to follow the Ionians in the face of the Persian threat. But the Ionians were disunited. Miletus made its own settlement with Cyrus, and the island cities were unafraid, for the Persians lacked a fleet. The Ionians showed little leadership or resolution now, nor ever in the *History*, until the very end. That fact, one suspects, may be a major reason for Herodotus's contempt.

The Ionians and Aeolians sent to Sparta for help, and their spokesman, a man Phocaea, made a speech imploring aid to the Spartans, who considered him long-winded. But Sparta did send one ship to Phocaea to reconnoiter, and a Spartan herald went to Cyrus to warn him that Sparta would not permit him to harm any city of the Hellenes. Cyrus first asked who the Spartans were, and then made a reply which both highlighted the difference between Greek and Persian, and defined Persia's imperial ambition. "I have never yet feared men of the sort that have a place set apart in the midst of their city for meeting to cheat one another by oaths" (1.153.1). The marketplace in the Greek city was the center of free speech, government by discussion and consensus, and free trade; there was no equivalent in Persia. "If my health continues, they shall not have the troubles of the Ionians to talk about, but their own." Cyrus was a world-ruler; no sooner did he learn that a nation existed than he thought of it as a future conquest. It was not a picture invented by Herodotus. The so-called Cyrus Cylinder introduces Cyrus thus: "I am Cyrus, king of the world, legitimate king. . . chosen by Heaven to be ruler of all the world."[25]

But for the moment, Cyrus had more important conquests to make, and thinking the Ionians of no account, he left for Ecbatana, taking Croesus with him. But the Lydians rose in revolt behind him, and the king was about to enslave them when Croesus deflected his intention with shrewd advice. Let Cyrus order the Lydians to give up their arms and learn to play the lyre and become merchants; then they would never rebel again. Cyrus liked the plan, and detailed a Mede named Mazares to carry it out. But as some Greek cities were involved in the revolt too, Mazares turned against them, and was pressing his attack when he took ill and died. Cyrus appointed in his place the Mede who had betrayed Astyages, Harpagus.

The first city he attacked was Phocaea, then the foremost naval power in Greece, whose trading ships plied the Mediterranean, and whose great walls were built with a subsidy from the king of Tartessos in Spain, with whom Phocaea had close mercantile connections. But the Phocaeans did not trust their walls and resolved to emigrate. Half of them turned back, homesick, but the rest sailed on, and eventually founded the city of Elia, later Velea, on the west coast of Italy. Another city, Teos, followed Phocaea's example and founded Abdera in Thrace. But the rest of the Ionians stayed, fought, and lost their separate battles and were subdued. "Thus for the second time was Ionia enslaved," wrote Herodotus (1.169.2), with a nice feeling for symmetry, for Ionia was also to rebel twice, and near the end of the *History* (9.104), he was to write, "Thus, for the second time, Ionia revolted from the Persians."

After their conquest, the Ionians met at the Panionion, and there one of the Seven Sages, Bias of Priene, advised them to emigrate to Sardinia, whose reputation for size and wealth quite outstripped reality. Herodotus thought it good advice (in a private way, he had followed it himself by emigrating to Thurii). Another of the Seven Sages, Thales of Miletus, had also given good counsel before the Persian attack: the Ionians should unite and set up a central government. Needless to add, the Ionians took neither counsel.

Harpagus next mopped up the non-Greek tribes in the area: the Carians, the Caunians, and the Lycians. The Carians were subdued without much resistance. The Lycians, however, who were Cretan emigrants called "Termilae," Herodotus (1.173) claims (in the Lycian language their name was *Trmmili*), fought desperately, and preferred death to submission; only eighty families survived. The Caunians receive brief mention; their greatest pleasure in life was to hold drinking contests, and like the Lycians, they died fighting.

The Conquest of Babylon

It was now Babylon's turn, and Herodotus attempts to describe the city as it was when it was taken, though when he saw it, Darius and later Xerxes had broken its walls, and Xerxes had pillaged the great temple of Marduk. Herodotus knows little about the neo-Babylonian empire of Nabopolasser and Nebuchadrezzar; for him, Babylon is an Assyrian city, which became the seat of the kingdom after the fall of Ninus (Nineveh). The last king was Labynetos, whose father bore the same name (1.188.1), and whose mother, queen Nitocris, was famous for strengthening the defenses of Babylon. Labynetos is Nabonidus, who seized the throne of Babylon in 556 B.C. in the period of turmoil after Nebuchadrezzar's death; his "father" of the same name must be Nebuchadrezzar himself (605–562 B.C.) and Nitocris, to whom Herodotus attributes some of Nebuchadrezzar's works, may be the Median princess Amytis who married him. Chaldaean Babylon had already passed into myth by the time Herodotus visited it, about a century after its fall.

There was a reason. Cyrus took care to present himself to Babylon as a savior rather than a conqueror; he restored temples, and installed as viceroy his son Cambyses, who clasped the hand of Marduk in the New Year Festival of 538 B.C., thereby affirming the ancient link between Marduk and the ruler of Mesopotamia. But Babylon made a bid for independence at the start of Darius's reign, and when Darius reorganized the empire, he made it a mere satrapy, tightly controlled and heavily taxed: Herodotus (1.192) comments with admiration on the revenues the satrap received in his day. Under Xerxes, Babylon revolted again (482 B.C.) and was brutally suppressed. The colossal gold statue of Marduk was taken from his temple, the Esagila. "Darius, the son of Hystaspes, planned to take this statue, but did not dare," Herodotus (1.183.3) wrote, "but Darius's son, Xerxes, took it, and killed the priest who forbade him to move it" (1.183.3). Xerxes cared nothing for Babylon's gods. "Perform religious service [only] for Ahuramazda and the *arta* [cosmic order] reverently": this proclamation of his, on a foundation tablet from Persepolis, betrays the character of the man.[26] Admittedly Xerxes did not enforce his proclamation, but he did abandon the politic religious toleration that Cyrus had practiced.

Babylon stagnated. The "Royal Road" from Sardis to Susa bypassed it, the cost of living increased, and Aramaic, which Darius adopted as the *lingua franca* of the empire, became the language of the street.

Scholars and temple scribes still knew Akkadian and Sumerian, and continued to copy cuneiform texts, but for most of the population, Babylon's past was locked away in an unknown tongue. Herodotus spoke to the "Chaldaean priests" of Marduk, or so he claims, but in fact, his sources of information must have been meager.[27]

But he had eyes. His visit was probably brief, but he had a sharp impression of a city of great size and symmetrical plan. It had a double circuit wall, with bitumen for mortar between the bricks, and a moat surrounding it. The Arahtum canal cut through the city, but Herodotus was clearly following the popular designation when he identified it as the Euphrates.[28] He mentions the palace of Nebuchadrezzar, and passes on quickly to the temple of "Zeus Belus" (Marduk Ba'al) on the same bank of the canal though Herodotus puts them on opposite banks.[29] But his description of the temple complex is essentially correct. The great tower with the shrine on top, containing a bed and a golden table, but no image, was the ziggurat, the *Etemenanki,* and the lower temple which contained the gold image that Xerxes took in revenge for the Babylonian revolt of 479 B.C. was the *Esagila,* "the temple that raises its head." But what he learned of the rites of Marduk was sketchy and he only half believed it.

According to Herodotus, Cyrus defeated the Babylonians. drove them within their walls, and then cut short the siege by diverting the Euphrates and entering the city by the riverbed. Oriental sources say nothing about this maneuver; they simply aver that the Persians entered the city without a fight.[30] The best that can be said is that Herodotus need not be wrong; the battle where Cyrus defeated the Babylonians was fought in September, 539 B.C., and Babylon did not fall until mid-October. There was time for Cyrus to divert the river, and the story that Herodotus relates may be true.

Before he leaves Babylon, Herodotus inserts a brief essay on its marvels and customs. One custom he thought wise: in every village, nubile girls were auctioned to would-be husbands one day each year, and the money which the beautiful, desirable maidens brought in was used to provide dowries for their ugly sisters. Another custom met his disapproval: every Babylonian woman had to go once in her life to the temple of Mylitta and there have intercourse with a strange man. In Cyprus, too, he noted, there was a similar custom: Mylitta of Babylon

was the Assyrian Ishtar, the Phoenician Astarte, and the Greek
Aphrodite, whose birthplace was Cyprus.

The Death of Cyrus

Once Babylon was conquered, Cyrus "conceived a desire to make
the Massagetae his subjects" (1.201). Thus Herodotus passes on to
Cyrus's last campaign and his death. The Massagetae lived almost
beyond the boundaries of Herodotus's geographical knowledge, on the
great steppe stretching to the east of the Caspian. Cyrus's motives were
many and powerful, and Herodotus names two: his birth, which made
him appear superhuman in men's eyes, and his success in war, for no
nation had been able to stop him. The truth may have been that a
tribe of Sakan (Scythian) nomads were raiding the northern territories
of Cyrus's empire that now stretched up to the Jaxartes where he had
built a powerful fortress,[31] and he resolved to counterattack. No
matter. As Herodotus presented him, the Great King embodied the
imperialism of his empire. He longed to increase the number of his
subjects, and he was as blind as Croesus had been to the mutability of
human fortune. He went forward to his death.

The Massagetae were ruled by a queen, Tomyris, whom Cyrus first
offered to marry, but she realized that Cyrus wooed her kingdom, not
herself, and refused him. Then Cyrus made ready to cross the river
that was the boundary of the Massagetic kingdom; Herodotus names
it the Araxes, which was, however, west of the Caspian. Whereupon
Tomyris made a proposal. She offered a trial of strength: the
Massagetae would allow the Persians to cross the river for a battle on
the Massagetic side, or, if the Persians preferred, they could let the
Massagetae cross and fight the battle on their own territory.

Cyrus's council thought it best to fight on Persian soil. But Croesus,
who was also present, disagreed. Wise counselors usually advised
caution and restraint, but here, though Croesus prefaced his advice
with a warning that human fortune was changeable, what he advised
was a stratagem to overreach the queen. Cyrus took the advice, and
the outcome was disastrous.

But before his death, Cyrus had a dream where he saw the young
Darius with wings on his shoulders overshadowing Europe and Asia.
Cyrus recognized the symbolism. Winged figures represented kingship

and the charisma that surrounded it; one still stands carved on a pillar in Cyrus's ruined palace at Pasagardae. Suspicious of a plot, Cyrus summoned Darius's father, Hystaspes, for Darius himself was too young to serve in the army, and ordered Hystaspes to bring his son before him. Then he pushed on with his ill-fated campaign.

The Persians and the Massagetae struggled hard; Herodotus judged this the toughest battle ever fought between barbarian armies. It ended in Persian defeat and Cyrus's death. Tomyris, who found his body among the dead, filled a skin with human blood and lowered his head into it, so that he could sate his thirst for it. Cyrus had shown himself capable of self-knowledge when he rescued Croesus from the funeral pyre, but he remained a king committed to extending his empire. He lived and died, a man of blood.

Chapter Three

Egypt

Cyrus died, and his son Cambyses inherited the empire, and with it, the Greeks of Asia. He considered them his father's slaves, and hence, when he resolved to invade Egypt, he made them contribute to his army. The subjection of the Greeks is the transitional idea that carries the narrative to the next topic: Egypt, which Herodotus describes on the eve of the Persian attack. The Egyptian section is the longest, most developed digression in the *History:* indeed it could stand by itself as an independent work. It falls into two parts. The first (2.2–98) deals with the geography and customs of Egypt, and is based, Herodotus claims (2.99), on his own observations and queries while he was in the country, and the second (2.99–182), on the history of Egypt, is based primarily on Egyptian accounts he had heard. At first glance, Herodotus appears to move from topic to topic without an underlying plan, but in fact, he follows a succession of themes and selects his material accordingly. The transition between topics is at times abrupt, but never illogical.

The Formation of the Land of Egypt

The section opens with a tale that Herodotus got from the priests at Memphis; it told how the pharoah Psammetichus (664–610 B.C.) showed that the Phrygians were older than the Egyptians by an experiment. Taking two infants, he had them raised without hearing human speech, so as to discover what language they would speak first. Their first word was *bekos,* which was Phrygian for "bread," and hence he concluded that the Phrygians were more ancient than the Egyptians.

The story is probably Ionian. A couple of generations before Herodotus, one of the visitors to Egypt had been Hecataeus of Miletus, a *logopoios,* as Herodotus calls him, without disrespect, for the term means merely a writer of prose. "I write what seems to me to be the truth," Hecataeus had begun, "for the stories of the Greeks seem to me numerous and absurd."[1] Hecataeus probably told the story of Psammetichus's experiment, and when Herodotus comments that his own version was corroborated by the priests not merely at Memphis but at Heliopolis and Thebes too, and that the Greeks relate many other absurd things about it (an echo of Hecataeus!), we may believe that he had his predecessor in mind.

But not merely Hecataeus. What interested Herodotus about the geography of the Nile Valley was what interested Ionian science: the formation of the land by the silting action of the river, the actual distances from one known point to another, and the appearance of shells and salt deposits on dry land, for example. The distances are exaggerated,[2] for Herodotus measured by the length of time it took to travel from one point to another, and this method assumes that one can always maintain a standard speed. Herodotus's distance between the Plinthinate Gulf (Arabs Gulf) and the Serbonian bog (Lake Bardawil) is about forty percent too great (2.6). But his dominant idea is that Egypt is the gift of the Nile. This was the Ionian view, shared by Hecataeus, that the Nile was formed by the river's silting action; but at the same time Herodotus develops a secondary theme, that the Ionians have made serious errors in their accounts of Egypt. He will present a corrective.

The section closes with a reference back to Psammetichus's experiment (2.15). This return to the initial idea of a piece is a characteristic feature of Herodotus's composition: the leading thought develops in its own direction, but then circles back to the starting point, so that the original context can proceed. Psammetichus's experiment was needless, Herodotus reasoned, closing the ring.[3] The Egyptians had always existed, but they could not move on to the land of Egypt until it had been created by the Nile's silting action.

The Nile

Having shown that the Nile created Egypt, Herodotus now moves to the geography of the river. How should we define Egypt? The Ionians were wrong who regarded only the Delta as Egypt, and the

Greeks equally wrong for whom Egypt was the Nile valley north of the first cataract, but the east bank was part of Asia and the west Libya. Egypt was the land peopled by Egyptians, just as Cilicia was the land inhabited by Cilicians. It was not geography that defined a country, but the ethnic group that inhabited it. The oracle of Ammon supported this view, for when people on the border of Libya inquired if they were Egyptian, the oracle replied that Egypt was the land the Nile flooded, and everyone north of the first cataract who drank its water was Egyptian.

The narrative flows easily on to the problem of the Nile flood, for which no Egyptian whom Herodotus questioned could give a reason. Nevertheless he gives three hypotheses propounded by the Greeks, though only to refute them. The Greeks are unnamed, but we can identify them. Thales of Miletus had argued that winds blowing from the north in summer backed up the water. Hecataeus's view was that the Nile connected with *Ocean*: the stream that flowed round the world—at least, the world of Homer and the epic poets—and the third hypothesis, that the Nile flooded from melting snow, belonged to Herodotus's older contemporary, Anaxagoras of Clazomenae, a teacher and friend of Pericles. Herodotus accepted none of them. Instead, he put foward an hypothesis of his own that was a little closer to the truth (2.24–25). He argued that the Nile shrank in winter because winds forced the sun southward where it parched the headwaters of the river. Hence the water was low in the Nile, for Egypt herself received no rain (rain does occur, in fact, but for practical purposes Herodotus is right). But in summer, the sun moved north, and there was abundant rainfall in the Nile's upper reaches, and hence the flood. In fact, the major cause of the flood is heavy precipitation from June to September in Ethiopia, which is drained by the Blue Nile,[4] though it is not a windblown sun that brings the rain.

As for the source of the Nile, Herodotus found no one who pretended to know, except for the *hierogrammateus* ("temple scribe") of Athena (Neith) at Sais. The *hierogrammateis* attached to Egyptian temples were the clergy most likely to have the information that Herodotus wanted, for they were experts in the priestly lore which passed for philosophy,[5] but there was a great difference between what a Greek savant and an Egyptian priest regarded as philosophy. The *hierogrammateus* of Neith told Herodotus that there were two peaks called Crophi and Mophi between Syene "in the district of Thebes" and Elephantine; the Nile rose from bottomless springs between these two peaks, and half the water flowed north and half south. Herodotus was incredulous; he thought the scribe was joking.

However, the story was probably based on a native tradition that the Nile issued from the earth at Gebel es-Silsila, about midway between Luxor and Aswan, where the river flows through a defile between two hills, which could have served as the original models of Crophi and Mophi. Even after the boundary of Egypt moved south to the first cataract, and the tale of Crophi and Mophi moved with it, there were great festivals in honor of the Nile god *Hapi* held at Silsila. The scribe of Neith was probably more ignorant of the topography of the Aswan area than Herodotus, who went up the Nile as far as Elephantine at the first cataract, and had a look at the river himself (2.29.1). But the scribe did know about the ancient traditions that belonged to the *Hapi*-festivals at Silsila, and based his tale upon them.[6]

For the Nile south of Elephantine, Herodotus had only hearsay. One morsel that he picked up in Cyrene illustrates the way stories filtered back from the edges of the known world to the Greeks. Cyrene got the tale from Etearchus, the ruler at the Siwa oasis, where there was the oracle of Zeus Ammon, and he had it in turn from the Libyan Nasamoneans who dwelt at the Awjila oasis. Some Nasamoneans had crossed the Sahara and come to a city at the edge of a river, inhabited by Negrilloes. In the river, which flowed eastward, were crocodiles. Etearchus thought it was the Nile, and Herodotus thought that likely enough. Modern scholars have identified it as the Niger, but it was more probably a river northeast of Lake Chad, now only a dry depression known as the Bahr el Ghazal, but in antiquity a tropical river fed by the overflow from Lake Chad.[7]

As to the sources of the Nile, Herodotus admits ignorance, but he is willing to argue by analogy. The Nile was comparable to the Ister (Danube), and thus its length should be about the same, for Herodotus's concept of the map of the world kept a nice symmetry between the northern and southern sectors. The section on the Nile terminates abruptly with the tag: "Now about the Nile, that's all I shall say" (2.34.2).

The Marvels and Works of Egypt

"But I am going on to deal with Egypt at some length because it possesses the most marvels, and has works beyond description compared with other countries. Hence I shall have more to say about it" (2.25.1). Thus Herodotus introduces a long ethnographic section on Egypt. He describes what an alert observer could have seen, and at the end, states that these are his own observations. He wrote of what he saw or reckoned to be true, and what he discovered with questions.

The proem reveals a common Greek attitude toward Egypt: it was a country of marvels greater than those found elsewhere. It was also a topsy-turvy society with customs the opposite of those found elsewhere, particularly Greece which was the norm for Herodotus. Women went to the market while men stayed at home and did the weaving. The gods were never served by priestesses but only by priests, and instead of allowing their hair to grow, they shaved their heads. The Egyptians practiced circumcision, which was to be found elsewhere, Herodotus knew, but he thought the custom derived from Egypt. The hint of *Erewhon* that we detect in the Persian-*nomoi* section is more apparent here, but the spirit is not utopian. What Herodotus is at pains to demonstrate is a point he will make again and again: that *nomoi* which one nation may regard as right and proper may be considered outlandish and even shocking by another.

At the same time, this review of Egyptian ethnography has to it a touch of "foreign enclave wisdom" about the "natives," as if some of the Greek-speakers whom Herodotus met and questioned knew Egypt in the same way that the "old China hands" knew China. The natives are an undifferentiated mass that can be described with sweeping generalizations which are based on insufficient contact. Herodotus's informants, for instance, knew that the favorite Egyptian beverage was beer, and proceeded to the dogmatic assertion that Egypt had no vines, which was untrue (2.77.4). However, wine was used in sacrificial rites (2.39.4)! *Pace* Herodotus (2.37.5), beans were cultivated in Egypt, but the Pythagoreans eschewed them, and Herodotus probably knew the tradition that Pythagoras got his wisdom from Egypt.[8] Hence it was easy to assume that Egypt shared the Pythagorean taboo against beans. Under the pharaoh Amasis, Greek merchants were concentrated at Naucratis, which became the window through which Greeks could view the strange world of Egypt.[9] But it did not allow the intimacy necessary for accurate observations, and the "foreign enclave wisdom" of Naucratis must have been replete with sweeping generalizations based on insufficient data of the sort that Herodotus makes. With the Persian conquest, restrictions on the movements of Greek traders were apparently dropped, but Naucratis remained a trading center of some importance, and the Naucratite perception of native life could still influence Herodotus.

However, when he moves on to his next topic, Egyptian religion, he has another theme that he articulates more than once: "The names of practically all the gods have come to Greece from Egypt" (2.50.1), and again, later, "These observances, and others besides these which I shall describe, the Greeks got from Egypt" (2.51.1). It seems clear that Herodotus meant these statements literally.[10] Equations between Greek and Egyptian gods had been made long before him, probably by the interpreters who formed a special hereditary class in Egypt (2.59.2; 2.156.5). If so, they were responding to the expectations of the Greeks, who required Egyptian customs to be put into terms they could comprehend, and both sides, Greek and Egyptian, collaborated in making analogies. The Egyptians said that Osiris was Dionysus (2.42.2); the Greeks said Isis was Demeter (2.41.2), though Herodotus noted that her images resembled those of Io (2.42.2). Zeus was Amun (2.42.5), Apollo Horus (2.156.5), Artemis Bubastis (2.156.5), and the Apis bull was equated with Epaphos, son of Io and Zeus (2.38.1; 2.153). Mendes was the Egyptian word both for a male goat and for the god Pan, Herodotus claims. The sacred animal of Mendes was, in fact, a ram, but it belonged to a native species (*Ovis longiceps palaeoaegyptiaca*) with long goatlike horns that had died out in the Middle Kingdom, and so Herodotus's error, which later Greeks shared, was understandable.[11] These were gods whose names in Greek were simply translations of the Egyptian, and consequently their Greek names sounded differently from their Egyptian ones.

In addition, however, there was a group of gods whom Herodotus knew only by Greek names. At Memphis, he met the priests of Hephaistos; this was Ptah, who in the theology of Memphis, created the elements of the universe by conceiving them in his mind.[12] At Sais, he thought Neith was Athena; the equation was natural, for Neith was a warlike goddess, who manifested herself in two arrows crossed over a shield.[13] Most baffling of all, not merely to Herodotus but the modern reader, is the Egyptian Heracles. He cannot be identified with certainty.[14]

However, that was not what puzzled Herodotus. His problem was that, while he had no doubt that the Greek Heracles derived from Egypt, he found that the Egyptian Heracles was one of the "Twelve Gods," whereas in Greece, he was a latecomer to Olympus, and except at Thasos where he had a temple, he generally received the cult appropriate to heroes. Herodotus's mind was firmly Greek, but nevertheless he tackled the Heracles-problem deftly. The Greeks had a canon of Twelve Gods; we can see them on the east frieze of the Parthenon: Zeus, Hera, Poseidon, Demeter, Apollo, Artemis, Ares, Aphrodite, Hermes, Athena, Hephaistos, and Dionysus. But in the Memphite and Heliopolitan theology, the original eight gods gave rise to the "Ennead," which was not, in fact, a rigidly fixed number of deities, and Herodotus or his informant evidently took it as the equivalent of the Twelve Gods of Greece. Herodotus (2.43.4) knew that a change had taken place; seventeen thousand years before the reign of Amasis (569–526 B.C.) the number of Egyptian gods had increased from eight to twelve, and Heracles was among the new gods.[15]

In pursuit of Heracles, Herodotus went to Tyre, where he found two temples dedicated to him, the first of which was a great temple with rich dedications, while the second belonged to Heracles of Thasos. The Tyrian "Heracles" was the Phoenician Ba'al, worshipped as Eshmun at Sidon and Melqart at Tyre, where his temple, probably built by Hiram I in the tenth century B.C., was famous in antiquity, though archaeologists have found no trace of it. The other temple, of "Heracles Thasios," attests a lively and quite unhistorical belief among contemporary Greeks that the "Heracles" of Tyre and that of Thasos were the same. There must be another explanation for the two temples Herodotus saw, and perhaps the truth is that the great temple belonged to Melqart in the guise of Ba'al-Shamin, lord of the heavens, while the second belonged to the tutelary deity of Tyre, for whom the Tyrians built a temple whenever they founded a new colony.[16] They founded one on Thasos, Herodotus believed, for he thought that the Phoenicians had explored the Mediterranean long before the Greeks: five generations, in fact, before the birth of the Greek Heracles who was the ancestor of the Spartan royal families and stood at the head of the Spartan king lists (2.44.4). It was at this time that Heracles came from Tyre to Thasos.

All this tells more about Herodotus's historical model than strict history. He was a diffusionist: Egypt was the source of knowledge about the gods, whence it spread to other countries. The Phoenicians and the mysterious Pelasgians assisted in the diffusion. The Egyptians themselves did nothing to diminish their reputation for ancient wisdom. On the contrary. "Except for Poseidon and the Dioscuri, as I have said before, and Hera, Hestia, Themis, the Graces and the Nereids, the Egyptians have had the names of the gods in their country time out of mind. *I am telling what the Egyptians themselves say"* (2.50.2). He inquired about the oracles and learned a fantastic story: two black pigeons had flown from Thebes in Egypt to the Siwa oasis in Libya, and Dodona in Greece, and bidden the natives establish oracles (2.55). Religious festivals were also of Egyptian origin, and Herodotus (2.58) cites proof: festivals seemed to have a long history in Egypt, whereas in Greece their introduction was recent.

This diffusionist model was Greek, and Herodotus brought it with him when he came to Egypt. But everywhere he met Egyptian priests willing to collaborate with it. Did they resent his questions and deliberately mislead him?[17] There is nothing in the *History* to suggest that they did not speak to him willingly and even volubly, though they must have spoken through one of the hereditary caste of translators who interpreted not merely words into Greek but ideas too: a more treacherous operation. Egypt was under the Persian yoke, which was all the more galling because of her own brilliant past, and it must have flattered the damaged ego of the priests to have a foreigner approach them as avatars of ancient wisdom. The details of Herodotus's diffusionist model may have been strange to them, but they, too, were convinced of Egypt's primacy, and were happy to collaborate. The strange story of how two black pigeons from Amun's temple at Thebes founded oracles at Siwa and Dodona may have come from a quick-witted priest who responded to a leading question with courtesy, humor, and cooperation.

Having established the diffusionist model to his satisfaction, Herodotus continued with the strange customs to which the Egyptians were devoted. They kept to the *nomoi* of their ancestors, and eschewed new ones, from Greece or anywhere else. Resistance to foreign influence interested Herodotus; the Persians, he noted (1.135), were the most receptive nation, whereas the Scythians were the least (4.76.1). Some of Egypt's *nomoi* were unique, such as her animal cults that had grown in popularity under the twenty-sixth dynasty, and the practice of mummifying the dead. Yet, he found some parallels. Like the Lacedaemonians (but no other Greeks), young men showed respect for their elders (2.81.1), and in spite of Egyptian resistance to Greek *nomoi*, Herodotus claimed that he found a temple to Perseus, near Thebes (2.91). It probably belonged to Horus.

The section ends abruptly. The account thus far, he states, is based on his own observations, judgment, and inquiries. What follows rests on accounts received from the Egyptians, supplemented, however, by his observations. Whereupon he turns to the history of Egypt (2.99).

The History of Egypt

The Early Kings

The first king of Egypt was Min, who built a dyke to protect Memphis from the Nile flood. The priests who told Herodotus this were reading from a king-list (2.100.1) and such a list survives, the so-called Turin Canon, where one Meni appears as the first pharaoh. As for the dyke, one may have existed in Herodotus's day, but we can hardly date it back to Min.[18] Next came 330 rulers, including one queen, Nitocris, homonymous with the Babylonian Nitocris. Herodotus has a lively tale to tell of how she took murderous revenge on her subjects because they slew her brother who ruled before her, and then killed herself so that she could not be punished for her crimes. But by and large, this was not a memorable group, and Herodotus moves on to Sesostris, a fabulous conqueror made up of traditions about several pharaohs who made foreign conquests, notably Thutmose III of the Eighteenth Dynasty, and Ramses II in the Nineteenth.[19] Next came Sesostris's son, Pheros, whose name is too close to "pharaoh" for accident. Next was the king known to the Greeks as Proteus, with whom Herodotus can connect Helen of Troy, for according to one version of the myth, apparently invented by Stesichorus, Paris and Helen came to Egypt on their way from Sparta to Troy, and Proteus detained Helen there. Paris took merely a wraith of Helen to Troy while the real Helen remained in Egypt. Herodotus asked the priests about this myth, and they obliged with a version of their own, in which the pharaoh Proteus was the very model of a just king. Or was the story shaped by a couple generations of interpeters, who knew what their Greek customers wanted?

Proteus's successor was Rhampsinitus, and about him Herodotus tells a folktale that has found its way into oral tradition across Europe and Asia, from Iceland to the Philippines. Rhampsinitus built a treasury, but the architect left a stone loose so that it could be taken in and out, and before he died, he revealed the secret to his two sons, who set about pilfering the pharaoh's wealth. The pharaoh set a trap, one son was caught, but the other cut off his brother's head so that he could not be identified, and when the pharaoh hanged the headless corpse, the thief outwitted the guards and recovered it. Then the king sent his daughter to a brothel, and told her to ask every man who slept with her to relate his wickedest exploit. When the thief came, he told how he had cut off his brother's head, and when she attempted to take hold of him, he gave her his brother's arm, which he had brought with him, and she clasped it, thinking she had secured the thief. Finally, the pharaoh so admired the clever thief that he gave him his daughter to marry.[20] Both Greeks and Egyptians admired sharp wits.

Then came the pyramid-builders, hopelessly misdated.[21] The Great Pyramid at Giza was built by Cheops (Khufu) whose reputation was black; his brother Chephren (Khafre) built the second pyramid, and the small pyramid belonged to Mycerinus (Menkaure), though Herodotus had heard, but disbelieved, a Greek tale that its builder was the courtesan of Naucratis, Rhodopis, whom Sappho's brother, Charaxus, loved. The tale may be based on legends surrounding the transition from the Fourth to the Fifth Dynasties where the connecting link was a queen whose tomb was built at Giza, for Manetho, the priest of Heliopolis who wrote a history of Egypt in Greek for the Hellenistic world, made the builder of the small pyramid the fair-skinned queen Nitocris.[22] Among the Greeks, the legend attached itself to the famous Rhodopis (*rosy complexion*), but Herodotus knew that she lived long after the pyramid builders.

After the pyramid builders came two kings we cannot identify, Asychis (Bokenranef, the Greek Bocchoris?) and a blind man, Anysis. Then the Ethiopian King Sabacos (Shabaka, 712–700 B.C.) invaded Egypt, and the blind pharaoh fled to the marshes, where he survived for fifty years on an island made of ashes, until Sabacos, warned in a dream, retired to Ethiopia. The island was found and reused in Herodotus's day by Amyrtaeus, one of the leaders of the mid-fifth-century revolt against Persia. The historical Shabaka united Egypt under him, but he supported a revolt of Judah and Sidon against Sennacherib, king of Assyria, and lost, after which he disappears from history.

After the blind pharaoh, there ruled a priest of Hephaestos called Sethos; the name probably comes from the Egyptian *Seti,* but we cannot identify either the pharaoh or the tale that Herodotus puts in his reign, though it does have a parallel in the Bible and is perhaps based on an historical incident.[23] Sennacherib invaded Egypt, but at Pelusium a swarm of mice overran his camp, devouring quivers, bows and shield handles, and leaving the Assyrian host defenseless. The tale was pious legend when Herodotus heard it, but it may have been based on some unrecorded defeat of Sennacherib, or his successor, Esarhaddon, who actually did invade Egypt. Herodotus reports that there was a statue of Sethos to be seen in the temple of Hephaestos; in his hand was a mouse, and the inscription read, "Whoever looks on me, let him fear the gods" (2.147.6).

The statue may have contributed to the development of the tale. It no doubt represented Horus, to whom the mouse was sacred,[24] and the story has the flavor of a cicerone's tale elaborated for Greeks, curious about this exotic representation. But the kernel of truth at its core is impossible to recover.

In conclusion, Herodotus returns to the beginning of Egyptian history. Like the Greeks, the Egyptians thought there was a time when the gods lived on earth. But the Greeks counted back only a few generations to the gods. Herodotus relates a story that he no doubt found in the writings of Hecataeus of Miletus: Hecataeus had visited Thebes, and for the edification of the priests there, traced back his own descent to a god in a mere sixteen generations. The priests took him into the temple and showed him statues of three hundred and forty-five high priests of Amun, all in succession and none a god or hero. The point of the tale is that Egypt's historical past was vast, and hence it was there that the earliest and truest knowledge of the gods could be found.

The Later Kings

Herodotus resumes his history of Egypt with the remark that what he has written hitherto was based on Egyptian tradition; now he can supplement this with the accounts of others and with his own observations (2.147). He has reached the last Egyptian dynasty before the Persian invasion: the twenty-sixth. He knew nothing about the Assyrian invasions of Esarhaddon and Assurbanipal, nor anything about the Assyrian period, except for the tale of Sennacherib's abortive attack. All this had been edited out of the "history" that the priests told Herodotus. The historical Psammetichus, who founded the twenty-sixth dynasty, began as an Assyrian vassal, but the story Herodotus received told that he was one of twelve kings who agreed to rule Egypt, and that he made himself pharaoh (this, at least, is probably true) with the help of "bronze men from the sea": Ionian and Carian mercenaries. The twelve kings were supposed to have left the Labyrinth as a memorial, and this structure Herodotus (2.148) locates "a bit above the lake of Moeris," in present-day *Faiyûm mudiriyeh*.[25] It existed intact in his day, though practically nothing remains now, for it served as a stone quarry from late Roman times until early in this century, when the last of its superstructure was removed to build a railway. It was, at least in part, a mortuary temple connected with the pyramid of the twelfth dynasty pharaoh, Amme- nemes III, the Moeris of Herodotus, and the story connecting it with the "twelve kings" has removed it from the Middle Kingdom and dated it nearly one and a half millenia too late. However, some of Herodotus's information seems to have come from the attendants at the Labyrinth, who took him through the rooms above ground, but refused to show him the underground chambers, because there lay the bodies of the twelve kings, and the sacred crocodiles, for the crocodile, *Sobk,* was the god of the Faiyûm.

Beside the Labyrinth was the "so-called Lake of Moeris," which Herodotus thought was artificially made, though he noted truthfully that he could not see the earth that had been excavated. Such a lake did exist in Herodotus's day, although the depression in which it lay was natural, and though Herodotus has exaggerated its size, there is no reason to doubt that he stood on its shores and asked some shrewd questions.[26] Ptolemaic irrigation engineering reduced its size even further, and all that remains now is the small, salt-water Birket el-Qarun in the northwest corner of the Faiyûm.

With the twenty-sixth dynasty, Herodotus's sources are more secure. He was no longer dependent on stories of the priests. Psammetichus's line continued until Apries, who faced a revolt led by Amasis. It was a nationalist reaction to the pharaoh's use of foreign mercenaries and his neglect of the Egyptian warrior class; however, the Greeks remembered Amasis as a friend, who gave them Naucratis as a trading post where they might settle. Herodotus was told that in his reign, Egypt reached its acme of prosperity (2.177.1). He made an alliance with Cyrene and married a Cyrenaean princess; Polycrates, the tyrant of Samos, was his *xenos* ("guest-friend"), and he conquered Cyprus and made it pay tribute. He was also the pharaoh whom Persia prepared to attack.

Chapter Four

The Growth of Empire

The Conquest of Egypt

Herodotus began his long excursus on Egypt by announcing Cambyses' intention to invade, and he concludes it by returning to the same point. "Against this Amasis, Cambyses son of Cyrus, made an expedition . . ." The blame lay at Amasis's door. Cambyses had wanted to add the pharaoh's daughter to his harem, and asked for her, whereupon Amasis sent the daughter of Apries instead. The girl revealed the trick to Cambyses, who took it as an insult. Herodotus identified the story as Persian; the Egyptian version claimed that Apries' daughter married Cyrus and Cambyses was her son.

Herodotus rejected the Egyptian story, for if Cambyses were the son of Apries' daughter, he could not have been legitimate, and the Persian royal line laid stress on legitimacy. It was a shrewd point, though it does appear that Cambyses regarded himself as Egypt's legitimate king, and treated Amasis as a usurper, whose corpse (he died just before the invasion) he ordered scourged and mutilated.[1] There was a third story too, which Herodotus rejected: that Cambyses invaded Egypt to avenge his mother Cassandane whom Cyrus neglected for his Egyptian princess.

About the invasion, Herodotus knew a tale that he may have learned as a boy. One of Amasis's mercenaries was a Halicarnassian named Phanes, who deserted to Cambyses and advised him to make the Arabs his allies and have them supply his army with water for crossing the Sinai desert. Thus the Persians reached Pelusium safely, where Amasis's son and successor, Psammetichus II, awaited them. The Greek and Carian soldiers in Psammetichus's army repaid Phanes by taking his sons into the front battle line, slitting their throats in full view of the Persians, and Phanes himself, and mixing the blood with wine and drinking it. Then the battle began, which ended in Egyptian defeat. Herodotus saw the battlefield, and though three quarters of a century had passed, he claimed that the bones of the Persians and Egyptians still lay in two piles where the opposing lines had been drawn up.

The Egyptians fled to Memphis which capitulated after a brief siege, and the rest of Egypt submitted. But Cambyses' appetite for conquest was not satisfied. He planned further expeditions: one by sea against Carthage, and two by land, one against the Ammonians at the Siwa oasis and the other against the "long-lived" Ethiopians to the south. Herodotus had already described the route up the Nile to Ethiopia, and given the name of the Ethiopian capital, Meroe, the first ancient writer to do so.[2] Here he goes on to describe the fabulous Table of the Sun at Meroe: a meadow stacked every day with cooked meat, where anyone could go and feast. The reference may be to the "Temple of the Sun" (so identified by its excavator) which was built early in the sixth century B.C., a short distance outside Meroe, but Herodotus's description was based on tales that were already half legendary.[3] Cambyses sent envoys there with gifts for the Ethiopian king, but the king recognized the envoys for what they were: spies. He gave them a great bow, saying that when the Persians could draw one of such a size as easily as he, then let them attack the Ethiopians. But he also showed them the wonders of Ethiopia, including a fountain of life, and when the spies brought their report back to Cambyses, he was filled with a mad desire to invade. He started out, but soon ran out of supplies, and when his army was at last reduced to cannibalism, he turned back.

A stranger fate befell the Persian detachment sent against Siwa. The force reached the El Khargeh oasis, where Herodotus claims there was a settlement of Greeks from Samos; the story is without proof, but it may be true, for Samos was one of the first Greek states to interest itself in Egypt.[4] From El Khargeh, the Persians headed over the desert to Siwa, but half way there, they were overwhelmed by a sandstorm. This was the story that the Ammonians at the Siwa oasis told, and it received confirmation in 1977, when an Egyptian archaeological team uncovered thousands of bones, together with Persian swords and spears, at the foot of the Abu Balassa in a region near Siwa known as the "sea of sand."

The naval expedition against Carthage never set sail. Carthage was a colony of Tyre, and still sent offerings to the Tyrian Heracles.[5] The Phoenician cities had submitted to Cyrus after the capture of Babylon, but it was a voluntary submission; they would not take part in an attack on a daughter city, and since they supplied the backbone of the Persian fleet, Cambyses abandoned the project.

It was after these unsuccessful projects that Cambyses began to show symptoms of madness, although Herodotus (3.30.1) noted that he was not fully sane earlier. When Cambyses returned to Memphis, he found a festival in progress, for a new Apis bull had been found, but Cambyses' paranoiac mind imagined that the Egyptians were celebrating his failure against Ethiopia. When he was shown the bull, he stabbed it in the thigh, so that it died, and he had the priests scourged. There followed other acts of madness; the first, which was to have far-reaching consequences, was the murder of his brother Smerdis. The theme of Cambyses' insanity ends the story of the Persian conquest of Egypt. "To me it is completely clear that Cambyses was utterly mad," Herodotus wrote, "Otherwise he would never have ridiculed shrines nor religious customs. For if someone were to propose to each man to choose the best customs of all that are, he would look them over and choose his own" (3.38.1).

The tradition of Cambyses' sacrilege and madness was taken as fact by the time Herodotus visited Egypt. A century after the conquest, the Jewish settlement at Elephantine recalled it: when Cambyses took Egypt, the Persians "knocked down all the temples of the gods of Egypt," but they left the Jewish temple intact.[6] Contemporary evidence, as far as we can recover it, reveals something different. One important clue is a naophoros statuette found in Hadrian's villa at Tivoli; it shows one Udjahorresne, admiral of the Egyptian fleet who had gone over to Cambyses and become his physician and companion, and who remained an important collaborator under Darius. Udjahorresne is not an impartial witness. But for what it is worth, this shrewd trimmer records favors that Cambyses did for the temple of Neith at Sais, and it is a fact that Cambyses adopted the titles of Egyptian royal protocol and tried to present himself as a true pharaoh of Egypt.[7]

As for the tradition that Cambyses slew the Apis bull, it is at variance with the evidence of a gravestone in the Louvre bearing the Apis bull's epitaph, and dating to 524 B.C. Herodotus never denied that the bull was buried, but the stone shows Cambyses in an attitude of devotion which would be out of place if Herodotus's story of a secret burial is well-founded. Moreover, the sarcophagus of this bull bears an inscription stating that Cambyses gave and dedicated it.[8] So much for Cambyses' impiety.

But not quite, for we also have the epitaph of the next Apis bull, which should have been born when its predecessor died. There could not be two bulls at the same time. But this second Apis, buried under Darius, was born fifteen months before the funeral of its predecessor. Something is out of place, though at this date, it is impossible to say what it was. After Cambyses' return from Ethiopia, he put down an uprising led by Psammetichus II, whose life he had spared, and the delay in burying the Apis bull may be connected with this revolt. Yet, the mad, impious Cambyses was in large part a myth of the Egyptian priests, who had grown rich under the twenty-sixth dynasty and saw their revenues curtailed under the Persians. No one had any interest in championing Cambyses' reputation after his death. Not the kings who succeeded him, for they belonged to a different branch of the Achaemenids. Not the Egyptians, for whom Persian rule grew increasingly oppressive. And certainly not the Greeks.

Cambyses' first insane act was to dispatch Prexaspes to kill his brother, Smerdis, for he had dreamed that a messenger came to announce that Smerdis was king. Then he slew his sister, who reproached him with Smerdis's death; thus far, there is no hint that the murder was secret. Then he committed other outrages, among them the murder of Prexaspes' son. Croesus tried to remonstrate. The fallen king of Lydia, playing the wise advisor, makes his last appearance, and nearly loses his life. Cambyses ordered Croesus killed, but his courtiers saved him, thereby losing their own lives, for though Cambyses repented of his command, he was not prepared to forgive his courtiers for disobeying it. Mad, Cambyses assumed the exaggerated persona of an Oriental despot, and by his whim, Croesus lived on and the men who saved him died.

The First Samian Story: The Luck of Polycrates

The bulk of Herodotus's third book tells how Cambyses took Egypt and Darius succeeded him as king, but three times he interjects excerpts of Samian history, like panels inserted into a larger diorama. The first is introduced with the excuse of synchronism: "While

Cambyses was invading Egypt, the Lacedaemonians too made an expedition against Samos" (3.39.1), and to conclude the digression, Herodotus offers a defense for treating Samos in such detail: "I have dwelt at length on Samos, because they have done the three greatest works of all the Greeks" (3.60.1).

But there is some logic to the plan. Herodotus's general theme is Persian expansionism, and while Cambyses was conquering Egypt, and Darius consolidating his position, Persia impinged on the Greek world only once. During this time, she installed a puppet tyrant on Samos. Moreover, Samos had a claim to fame for three great engineering works: an aqueduct designed by Eupalinus of Megara, a harbor mole, and the great temple of Hera "whose first architect was a native son, Rhoecus son of Philes." In fact, Rhoecus's temple had burned down long before Herodotus's day, and the structure built to replace it was unfinished. Just as Herodotus preferred to describe Babylon as it was when Cyrus captured it, he presents the Hera temple as he imagined it, intact, in the time of Polycrates, the magnificent tyrant of Samos.[9]

Early Samian history followed a pattern familiar in other Greek states: a landowning aristocracy squeezed out a hereditary monarchy in the early archaic period, and fell in turn to a *coup d'état* about 600 B.C.[10] In the following years, Samos had several tyrants; lack of evidence makes reconstruction tentative, but Polycrates' family wielded substantial power, and possibly Polycrates' father was tyrant before he was. In the 540s, Persia gobbled up the Greek mainland states, whereupon, according to Herodotus (1.169.2), the offshore islands hastened to submit, although Thucydides (1.13.6) indicates that they put up resistance. The Persian conquest ended the seapower of one of Samos's rivals, Phocaea, but another rival, Miletus, fared better, for she came to terms voluntarily with the Persians. At Samos, Persian rule was felt lightly, for there was no regular tribute before Darius; instead subjects sent "gifts" to the king, the value of which varied, no doubt, in proportion to the danger of Persian intervention (3.89.3). The king could demand military aid too, and Cambyses did ask Polycrates to contribute a contingent to the fleet that he mustered against Egypt. Herodotus (3.44.1–2) reports that Polycrates sent heralds to Cambyses to invite him to make the demand, but the heralds were probably taking Polycrates' gifts to the king, and the king's demand was quite in order. Polycrates seems not to have broken with Persia before Cambyses' death, nor did he follow a consistent anti-Persian policy. He was, on Herodotus's showing, simply an immensely successful pirate chief whose luck ran out at last.

Polycrates' two brothers helped him in the *coup* by which he seized power, but once established, he killed the one and exiled the other, Syloson, who went off to join the Persian army. Polycrates made a treaty of friendship with the pharaoh Amasis, and on that hangs a folktale: the story of Polycrates' ring.[11] Alarmed at Polycrates' consistent good fortune, Amasis wrote Polycrates to warn of the jealousy of the gods, and to counsel him to inflict some loss upon himself. Polycrates thought the advice sound, and ordered a valuable ring to be thrown into the sea. But a few days later, a fisherman came to present Polycrates with a fine fish, and in its belly was the ring. Whereupon Amasis knew Polycrates was destined for a bad end, and revoked his treaty with him, for he did not want to mourn the fall of a friend. The story indicates that Amasis took the initiative in breaking off the friendship, and it may be right, for Polycrates had become an embarrassing ally. He was, perhaps, preying on those Greek cities where Amasis needed to recruit mercenaries against the impending Persian invasion.[12]

When Polycrates received Cambyses' demand for a naval contribution to his expedition against Egypt, he manned forty ships with his enemies and dispatched them to the king, asking him not to return them. Traditions differed about what happened next. But in any case, the Samian exiles came to Sparta to ask for help to attack Polycrates, and the Spartans gave it.

From this point on, Herodotus had at least two sources for his story, one Samian, and another Spartan; indeed Herodotus names his Spartan informant, Archias, whose grandfather of the same name fought at Samos against Polycrates. Possibly too, at Corinth or Corcyra, Herodotus learned that Corinth had supported the attack on Samos, and why. The Samians had intervened much earlier between Corinth and her erstwhile colony and present enemy, Corcyra, when Periander was Corinth's tyrant, and here Herodotus pauses for a story within a story. He tells how the Corcyraeans slew Periander's son, and Periander took vengeance by seizing the sons of Corcyraean nobles and sending them to Lydia to be made eunuchs. But the Samians saved the boys, and now Corinth was anxious to retaliate. But their support for the expedition must have been largely moral, for Herodotus mentions no Corinthian participants.

The expedition failed. Herodotus dismisses a story he heard that Polycrates bought off the Spartans with coins of lead covered with a gold wash, but his skepticism may be too great, for five coins have survived from this time, four with a lead core and the fifth with copper, and plated, not with gold but electrum.[13] The Samian exiles had to depart. First they plundered Siphnos in the Cyclades, a rich prey, for her gold and silver mines were not yet exhausted. Then they moved to Hydrea (Idhra) and thence to Crete, where they prospered briefly until the Aiginetans enslaved them, alleging an ancient wrong as justification.

The Accession of Darius, and his Empire

The narrative switches abruptly back to Persia (3.61), to the revolt of Smerdis, and Cambyses' death, and goes on to tell how Darius became king. Then comes the presentation of the Great King's realm, for he made his power felt everywhere (3.88.3). The Persians called Darius a shopkeeper, for he organized the empire into satrapies, and assigned each assessments of tribute instead of the "gifts" that the king's subjects had paid in the past. From the empire, Herodotus moves easily into a digression on the wonders of the remote parts of the world, which "surround the other countries and enclose them" (3.116.3). Finally, we have two brief stories as pendants to the whole, before returning to the vicissitudes of Polycrates. Both illustrate the Great King's power: the first tells how he built a reservoir to control the water supply in central Iran, in the basin of an unidentifiable river called the *Akes*,[14] and the second relates the death of Intaphrenes, one of the seven conspirators that overthrew Smerdis. Intaphrenes brings the section back to Smerdis's revolt, closes off the ring-cycle, and concludes the section.

The Usurpation of Smerdis

As it happens, we have an official version of Smerdis's revolt, promulgated by Darius himself, and inscribed in three languages on the rock face of Behistun, high above the main highway between Iran and Babylon. Herodotus could not have read it, for it was inaccessible, though impressive, but it was translated in the imperial chancery and copies circulated through the empire, and it is more than possible that a copy reached Ionia, for though Herodotus's narrative has been assimilated to folktale motifs, the outlines of the official version are recognizable. Herodotus speaks of two conspirators: Smerdis and his brother Patizeithes whereas Darius mentions only one, the *magus* Gaumata, who claimed to be Cambyses' full brother, Bardiya. Both Herodotus and the Behistun inscription name seven conspirators who slew the usurper, and with one possible exception, the names tally.[15] However, the inscription does indicate, as Herodotus does not, that after Darius slew the usurper, he had to face a general revolt, which he claimed to have suppressed within the year.[16] An historian need not be overly suspicious to wonder if Darius's Gaumata was not, in fact, who he claimed to be: Bardiya, the brother of Cambyses. The Behistun inscription is propaganda, and Darius's Gaumata, the false Smerdis of Herodotus, was created to justify Darius's own usurpation.

Herodotus had left Cambyses bordering on madness. Word came that his brother Smerdis had revolted. The *magus* Patizeithes had been left in charge of the royal household, and he had a brother who not only looked like the brother whom Cambyses had killed, but had the same name: Smerdis. On this identity of name hinged Cambyses' recognition of the truth and his own folly, for when he interrogated Prexaspes to discover if he had carried out the order to kill his brother, Prexaspes had only to suggest that Patizeithes and Smerdis were the rebels, and Cambyses divined the truth. His dream that Smerdis would be king had come true. A Smerdis was king, but it was another Smerdis.[17]

Thereupon Cambyses leaped on his horse, intending to lead an immediate attack on pseudo-Smerdis, and accidentally cut open his thigh with his sword, "in the same place where he had himself earlier smitten the Egyptian god Apis" (3.64.3). Then he asked the name of the place where he was, and was told it was Ecbatana. This final coincidence overwhelmed Cambyses, for an oracle had foretold his death in Ecbatana, which he had imagined was the Median capital. All unknown to him, Fate had dogged his footsteps, and now moved in for the kill.

Still there remained the usurper. On his death bed, Cambyses summoned the Persian nobles and revealed that he had killed his brother and the Smerdis on the throne was a pretender; the revolt was an attempt by the Medes to recover their hegemony in Asia. The nobles wept with their king, but they did not believe him. When Cambyses died, they accepted pseudo-Smerdis, and Prexaspes, who now feared for his life, denied that he had killed Cambyses' brother. Cambyses ruled for seven years, five months, and pseudo-Smerdis filled out Cambyses' eighth year before he was found out. He was a benevolent ruler, greatly missed by all his subjects, except the Persians themselves.

The story of how the *magus* was unmasked proceeds with folktale logic. One noble, Otanes, himself a scion of the royal house, grew suspicious, and he had an agent able to test his surmise, for his daughter had been Cambyses' wife and had passed on to pseudo-Smerdis along with the rest of the harem. Otanes knew that Cyrus had cut off the ears of Smerdis the *magus* for some crime, and now he asked his daughter to discover if her husband had any ears. The girl waited for her turn to share the the *magus*'s bed, and as he slept, she felt his head and found no ears. The truth was out. Otanes put together a plot, that Darius was the last to join. The conspirators decided to act immediately, but while they debated, coincidence intervened: the *magi* decided to have Prexaspes proclaim the legitimacy of pseudo-Smerdis from a high tower. However, Prexaspes chose to reveal the truth, and then leaped from the tower to his death. When the conspirators, ignorant of Prexaspes' act, made their way into the palace, the eunuchs were alarmed and tried to detain them, but they cut their way in, and it was Darius who drove his dagger into the false Smerdis. When the Persians discovered the truth about the Magian Revolt, they slew every *magus* they could find, and the anniversary of this mass murder became the festival known as the *Magophonia*, when *magi* avoided appearing on the streets. The tale may be based on an actual massacre, but there is no evidence of a festival to commemorate it, and it is not clear where Herodotus found his information about it.[18]

The Choosing of the King

Five days after the assassination, the conspirators met to discuss the succession. They decided to continue the monarchy and to recognize as king whichever conspirator of the six (Otanes withdrew from the contest) whose horse neighed first after sunrise. Darius consulted his groom, who devised a strategem to make his master's horse neigh. So Darius became king, and like Deioces, first king of the Medes, he owed his throne to a trick.

However, the first act in this process of carrying on the empire is a remarkable debate on the forms of government among three of the conspirators, Megabyzus, Otanes, and Darius. Herodotus believed that such a debate had taken place (it is clear that not all his contemporaries agreed) and some sort of debate may have, in fact, occurred, for Darius's hereditary claims to the throne were weak and, in addition, the death of Cambyses without an heir may have provoked a reaction against the monarchy among the Persian nobility, for Cambyses had curtailed their prerogatives.[19] Herodotus probably based his debate on some incident that did take place. But the debate he produces is his own composition, that uses ideas belonging to the thought-world of contemporary Greece. The idea of dividing government forms into three types—democracy, oligarchy, and monarchy—had been in the air earlier, but here for the first, the division is explicit.[20] The political concepts voiced in the debate are borrowed from the sophists, particularly Protagoras,[21] but the composition is Herodotus's own, and one of his motives for it (not, perhaps, the only one) was to tease his culture-bound Greek audience. Here were barbarians discussing the latest ideas of political science long before the Greeks thought of such matters!

Otanes led off, arguing for rule by the people. Democracy. Herodotus rarely uses the term *demokratia*, and he does not allow Otanes to use it here, but it is what he means. Moreover, it is a democracy like that of Athens, where offices were filled by magistrates held responsible for their conduct and issues were decided by public debate. But most of Otanes' speech is directed against monarchy, which he contrasts with democracy, and the nub of his argument is that the absolute ruler is corrupted by power and puts himself above the law. Otanes' monarch is the tyrant of Greek tradition, and his characteristics, particularly his lust, and disregard for established customs, remained remarkably stable up to the age of Justinian, when Procopius painted the emperor with similar colors in his *Secret History*.

Next Megabyzus spoke against democracy, and in favor of oligarchy. Kings, he agreed, might well rule badly, but at least their rule was rational, whereas the mob's actions were governed by caprice and ignorance. The Persians should choose a company of the best men and let them rule, for one would expect the best men to produce the best policies.

Darius spoke last for monarchy, but his monarch was an ideal king, quite unlike the tyrant of Otanes. In oligarchy, competition for distinctions among the oligarchs led to schism and eventually civil strife, until the only solution was rule by one man. In addition, Darius had a final argument that was, I suspect, Herodotus's own: monarchy was the ancestral constitution of Persia. Persia had won liberty under monarchy; why change now?

The debate hinges on a series of simple contrasts that rebut each other. In a monarchy, one man is above the law, whereas the distinguishing mark of democracy is equality before the law (*isonomia*). Megabyzus gives the opposite side of the coin: in a democracy, power resides with the people who lack knowledge and judgment, whereas in an oligarchy, the best people will govern best. Darius, however, introduces the concept of political evolution: oligarchies generate internal strife and as a result, evolve into monarchy. There is a hint of a parallel argument in Otanes' description of a tyrant: power corrupts the monarch and eventually corruption rots the monarchy itself. Herodotus's types of government are in a state of flux.[22] The arguments cancel each other, and in the end, Darius won by an emotional appeal to the ancestral customs of Persia. Monarchy and the Persian Empire went together. The rest of the conspirators agreed.

The Dominion of Darius

Herodotus knew nothing about the revolts that Darius had to suppress in order to secure his throne. But he did know that Darius reformed the administration of the empire, and he attributed to him a system of satrapies, each with a tribute quota. There were twenty of them, starting in the west with the first satrapy of the Ionians and their neighbors, and ending with India in the east. We have seven inscriptions giving "satrapy lists," including that of Behistun, and none can be quite correlated with Herodotus's roster, but that need not discredit him, for the lists that the Great Kings put on their monuments may not be administrative documents, but merely catalogs of subject peoples.[23] Hence attempts to reconcile the monuments with Herodotus's satrapy list are likely to be unproductive. The ultimate source of Herodotus's information may not have been an administrative document either, but rather an eyewitness of the scene at Persepolis where the various peoples of the empire gathered at the time of the New Year's festival (probably in the spring) to pay homage and tribute to the king of kings. Persepolis was a ritual capital of sorts,[24] about which Greek sources are strangely quiet, but Greek artisans helped build it, and Ionians were among the subjects who brought tribute there. The assessments that Herodotus records are probably only estimates in Greek currency. But it may be more than coincidence that his list has the Ethiopians, who had no regular quota, pay two "quarts" of unrefined gold, twenty elephant tusks, and two hundred ebony logs, while on the reliefs showing subject peoples bringing tribute, on the East Staircase of the Audience Hall (Apadana) at Persepolis, the Ethiopians carry an elephant tusk and a vase, perhaps filled with gold.

Gold takes Herodotus from the revenues of Persia to a fabulous account of the sources of gold. In India, it was mined by giant ants, who protected it fiercely; the Indians who stole it filled their saddlebags and rode for their lives, for the ants gave hot pursuit. Remote parts of the world produced the most splendid things, Herodotus (3.106.1) observes, whereas Greece had the most temperate climate, and with this remark, that implies a sort of balancing mechanism in nature, he passes on to describe other items, equally fabulous, from the world's far corners. This is a fascinating section that mingles fiction with a good deal of fact. But it is only a pendant to the description of Darius's empire.

The Death of Intaphrenes

The folktale that relates the death of Intaphrenes concludes Darius's accession. Darius suspected one of the seven conspirators, Intaphrenes, of plotting against him, and imprisoned him, his children, and relations. But he was moved to pity by the weeping of Intaphrenes' wife, and promised her the life of one prisoner. She chose her brother.

She could get another husband and children, she explained, but never another brother.

Since the motif has an echo in Sophocles' *Antigone*, produced in 443[25] or 442 B.C., the whole account of Darius's accession may have been written and recited in Athens shortly before Herodotus left for Thurii. For the tale of Intaphrenes is an integral part of the accession story. It means that Darius is now master and the confederates who helped him to the throne are his subjects. "Of the seven, one died forthwith in the manner I have told," Herodotus sums up, and with that he returns to the history of Samos.

The Death of Polycrates

As Herodotus picks up the thread of Samian history, he moves backward to the point where he had dropped the subject. "At about the time of Cambyses' illness, this happened" (3.120.1): with that, Herodotus concludes the story of Polycrates' ring by telling how he died. Oroetes, the satrap of Sardis, determined to slay him. Herodotus had two accounts of Oroetes' motive; the one that "most people" told, had it that Oroetes' rival, who governed the northern (Phrygian) satrapy, had taunted Oroetes with failing to take Samos. However, Herodotus leaves us with the impression that Polycrates' ambition to rule the sea had something to do with his removal. For Oroetes sent a Lydian to Polycrates with the message that he was planning to rebel, and if Polycrates joined him, he would pay him well. Polycrates loved money. He sent his secretary, Maeandrius, to investigate, but Maeandrius was deceived by a simple trick, and returned with exaggerated reports of Oroetes' wealth.

Polycrates determined to go to Sardis himself. Cassandra-like, his daughter tried to dissuade him, for she had dreamed she saw her father hanging in the air, washed by Zeus, and anointed by Helios. But Polycrates rushed on blindly to his doom. For Oroetes had him killed and his body hung on a cross, so that he was washed by the rain of the sky-god, Zeus, and anointed by the sun, Helios. Thus the jealousy of the gods that Amasis had feared brought down Polycrates.

The Death of Oroetes and the Story of Democedes

Polycrates' death began a chain of events that culminated in Darius's first hostile move against Greece. One companion of Polycrates on his last voyage had been Democedes, a doctor from Croton in south Italy, and Oroetes enslaved him along with the other non-Samians in Polycrates' company; the Samians he let go free. After Cambyses' death, Oroetes did, in fact, rebel, and once Darius secured the throne, he put him to death and confiscated his property. Thus Democedes was taken as a slave to Susa.

It so happened that Darius injured his ankle one day in a hunting accident, and the Egyptian doctors who treated it only made it worse. The tale proceeds from coincidence to coincidence; nevertheless it may go back through several storytellers to Democedes himself, who was probably well remembered by the medical fraternity at Croton. A courtier recalled that he had heard of Democedes, and Darius ordered him fetched. He was found in chains, among Oroetes' slaves. He cured the king, and was richly rewarded, but now the king valued him too much to let him leave.

But soon there came a second chapter to the tale. Democedes cured Atossa the queen of an abscess on her breast, and in return, requested a favor. She was to suggest to Darius that he invade Greece, and that Democedes would be well-qualified to guide a reconnaissance mission there. Darius liked the suggestion, and thus the Crotoniate doctor led a Persian convoy of two warships, and a merchant vessel westward as far as Taras (Taranto) in south Italy. There he escaped. The Persians pursued him to Croton, but the Crotoniates would not let him be taken, and the Persians had to go back empty-handed. Thus through Democedes' initiative, Persia made her first imperialist gesture toward Greece.

The Subjugation of Samos

Persia took Samos soon after Polycrates' death. The Greeks perceived Polycrates (as do modern scholars) as an anti-Persian tyrant whose fleet secured his island against attack until Persia herself became a naval power in the eastern Mediterranean, but the Persians may have regarded him merely as a wayward vassal, and the subjugation of Samos after his death was only part of Darius's ordering of his empire. Herodotus, however, looked for a personal motive.

Polycrates' brother, Syloson, had met Darius in Egypt, and had done him a small favor. Once he heard that Darius was king, he rushed to Susa and asked a favor in return. He wanted Samos, for now that Polycrates was dead, it was ruled by Maeandrius.

Maeandrius had a talent for bringing disaster on those around him. He had been Polycrates' trusted secretary, whose naive assessment of Oroetes' wealth had lured Polycrates to his doom. After Polycrates' death, he found himself left in power, and his first impulse was to return sovereignty to the people and establish equality before the law. At once a leading Samian used the freedom that was offered to demand Maeandrius's accounts. Realizing that if he abandoned the tyranny, someone else would seize it, Maeandrius arrested the chief men of Samos and put them in chains, and shortly afterward, while Maeandrius was ill, his brother Lycaretus, later to reappear as Persian governor of Lemnos, put them to death.

Consequently, when a Persian force led by Otanes arrived to restore Syloson, the Samians were glad to have him back, and Maeandrius left the island, putting up no resistance himself. But his demented brother, Charilaus, armed soldiers—with Maeandrius's approval, Herodotus thought—caught some Persians by surprise and massacred them. Otanes took terrible revenge, and put to death every Samian man or boy he captured.

Greek tradition remembered Syloson as a harsh ruler and blamed him for the depopulation of the island.[26] But as Herodotus told the story, Syloson was blameless. When he asked Darius for Samos, he stipulated that no Samian should lose his life (3.141), and Darius passed on the stipulation to Otanes. It was only the treachery of Maeandrius and his brother's madness that brought on the catastrophe. Maeandrius himself went to Sparta and tried to bribe the king, Cleomenes, to help him. We do not know what he planned to do; a return to Samos was surely out of the question. But Cleomenes expelled him, and Maeandrius sailed away. His family had Persian connections, and his brother Lycaretus reappears in Persian service, all of which makes Herodotus's story of the massacre difficult to accept in all its details. The tradition that blamed Syloson for Samos' depopulation may merit greater credence than Herodotus gave it.

The Revolt of Babylon

After the subjugation of Samos came the revolt of Babylon, for which the Babylonians had begun to prepare under the reign of pseudo-Smerdis, and its suppression is the last chapter of the tale of how Darius consolidated his power. There were, in fact, two revolts of Babylon, the first belonging to the last three months of 522 B.C., and the second a year later;[27] Herodotus has combined them, and transformed the siege into a folktale telling of the heroism of Zopyrus, son of Megabyzus, who had been one of Darius's confederates in the plot against the *magus*. Zopyrus's grandson came to Athens in 441 B.C., after an abortive revolt against Artaxerxes I, and Herodotus may have interviewed him, but whatever his source, he has turned the siege of Babylon into a product of the storyteller's art.

The tale relates that the siege was in its twentieth month, when one of the mules in Zopyrus's pack train foaled, and Zopyrus, remembering a Babylonian saying that the city might be taken when mules had young, was convinced that Babylon was ripe to fall. He mutilated himself and appeared before Darius with a proposal: he would desert to Babylon, pretending that Darius had punished him horribly for advising an end of the siege. Then, when he had wormed his way into the confidence of the Babylonians, he would betray the city. The plan turned out as Zopyrus hoped, and at an agreed time, he opened two of Babylon's gates to the Persian army.

The motif is that of the Sinon legend that probably appeared in the lost *Little Iliad,* but the modern reader knows it best from Vergil's *Aeneid.*[28] Sinon, like Zopyrus, persuaded the Trojans that he was a bona fide deserter, and induced them to bring the wooden horse inside the city walls. Then, at night, he released the Greek warriors concealed in the horse. Long after Herodotus, the Roman historian Livy (1.53.4) used the same motif to tell how the Tarquins captured the Latin town of Gabii. It was, remarked Livy, an un-Roman trick. Darius felt no such scruples. He loaded Zopyrus with honors, freed him from taxes as long as he lived, and made him governor of Babylon (3.160.2).

Chapter Five

Persian Expansion into Europe

The Scythian Expedition of Darius

After Darius took Babylon, he made an expedition against Scythia, the date of which we put at 513 B.C. on the somewhat defective evidence of a Roman inscription, the "Capitoline chronicle."[1] Following the logic of his organization, Herodotus inserts a digression here on the Scyths. They had appeared earlier in the *History* (1.103–7) as invaders of Asia, whither they had pursued the Cimmerians, and by way of introduction, Herodotus refers back to this first mention of them here. But the plan of the *History* required that they be described not when they first appeared, but when the Persian appetite for empire impinged upon them. So Herodotus turns to the *nomoi* of the Scyths.

Scythian Nomoi

The section on Scythia is comparable to that on Egypt; both essays could stand by themselves, and both are based to some extent on Herodotus's own travels. The Scythian essay is a remarkable description of nomad life, unique in ancient literature, and to a great extent confirmed by archaeology. The story of the royal Scythian burial rites sounds like an eyewitness account—though the eyes need not have been Herodotus's own. Excavations of the Scythian tombs have corroborated the main points,[2] and even a detail that Herodotus did not understand: that, after the burial, the Scyths purified themselves in a sauna where they threw hemp seed on hot stones, howling with delight as they did so, was confirmed in 1952, when both hemp and hemp-burning equipment were found refrigerated in ice in Scythian barrows at Pazyryk in Siberia.

The essay starts with a fable of how the Scyths returned from their invasion of Asia, which they ruled for twenty-eight years, and found that their wives had mated with slaves, and a generation of young men had grown up in their absence to oppose their return. But the Scyths hit upon the happy idea of riding into battle with whips rather than spears and bows, whereupon the slave-born young men recalled their status and fled. It is a nice story that illustrates the tenet which Aristotle was later to propound: that slavery was natural, and thus the conduct befitting slaves was inherent in certain classes or races of people. Herodotus represents Darius's expedition as an act of vengeance: the Scyths had invaded Asia and hence Darius invaded Scythia.

Having thus introduced the Scyths, Herodotus proceeds, topic by topic. As with Egypt, the first subject is the antiquity of the nation, and next, the geography of Scythia.

Scythian origins

Herodotus has three tales about Scythian origins. The first (the Scythian version) is a legend with a motif of predestined election. In the reign of Targitaus, son of Zeus, a thousand years before Darius's expedition, gold objects fell from the heavens, and only the youngest of Targitaus's sons could pick them up. He became the progenitor of the Royal Scyths. The Greeks of the Black Sea had a myth connecting the Scyths with Heracles, who in Greek legend wandered all over the areas where the Greeks settled or traded, and left offspring behind. The third story, which Herodotus himself considered the most probable, told how the Scyths migrated across the Araxes (Volga) into Cimmerian territory, and the Cimmerians, instead of fighting the invaders, fought among themselves until all the royal clan was dead. Then the people buried them by the river Tyras (Dnester) and withdrew into Asia.[3]

More information came from a source which is now lost to us, except for a few fragments that are probably not genuine.[4] Aristeas of Proconnesus, Herodotus tells us, was a Greek who, inspired by Apollo, traveled as far into central Asia as the country of the Issedones, who told him that beyond them lived the one-eyed Arismaspians, and further still, griffins that guarded gold. Beyond the griffins were the Hyperboreans, Apollo-worshippers whose lands bordered the sea, and who had probably been the objective of Aristeas's journey.

Aristeas's story was a strange one, and his trip sounds more like a psychic journey of the soul than a genuine voyage of exploration. He fell down dead while in a shop in Proconnesus, but while the shopkeeper hurried off to inform his relatives, the body disappeared. Meanwhile, a man of Cyzicus arrived, who insisted that he had just met Aristeas on the road. Seven years later, Aristeas reappeared at Proconnesus, recited the *Arimaspeia,* a poem in hexameters, and again disappeared. Herodotus was familiar with the poem, as he was familiar with a good deal of literature that must be classed as the semioccult,[5] but many of his readers were not, for otherwise he would not have summarized the *Arimaspeia* as freely as he did. He also knew that two hundred and forty years (or *three* hundred and forty, according to a variant reading) after Aristeas vanished for the second time, he reappeared at Metapontum, Thurii's neighbor in south Italy. Herodotus may have seen in the marketplace there the statue of Aristeas, which this apparition had demanded.

The scraps of information that survive about the *Arismaspeia* indicate that it was soundly based, dimly understood as it is by us, and even by Herodotus himself.[6] Beyond the Scythians were the Sauromatae; beyond them were the Budini, probably a Finnish tribe, and next were the Thyssagetae and their neighbors, the Iyrcae, two tribes that lived by hunting. Aristeas pressed forward, heading into the north wind as he thought, but since the dominant cold wind on the Russian steppe is not northern but eastern, he may have been traveling in an easterly direction.[7] He reported another isolated tribe of Scyths, perhaps at the southern end of the Urals where Scythian tombs have been found. Then came the bald-headed Argippaei, probably Mongols, who drank cherry juice. Beyond them were the Issedones. As for the country beyond, Aristeas said honestly (he was no charlatan) that he knew it only by hearsay.

Hereupon Herodotus digresses, with the remark (4.30.1) that the plan of his *History* required digressions. He does not return to the Scyths until he has rambled over a number of topics. Mules could not be bred in Elis, which piqued Herodotus's interest in the effects of environment, but he knew no reason for this phenomenon. The Scyths reported that in the far north, the air was filled with feathers, which Herodotus thought were snowflakes. At last he reaches a major digression, on the Hyperboreans.

The Hyperboreans

The Hyperboreans were well-established in myth before Herodotus. They were Apollo-worshippers who inhabited a remote Utopia beyond Boreas, the north wind, and they cannot be dismissed as figments of imagination, for they sent offerings regularly to Delos, transshipping them along a route that went via Dodona to Carystos on Euboea, and from there directly to Delos. The offerings were wrapped in straw, and what they were is not known, though there have been modern attempts to connect the Hyperboreans with the Mycenaean amber trade from the Baltic to the Aegean and to make the offerings amber.[8]

Herodotus treats the legend with circumspection. He does not deny that Hyperboreans existed, although a Hyperborean Utopia with clement weather does not fit the principle he pronounced earlier: that the fringes of the world had splendid things but Greece had the fairest climate (3.106.1). But he remarks that if there were Hyperboreans in the north, there should be dwellers beyond the south wind (Hyperno-tians) in the south. The statement betrays Herodotus's perception of geography: the world was symmetrical with the northern half balancing the southern. On that note, Herodotus moves to his next digression.

Maps of the World

Herodotus (2.23) had already signaled his contempt for mapmakers who borrowed their geography from Homer; now he presents his own map. It was rectilinear and symmetrical to north and south, presumably along an undefined east-west axis.[9] Asia consisted of a body of land bounded to the north by the Black Sea and to the south by the Persian Gulf, and from it, running westward, were two promontories. One corresponded roughly to Asia Minor, the other Arabia, if we can imagine it as a rectangle of land with its long side running east-west, and terminating in the west with the Red Sea.

Egypt was a narrow neck of land that broadened into Libya, and Libya was circumnavigable. An Egyptian fleet manned by Phoenicians had sailed around it at the command of the twenty-sixth dynasty pharaoh, Necho. The voyage took two full years; twice the crew had replenished supplies by landing on the coast, planting grain and waiting to harvest it, and only in two areas of Africa would climatic conditions have allowed this: near the Cape of Good Hope and in the Maghreb.[10] One detail that Herodotus reported, but disbelieved, lends credence to the story. As the Phoenicians sailed around the Cape from the east, they saw the sun on their right. Herodotus, who knew nothing of the equator, could not credit this, but, in fact, mariners sailing from east to west around the Cape do have the sun on their right, and this detail shows that the story is more than fiction.

Asia had been explored by Scylax of Caryanda, a neighbor of Halicarnassus. Scylax had led a Persian expedition down the Indus River, coasted along the shores of Iran and Saudi Arabia, apparently missing the Persian Gulf, and had finally sailed up the Red Sea to Suez. The far eastern part of Asia remained unexplored, but Scylax had shown that the continent was in part circumnavigable, and Herodotus thought it must bear a general similarity to Libya.

Europe, however, was different. Its bulk filled the northern sector of the map, and its length matched that of Asia and Libya combined. No one knew if it was circumnavigable.

This is a diagram rather than a map, but from occasional references elsewhere in the *History,* we can flesh out details. The course of the Nile River in the south matched that of the Danube in the north, which rose among the Celts *west* of Gibraltar. A line drawn south from the mouth of the Danube would pass through Sinope on the south shore of the Black Sea, and eventually reach the Nile (2.33–34). Later (5.49) Herodotus mentions a map engraved on bronze that Aristagoras of Miletus brought to Sparta, but it seems to have been a route map, based on the Royal Road from Sardis to Susa. The diagram here is different. It should remind us that the *History* is played out in a world where the points of the compass do not exist as they do for us.

The Geography of Scythia

Herodotus moves from the general to the specific: from the world diagram to the geography of Scythia, and the contrast with its southern counterpart, Egypt, is implicit. The Scyths were nomads and hard to conquer, and their way of life suited their environment, for Scythia was a well-watered land, with rivers almost equaling Egypt's canals in number. On its border was the world's greatest river, the Danube, fed by many tributaries (unlike the Nile) and never varying its flow, summer or winter. The second largest river of Scythia was the Borysthenes (Dnepr); Herodotus knew it as far north as the land of Gerrhus, near modern Nikopol[11] between Kherson and Dnepropitrovsk, but he knew its source no better than he knew the Nile's, nor did any Greek (4.53.5). But not all of Herodotus's rivers are readily identifiable. Much of his knowledge was second- or thirdhand, and inexact.

Anthropology of the Scyths

It is particularly Herodotus's treatment of Scythian customs that has made his reputation as an anthropologist. His descriptions of Scythian sacrifices, soothsaying, and especially royal burial rites sound as if they were based on primary research. The section concludes with two tales that illustrate a trait which both Scyths and Egyptians shared: intolerance of foreign customs.

The first anecdote told of Anacharsis, a favorite barbarian of Greek storytellers, for he was included among the Seven Sages. Anacharsis had learned the rites of the Great Mother, Cybele, in Cyzicus, and tried to introduce them into Scythia. The Scythian king, who, as Herodotus interpreted the family tree, was Anacharsis's brother, learned of Anacharsis's activities and slew him. This was the simple truth behind the Anacharsis-legend, though the Peloponnesians had a different version.

There was a similar tale about the Scythian king, Scylas, who had received a Greek education as a youth. He maintained a house in Olbia, where he kept a Greek wife and lived as a Greek for brief periods. There he was observed participating in Dionysiac rites, and the Scyths rose in rebellion. Scylas fled to Thrace, but the Thracian king exchanged him for his own brother who had fled to Scythia, and Scylas was repatriated and slain.

The Scythian digression ends with two travelers' tales. The first was intended to show how numerous the Scyths were. Four days' sail up the Hypanis (Bug) River, at Exampaeus, (the name meant "Sacred Ways," as Herodotus [4.52.3] had already noted) stood a monument in the shape of a great bronze bowl, six fingers thick, that could hold 600 amphoras: about 5,000 gallons![12] Every Scyth, by royal order, had contributed a bronze arrowhead for the making of this bowl, and thus it was a measure of the Scythian population. The round number is suspicious; "six hundred," also used to define the size of the Persian fleet at Marathon, probably indicates merely indefinite and somewhat exaggerated bigness, but this story deserves greater credence than what follows. Heracles left a footprint in Scythia; the natives showed it to visitors on the banks of the Tyras (Dnester). This is a cicerone's tale, but even serious historians must divert their audience at times.

The Invasion of Scythia

As Herodotus (4.83–112) tells it, Darius's campaign against the Scyths parallels the campaign of his son, Xerxes, against Greece in 480 B.C. Darius's brother, Artabanus, advises against both ventures. In both, a subject asks that one of his sons be excused army service, and the king exacts a fearful penalty for the request. Both kings yoked Europe and Asia with a bridge. But these are preliminaries which Herodotus passes over swiftly; they foreshadow the expedition of 480 B.C. that is the climax of the *History,* and once Darius crosses into Europe, the parallels cease.

The king commanded the Ionians in his fleet to sail ahead to the Danube and bridge it, while he himself led his army overland through Thrace, conquering the various tribes that he encountered. The first were the Getae, who believed themselves immortal. When they died, they went to join Salmoxis, and indeed every five years they sacrificed a man chosen by lot to their god. The Greeks in the area had a story that connected Salmoxis with Pythagoras, but Herodotus could not vouch for the truth of it. In any case, the Getae were forced to join Darius's expedition.

Once across the Danube bridge, Darius ordered the Ionians to destroy it, and follow him into Scythia. Hereupon Coes, who commanded the contingent from Mytilene, suggested that the bridge be left intact, under guard. His speech was a masterpiece of tact, and the king heeded it, and left the Greek commanders, most of them vassal tyrants, to guard the bridge, but his orders were curious. The Greeks were to remain for sixty days, and if the king had not returned by then, they were free to go home. It is hard to imagine an experienced general marching into an unknown land, leaving orders to have his retreat cut off if he did not return within a fixed period! Darius set forth like a folktale hero, prescribing for himself victory or death. In the sequel, he avoided both.

Now, as Darius marched into Scythia, the Scythians tried to make alliances with their neighboring tribes, and these merited description. There were the Tauri, connected in Greek minds with the daughter of Agamemnon, Iphigeneia, and the Agathyrsi, who promoted the brotherhood of man by having wives in common, the Neuri who were werewolves, and the Man-Eaters who were complete savages. The Budini, who had grey eyes and red hair, and may have been Finnish, lived in a town built of timber that resembled the palisaded settlements of early Russian colonists in Siberia.[13] The Sauromatae were the Sarmatians, whom the Romans were to find occupying the Ukraine. They sprang from a union of Scyths and Amazon women, and their language was debased Scythian, for the Amazons never mastered the tongue of their husbands!

The Scyths sought help from these tribes, but they got a mixed response. Thereupon they planned a defense typical of nomad tactics of the steppe. With one division, they drew on the Persians as far as the river "Oarus" and then disappeared. Darius swung around and headed back for the Scythian heartland, where he met the other, larger division, that likewise retired before him. The tough Scythian horsemen on their steppe ponies outclassed the Persian cavalry, and the Persian infantry, which might have defeated them, could not get close enough. Darius could not counter these tactics, and supplies begàn to run low.

Herodotus's source here is exceptional. It shows an understanding of nomad tactics that would not come naturally to an Aegean Greek. It could also report that the remains of the eight forts which Darius began to build on the banks of the "Oaros" (4.123–24) still existed "in my day." Indeed, the "Oaros" itself is new; it may be the Volga, but elsewhere the Volga is called the Araxes. From this source, too, comes a strange story: Darius received a cryptic gift from the Scyths: a bird, a mouse, a frog, and five arrows. It was the Scythian way of telling the Persians they were doomed.

Thereupon Darius determined to break camp under cover of night and retreat swiftly to the Danube. The Scyths had already contacted the Ionians there, urging them to demolish the bridge, and they imagined that the Ionians agreed. But not so. The tyrants in command of their various contingents had discussed the matter, and Miltiades the Athenian, tyrant of the Thracian Chersonese, argued that they should leave Darius to his fate and so free themselves from Persian rule. But the tyrant of Miletus, Histiaeus, pointed out that the tyrants present—Herodotus lists them—owed their positions to Persia, for all their cities would prefer democracy to tyranny, and if Darius fell, so would they. So the Ionians decided to pretend agreement with the Scyths, but to remove only a part of the bridge and await developments.

Darius evaded the Scyths and reached the Danube safely. Histiaeus swiftly repaired the bridge and the Persians crossed, to the disgust of the Scyths, who henceforth considered the Ionians a slavish, cowardly lot. Darius then marched south to Sestos in the Chersonese, through Miltiades' territory, but we hear of no reprisals against him, which is odd if his treasonous counsel was known. From Sestos, Darius crossed to Asia, leaving a Persian noble, Megabazus, behind to command his forces in Europe.

The incident at the Danube bridge introduces two Greeks who are to play important roles in the *History*. Histiaeus was to ignite the Ionian Revolt that was the first link in a chain of events leading to Xerxes' invasion of Greece. Miltiades was to be the architect of victory at Marathon in 490 b.c.. Did the incident actually take place?[14] It is likely that it did, but equally likely that the tradition was colored by Miltiades' later career as an Athenian politician anxious to claim that he had never been a Persian collaborator, even though he may have taken part in the Scythian expedition as a vassal of Darius. These are questions we must defer. But let us note that the incident at the bridge has special relevance for Herodotus's great theme.

We cannot say the same for the *logos* that follows. It tells the story of a parallel thrust along the southern arm of Asia against Libya. Persian expansionism moved in a symmetrical pattern: while Darius operated in the northern sector of the map, in the south, another Persian force marched against Cyrene, and was no more successful. The expedition, however, provides an occasion for a digression on Libya.

The Libyan Logos

The *logos* begins abruptly (4.145). Herodotus notes that the Libyan campaign coincided with that against the Scyths, and forthwith launches into a story that is structurally independent and neatly rounded. First there is an account of how Cyrene's history began and reached the point when the expedition took place. Next comes a description of Libya. Finally Herodotus disposes briefly of the Persian attack. Barca was taken and its people deported to Bactria where their descendants still lived in Herodotus's day. Queen Pheretime, the regent of Cyrene who had brought in the Persian army to avenge the assassination of her son by the Barcaeans, died horribly, devoured by worms while still alive. The gods, it seemed, punished mortals who exacted excessive vengeance.

Cyrene (modern Shahat) lies in the narrow plain along the coast of Libya between the sea and the mountain ridge of Jebel Akhdar (Green Mountain). Rain falls in winter along the coastal fringe, but the interior is desert, inhabited by Berbers in Herodotus's day, for the Arabs who have intermingled with them did not arrive until the Moslem invasion of 643. To the east stretched more desert for some 700 kilometers to the Nile Delta. But Crete lay only some 300 kilometers away, and mainland Greece 400, and connections with Greece went back as early as the Minoan period.

Cyrene was founded by Thera, and Thera by Sparta, and Herodotus's story derives from traditions from the three places. The royal house of Cyrene claimed descent from one of the Minyans who sailed with Jason on the *Argo* in quest of the Golden Fleece,[15] and Herodotus acknowledged the connection. The core of the story, telling how Thera was colonized by Sparta, was probably traditional in the great Laconian clan of the Aigeidae, that claimed descent from Theras and was prominent both at Sparta and Thera; Herodotus (4.150.1) claims to have found the story at both places.[16] It related that the Greeks joined a Phoenician settlement on Thera that had lived there for eight generations, but if so, these Phoenicians left no trace behind,[17] and we can be skeptical. It was a descendant of the oecist Theras whom the Delphic oracle bade found a colony in Libya.

According to a Theran story, not corroborated at Sparta (4.150.1), Grinnus, king of Thera, came to Delphi to sacrifice, and as he consulted the oracle, it bade him to found a city in Libya. But Grinnus was old, and pointing to one of his retinue, Battus, he urged that the commandment be laid on a younger man. The story of Apollo's command was genuine enough, for it appears on a fourth-century inscription found at Cyrene that gives the oath of the first colonists who were drafted to found the colony.[18] The inscription reflects the official tradition of Cyrene, whereas Herodotus has used an oral source at Thera, and has supplemented it with details from Cyrene. It is a strange story. Corobius, a trader in purple dye from the Eteocretan city of Itanos, led a shipload of Therans to the island of Plataea off the Libyan coast. There they left him with provisions, while they sailed home to announce that they had founded a colony. Corobius, meanwhile, exhausted his supplies and was saved from starvation by the fabulous mariner, Colaeus, who was driven to the island by contrary winds as he tried to make for Egypt. After restocking Corobius's larder, Colaeus continued his voyage, and the wind blew him westward beyond Gibraltar, until he put in at Tartessos. It was Phocaea that profited most from the Tartessian trade, but a bronze cauldron stood in the temple of Hera at Samos to attest Colaeus's exploit, and a bond of friendship survived between Samos, Thera, and Cyrene.

Thus far, the tradition derived from Thera, but for the rest of the tale, Herodotus has Cyrenaic sources. The colony moved to the mainland and suffered various vicissitudes. Under Battus II, the third descendant of Battus the founder, an oracle from Delphi urging emigration to Libya brought about a new influx of settlers, and their hunger for land provoked a clash with the natives, who appealed to Egypt. But the Greeks routed the Egyptian army that tried to intervene; this was the first time, Herodotus noted, that Egyptians met Greek fighting men in the field . Under Battus III (the Lame), Cyrene got a constitution limiting royal power, but the next king, Arcesilaus III, determined to recover the royal prerogatives, and thus brought disaster on Cyrene. For a popular revolt forced him to flee, along with his mother, Pheretime, but Arcesilaus went to Samos (the date is uncertain, but it may have coincided with the Persian rape of the island),[19] raised an army, and won back his kingdom.

But a folktale motif intervenes.[20] Delphi had warned Arcesilaus that if he found an oven full of jars, he should not bake them, for if he did, he would not enter the sea-girt place. But he trapped some of his foes in a tower, and burned them out, and only later realized that he had baked the "jars." So he went to live at Barca, modern el-Merj,

which had been founded by dissidents from Cyrene about 570 B.C.
There some refugees from Cyrene assassinated him.

Pheretime acted as regent at Cyrene until she heard of her son's
death. Then she hurried to Egypt and begged the Persian satrap to
avenge her, for her son, she claimed, had died because he was a
Persian sympathizer. So vengeance was the ostensible reason for the
Persian attack. "But," remarks Herodotus (4.167.3), "the expedition
was dispatched, I think, to conquer Libya."

Now Herodotus describes the tribes, fauna, and geography of Libya,
starting from the borders of Egypt and moving west.[21] Some of his
information he found at Cyrene, but not all, for at one point he quotes
the Carthaginians as a source (4.196.1). They reported that there was
a part of Libya west of Gibraltar where they went to trade with the
natives. They spread their goods on the beach and withdrew; the
natives then came, laid gold beside what they wanted to buy, and
withdrew in turn, and the Carthaginians came back to see if the gold
was enough, and so on, until a bargain was struck. Herodotus also
knew about the Garamantes who were charioteers, and are found
depicted in rock engravings in the Fezzan.[22] With their chariots, they
hunted down the fleet-footed Ethiopian troglodytes, who spoke a
strange language of squeaking sounds (4.185.5), that must remind us
of the Bushmen, whose range once extended much further north than
it does now. Then there was the Libyan fauna: the cattle (aurochs?) of
the Fezzan with horns pointing forward (4.183.3), great snakes
(pythons), the Berber lions, now extinct, and North African elephants,
which he is the first author to mention (4.191–92). There were three
species of Libyan mice, and the Libyan name that Herodotus gives for
one of them, *zegeries,* still persists as a word for "rat" in the Berber of
the Awjila oasis.[23] He remarks, with the aplomb of a world traveler,
that the weasels living in the silphium (an unidentified vegetable that
was Cyrene's richest export) were very like the ferrets of Tartessos.
Mingled with all this are references to Greek myths: the Argonauts
had come to the mysterious "Lake Tritonis," according to the
Cyreneans (the Battiad royal house may have been responsible for this
version, for it gave the dynasty an ancestral claim to the place), and
Odysseus had visited the land of the Lotus-Eaters and had eaten the
jujube fruit (4.178).

But only once was Herodotus ready to be impressed: the fertility of Tripolitana was comparable to that of Babylon.[24] However, Cyrene possessed one marvel. There were three distinct harvest times. The crops of the coastal plain were harvested before those on the plateau further south, and last of all, those further up the slopes of Jebel Akhdar were ready for reaping. But enough, Herodotus concludes, and returns to his main story.

The Persians sent by the satrap of Egypt to avenge Queen Pheretime, took Barca by a stratagem, and the queen crucified her son's assassins along the circuit wall of the city. The Persians enslaved those who were left. As they returned home, the Cyreneans let them pass through their city, acting in obedience to some oracle, Herodotus thought, for there was no reason why the Persians had to pass through. In any case, having traversed the city, the Persians repented of not having plundered it, and tried to return, but the Cyreneans would not admit them, and the Persians, for some reason, fled in a panic. In 1966, there was found outside the walls of ancient Cyrene a cache of broken archaic sculpture, which may be mute evidence of Persian rapacity at this time.[25] But absolute proof is lacking.

Persia's first subjects in Europe

Darius's Scythian expedition may have failed, but he had established a bridgehead in Europe, and the Persian army left behind under Megabazus was under orders to reduce every city and tribe in Thrace. The first to fall was Perinthos, a colony of Samos founded in the Hellespont about 600 B.C. It had already suffered at the hands of its neighbors, the Paeonians, but the Perinthians put up a brave, if hopeless fight, nonetheless. Megabazus turned next to Thrace, and Herodotus digresses to describe Thracian customs.

The population of Thrace numbered second only to India's, but the tribes were disunited and hence weak. Herodotus's description is brief, perfunctory, and marked by the familiar touch of *Erewhon*. The Trausi had customs which were the inverse of the Greek: they wept at birth and rejoiced at funerals, for birth marked the start of man's sufferings, and death his release. The Thracians beyond Creston had numerous wives, and when their man died, the wives competed for the honor of being his favorite. The winner of the competition was greatly praised, and then slain over her husband's tomb. On Thracian religion, Herodotus is unhelpful. The people worshipped Ares, Dionysus, and Artemis, and the kings, Hermes. The Thracian god who has left the most abundant archaeological evidence appears as a mounted warrior, but of this rider-god, Herodotus says nothing.

Now Herodotus touches again on his main theme. Histiaeus of Miletus, who had saved Darius at the Danube, and Coes of Mytilene, who had offered sound advice, received rewards. Histiaeus got Myrcinus in the Strymon river valley, close by the silver mines of Mt. Pangaeus, and Coes became tyrant of Mytilene. All this took place while Darius was still at Sardis, and coincidentally, he ordered Paeonia invaded and the Paeonians deported to Asia, probably because they menaced the coastal road that the Persians wanted to secure, but Herodotus prefers a personal reason. Two Paeonians in Darius's train cherished the hope of becoming rulers of Paeonia as Persian vassals, and so they produced an elaborate charade to impress the king with the beauty and industry of the Paeonian women. They succeeded so well that Darius sought them as immigrants to Asia.

Next was Macedon's turn. Persian envoys arrived at the court of the Macedonian king, Amyntas, and received earth and water, the symbols of surrender to Persia. Amyntas entertained them at a splendid banquet, but there an incident occurred that Macedonian tradition must have cherished, for it showed Macedonians were not prepared for servility, even in the face of Persian might. The envoys insulted the Macedonian women at the banquet, and the crown prince, Alexander, contrived their assassination. Then when a Persian force arrived in search of the dead envoys, Alexander hushed up the incident with bribes, giving his sister as wife to the commandant of the force, Bubares.

Once again Herodotus returns to the tale of Histiaeus, that runs like a thread connecting the Scythian expedition to the next great event: the revolt of Ionia. When Megabazus returned from Paeonia to Sardis he urged Darius to remove Histiaeus from Myrcinus, which was too strategic an area to entrust to a Greek. Convinced, Darius summoned Histiaeus and told him that he needed him as his advisor at court. So Histiaeus went to Susa with the king. In the north Aegean, the power of Persia quietly expanded, but Ionia was at peace.

Chapter Six

The Ionian Revolt

The Beginning

Croesus's subjugation of the Greek cities of the Aegean littoral may have begun the strife between Europe and Asia, but the revolt of Ionia against Persia marked a new stage in its escalation. There are, in fact, structural parallels between the Croesus-*logos* and the Ionian Revolt. When the Lydian planned his attack on Cyrus, he sent missions to Sparta and Athens to seek allies, and this provided the occasion for digressions on both states. Similarly, the instigator of the Ionian Revolt, Aristagoras, visits Sparta and Athens to look for help, and again, Herodotus digresses on them both. Croesus found an ally in Sparta but none in Athens, whereas Aristagoras is expelled from Sparta, but got twenty warships from Athens. These ships, Herodotus remarks (5.97.3), using words reminiscent of those with which Homer described the ships of Paris that bore Helen to Troy,[1] were the beginning of evils for both Greeks and Persians.

One protagonist in the Ionian Revolt, Histiaeus, made his entry in the Scythian Expedition. When he went to Susa, he left his son-in-law, Aristagoras, as his deputy in charge of Miletus, and possibly, his project at Myrcinus in the Strymon valley as well.[2] At least, when the Ionian Revolt faltered, and Aristagoras's popularity in Miletus waned, he retired there, and died in battle with a native tribe, the Edoni, These two enigmatic leaders, Histiaeus and Aristagoras, dominate Herodotus's story of the revolt. They appear as selfish schemers, willing to sacrifice public good for their own ends, and Aristagoras, at least, was a coward (5.124.1). Their whole venture met with Herodotus's disapproval.

The opening move was an expedition against Naxos. The plebs there had expelled the rich oligarchs, who came to Miletus for help. Aristagoras was sympathetic, for he recognized a chance to acquire

Naxos for himself, and he approached the satrap at Sardis, Artaphrenes, with a proposal. If the Persians would send a force against
Naxos, Aristagoras would pay the cost. He won over the satrap so well
that he offered double the fleet that Aristagoras had requested, subject
to Darius's approval, which was readily given.

Thus, by Persian command, a fleet was mustered against Naxos
from the Ionian cities. There is some irony in this, for Persia was
imposing a unity on the Ionians that they had never achieved
themselves, and once together, they found that they shared common
discontents. The Persian admiral, Megabates, was a martinet who
inspected the fleet in person, and when he found a ship from Myndos
without a watch posted, he arrested the captain and punished him
severely. But the unlucky captain was Aristagoras's friend, and he
intervened on his behalf. The incident led to a bitter quarrel between
Aristagoras and Megabates, who, out of spite, sent a ship to alert
Naxos. Herodotus does not add that Aristagoras must have won
popularity among the Ionians from this incident, for he had champi-
oned a fellow Greek against a commander who was not only Persian,
but rigid and disliked as well. The tale of Megabates' treachery was
probably based on a rumor which was a product of the friction
between the Ionians and their Persian officers, for the Naxians could
have learned of the attack without Megabates' help. But the expedition
did fail, and popular tradition in Ionia laid the blame at Megabates'
door.

Naxos repulsed the attack, and she added a wreath to the emblem
on her coins to celebrate the victory.[3] But, back in Miletus, Aristagoras, faced with the consequences of failure, planned revolt. By
coincidence, at this juncture a slave arrived from Histiaeus in Susa,
with a message tattooed on his scalp, that bade him revolt. Consequently, before the Ionian fleet could demobilize, Aristagoras gathered
a group of men he could trust, including the writer Hecataeus, and
laid his plans for revolt before them.

A good deal of this sounds like legend. But with the council of war,
we are on firm ground, for Herodotus read Hecataeus, who took part
in it, and argued against the revolt. But the council resolved to go
ahead; the argument that prevailed must have been that the fleet was
disaffected, and that the conspirators should act before it disbanded.

At any rate, their first move was to send an agent to the fleet to raise it, and then Aristagoras broke into open revolt.

The rebels went out of their way to win popular support. The puppet tyrants, through whom Persia had ruled the Ionian cities, were handed over to their subjects, most of whom let them go into exile, but Coes of Mytilene was so hated that he was stoned to death. Then Aristagoras touched off a democratic revolution. He abdicated his own tyranny, though Herodotus (5.37) remarks that that was mere pretence. Since Aristagoras ruled Miletus as Histiaeus's deputy, presumably it was Histiaeus who was the loser. Herodotus makes the two men collaborators, but as the story progresses, there is a hint of rivalry.[4]

Then Aristagoras went to Sparta and Athens for help, and Herodotus breaks off his narrative for two digressions (5.39–97).

Sparta and the Story of Cleomenes

Herodotus (3.148) had already introduced Cleomenes. He was the king of Sparta whom Maeandrius of Samos tried to bribe, and who retorted by having Maeandrius banished lest he corrupt him and other Spartans. That was just after Darius had secured the throne of Persia, and Cleomenes was to rule until shortly before the Battle of Marathon in 490 B.C. For a generation, he dominated Spartan policies. Yet, Herodotus speaks of him slightingly. It was not by merit that he gained the throne (5.39.1); his mind was unbalanced (5.42.1) and his reign was short (5.48). The verdict seems to fly in the face of the evidence.

There was a reason. Cleomenes' father, Anaxandrides, had had no children by his first wife, and the Spartan ephors and the council of elders insisted that he take a second wife, by whom he begot Cleomenes. After his birth, Anaxandrides got three sons by his first wife: Dorieus, Leonidas, and Cleombrotus. But the throne passed on Anaxandrides' death to Cleomenes, not Dorieus.

The slighting judgment on Cleomenes is an echo of the bitterness that Dorieus and his branch of the royal family felt against an unwanted half-brother. Dorieus preferred to leave Sparta to found a colony in Libya, and when that venture failed, he tried again in Sicily. Here tradition became muddied, though Herodotus tried to sort it out at Thurii. Dorieus's end was certain enough: he seized the tyranny of Selinus in Sicily, and died when the Selinuntines rose against him and slaughtered him as he clung to the altar of Zeus in the marketplace.

Cleomenes' successor was Dorieus's full brother, Leonidas, who was to die at Thermopylae in 480 B.C. It was Dorieus's branch of the family that was to control the traditions of the royal house. However, Cleomenes' only daughter, Gorgo, did not share her father's reputation, for she became Leonidas's wife; and was remembered as a shrewd, very Spartan lady.

Aristagoras arrived in Sparta, bringing a map engraved on a bronze tablet. He appealed to Spartan idealism and cupidity almost in the same breath: it was a shame that Greeks should be Persian subjects, and also the Persian Empire was rich and extensive, as the map showed, and there was profit to be had from an attack on her. Cleomenes took two days to reflect, and then asked how long the journey was from the coast to the Persian capital. At this point, Aristagoras's cunning failed him. He did not lie. The journey, he said, took three months, and Cleomenes ordered him out of Sparta before sunset.

In fact, the journey took three months and three days, Herodotus remarked, and attempted to prove his point by a description of the Royal Road from Sardis to Susa, along which there were one hundred and eleven post stations where the king's messengers could change horses. Like the Romans later, the Persians bound their empire together with military roads, and the Royal Road was the one that the Greeks knew best. Herodotus may have known the western part at firsthand, but not all of it. Still, he can correct Aristagoras, and conclude the adventure in Sparta by focusing briefly on the vastness of Persia.

Athens and the Expulsion of Tyranny

The digression on Athens is longer. When Croesus's envoys investigated Athens, they found Pisistratus newly reinstated as tyrant. Now Aristagoras found the tyranny overturned, and a new constitution established by Cleisthenes, with the result that Athens's power had increased. Herodotus begins with the story of how the tyrant fell.

It was already legend. In the Athenian *agora* stood a statue-group of the tyrannicides, Harmodius and Aristogeiton, and their descendants received special honors from the state long after Herodotus's death. Thucydides (1.20) was to protest that Harmodius and Aristogeiton never slew the tyrant nor did they free Athens; their victim was Hipparchus, brother of the tyrant Hippias, Pisistratus's eldest son and successor. Herodotus was more interested in the story. He looked into the traditions of the clan to which the tyrannicides belonged and satisfied himself that they were descended from Phoenicians who came to Greece with Cadmus. In fact, he devotes more space to this antiquarian research than to the glorious deed itself. The night before the Panathenaic Festival, when Hipparchus was slain, he was forewarned in a dream. Next morning, he disclosed the dream to interpreters, but then he forgot the matter, and went off to meet his death in the Panathenaic procession.

For what came next, Herodotus relied heavily on the traditions of the Alkmaeonid family, to which Cleisthenes belonged, though not exclusively. Later, when Herodotus undertakes to defend the clan against the charge of medism at the Battle of Marathon (6.123), he is to say outright that the Alkmaeonids had a better claim to be liberators of Athens than the tyrannicides, but here his Alkmaeonid leanings are more muted. Hippias's rule became harsher after his brother's death, and the Alkmaeonids, who had lived in exile ever since Pisistratus seized power (Herodotus overstates, for an archon-list fragment from the Athenian *agora* shows Cleisthenes as archon in 525–24, early in Hippias's tyranny), tried to fight their way back, and were routed. So they turned to Delphi and bribed the Pythia to command Sparta to free Athens.

The Spartans eventually discovered the trick and there was a scandal (5.90.1), but for the moment, they were gulled. They sent a "notable man," Anchimolius, to expel the tyrant, but his force was cut to pieces and he lost his life. Then they sent a larger army under king Cleomenes, who beleaguered the Pisistratids on the Acropolis. There they might have outlasted Cleomenes, except that the Spartans captured their children and forced them to leave Athens in order to get them back. Thus thirty-six years of tyranny ended.

Herodotus turns next to relate the "most memorable of the deeds and sufferings" of the Athenians down to the Ionian Revolt. Athens became a democracy. Later (6.131), Herodotus states bluntly that it was Cleisthenes who divided Athens into ten tribes, replacing the old four Ionic tribes, and established the democracy. Here he presents Cleisthenes less as a statesman than as a shrewd politician who sought political supremacy by espousing a popular cause.[5] He made the common people his allies against his rival, Isagoras, who won the archonship of 508 B.C.,[6] and his division of the Athenians into ten tribes, opined Herodotus, betraying his own anti-Ionian bias, was intended to mark them off from the Ionians, whom he despised. Also, he was following the example of his grandfather and namesake, the tyrant of Sicyon, who had pursued an anti-Dorian policy, renaming the three ancient Dorian tribes in his little *polis* "Hog-men," "Ass-men," and "Pig-men," and grouping the non-Dorians into a tribe dubbed "Rulers of the People." It was, in Herodotus's view, very reasonable that a statesman's public policy should follow the pattern set by his grandfather. But there is only tepid praise for Cleisthenes here.

Now it was Isagoras's turn to face defeat, and he turned to the king of Sparta. Cleomenes sent a herald to proclaim the expulsion of the Athenians who were under the curse. Herodotus's explanation was brief, for Sparta had resurrected the same story as a weapon against Pericles on the eve of the Peloponnesian War. Cylon, who had won an Olympic victory in 640 B.C., attempted a *coup d'état*, failed, and the conspirators took refuge with Athena. The "presidents of the *naukraroi*," whose identity eludes us,[7] seized the suppliants and killed them. The Alkmaeonids were held responsible, and a curse hung over them, ready to be resurrected whenever politics demanded it. Cleisthenes went into exile.

Then Cleomenes came himself, with a small force, expelled seventy families hostile to Isagoras, and tried to set up an oligarchic government controlled by Isagoras and his friends. But the *boule* fought back. Herodotus's account bristles with difficulties; suffice it to say that he must mean by this *boule*, which he mentions without definition, the Council of Five Hundred established by Cleisthenes, and that he cannot be right. There could have been no Council until there were ten tribes, for it consisted of fifty members from each, and it is clear that these tribes were the result of careful, sophisticated planning.[8] So the *boule* was probably the ancient council of the Areopagus, made up of former archons, which rallied against the Spartan invader, and shut Cleomenes up on the Acropolis for two days. On the third, the Spartans were allowed to depart (Isagoras also got away), but their Athenian collaborators were put to death. Cleisthenes and the families that Cleomenes had banished were called home.

But Cleomenes planned revenge, and Athens sent envoys to seek help to the satrap at Sardis, Artaphrenes, who stipulated that the Athenians give earth and water first. This was Athens's first brush with Persian imperialism, and possibly the envoys were unfamiliar with these symbols of submission. For they gave them, and presumably got their alliance, though nothing came of it, and Herodotus refers with enigmatic brevity to the recriminations they encountered when they returned home.

The attack soon came: a three-pronged invasion by the Boeotian League and Chalcis in the north and the Peloponnesians from the south, and Athens survived handily. Cleomenes led his allies as far as Eleusis, but there, before a battle could take place, the Corinthians decided to have no part in restoring tyranny in Athens and went home, and Cleomenes' co-king, Demaratus, did likewise. Cleomenes' army fell apart. Athens then turned on her other enemies and routed them. The immediate danger was over. But the Thebans consulted Delphi, which counseled them in suitably veiled terms to seek an alliance with Aegina. Aegina had a feud with Athens, and to explain why, Herodotus relates a tale of war that unfolds like a primitive myth. The Aeginetans were happy to ravage Attica in response to the Theban appeal, and the Athenians were equally willing to retaliate, but new danger from Sparta held them back.

The Intervention of Corinth

The digression on Athens ends with a story full of allusions to the Greek world in which Herodotus lived. In the 430s, Corinth was a "hawk" and the then king of Sparta, Archidamus, a "dove." The growth of Athenian power that roused Corinth's hostility dated from the overthrow of the tyranny and Cleisthenes' subsequent reforms. At least, so Herodotus thought. Yet, it was Corinth that saved Athens from renewed tyranny, and her motive was simply that she believed tyranny was evil. The Corinthians knew, for they had had a tyrant themselves.

The Spartans were by now convinced that they had blundered when they expelled Hippias from Athens. They saw Athens as a threat; indeed, Hippias's archive of oracles had fallen into their hands and they prophesied Athens' future greatness. Summoning an assembly of allies, the Spartans brought Hippias before it, and proposed that he be reinstated. But the allies sat in glum silence until the Corinthian delegate spoke up.

Nothing was more unjust or bloodier than tyranny, he said, and it was shameful that Sparta should wish to destroy political equality (*isokratia*) and set up tyranny in its stead. He illustrated with a circumstantial story of Corinth's tyranny,[9] founded by Cypselus, and outlasting every other tyrant dynasty except that of Sicyon. The Corinthian tyrants performed the stock tyrannical atrocities, but the delegate made his point, and all Sparta's allies agreed with him.

So Hippias returned to Sigeum on the Hellespont, but now he contacted Artaphrenes, and worked to get his support. Whereupon Athens sent a second embassy to Sardis to counteract Hippias, but he now had the satrap's ear. Athens was ordered to reinstate him. The Athenians received the directive with anger, and there was still a large residue of anti-Persian feeling when Aristagoras arrived. Thus they voted to send twenty ships to help the Ionian fight for freedom. "It is clearly easier to mislead many than one," remarked Herodotus sourly, for whereas Cleomenes resisted Aristagoras's blandishments, thirty thousand Athenians were taken in.

The Revolt Concluded

The End of Aristagoras

The combined Ionian force, including Athens's twenty ships, and five triremes from Eretria as well, sailed to Ephesus, landed, and marched inland to Sardis, which they captured and set ablaze. But the Lydians joined the Persians to resist the Greeks, who had to withdraw, and suffered a massive defeat at Ephesus before they could reimbark. Thereupon Athens deserted the Ionians and remained deaf to all further appeals from Aristagoras.

However, the revolt spread. Byzantium on the Dardanelles joined, as well as most of the cities in the area, and so did most of Caria and Cyprus. As the revolt reached its climax, Herodotus switches the narrative to Darius's court at Susa. When the king learned that Sardis had been burned by the Ionians and the Athenians, he cared nothing for the Ionians, for he knew he would defeat them, but he vowed vengeance on Athens. Then, summoning Histiaeus, he demanded an explanation of Aristagoras's actions, for Aristagoras was Histiaeus's son-in-law and deputy. But Histiaeus was ready with a smooth reply. Let the king send him to Ionia and he would set things right; why, he would even capture Sardinia for Darius, who must have known little about Sardinia, but was expected to appreciate the figure of speech.

Meanwhile, the Persians got a counteroffensive underway. They recovered Cyprus, where Herodotus admits that the Ionians fought bravely, notably the Samians (5.112). So did the Carians, who lost two bloody battles to the Persians, in the last of which, the Milesians, who fought alongside the Carians, suffered dreadfully (5.120). Even so, the Carians rallied, and destroyed a Persian force, leaders and all, in a surprise attack. But new Persian commanders took over: Artaphrenes himself, and Otanes; the Ionian Revolt reached its last phase. Aristagoras abandoned his city to its fate, and went off to Myrcinus, where, it seems, Miletus still had an interest. His motive is hard to determine, but in Herodotus's eyes, it was lack of courage. He had stayed behind when the Ionians had attacked Sardis (5.99.2), though he was responsible for that expedition, and now he preferred not to share the fate of the city he had induced to revolt. He left for Myrcinus and died there, fighting the native Thracians.

The End of Histiaeus

When Histiaeus reached Sardis, Artaphrenes received him with suspicion, for he thought him implicated in the revolt, and in any case, he was committed to a military solution, and had no use for a glib, ambitious Greek. So Histiaeus left hastily and got to Chios, where the Chiots arrested him. However, he satisfied them that he was on their side, and they ferried him to Miletus, but his old subjects would not have him. Back he came to Chios, but he got no help there, and went on to Mytilene on Lesbos, where he was given eight triremes. With these he sailed to Byzantium, and, surely with the support of the Byzantines, blocked the Dardanelles to all but friendly ships. There he remained, until word came that the Ionian fleet was destroyed at the Battle of Lade (494 B.C.), whereupon he led an attack on Chios. The Chiots had fought hardest of all the Ionians at Lade, and Histiaeus's attack coming in the wake of that disaster brought them to their knees. Next, he attacked Thasos, but broke off his siege when he heard that the Persian fleet was advancing, and sailed for Lesbos, directly into its path. Finally, forced by lack of supplies to forage on the mainland, he unexpectedly encountered a Persian force and was captured. Yet, he identified himself confidently to the Persian commander, Harpagus, expecting no harm, but he fell into the hands of his old enemy, Artaphrenes, who executed him swiftly, before Darius could save him, as he certainly would have done, or so Herodotus thought.

Histiaeus left a strange, contradictory tradition behind him, probably because, during his last months, he was trying to pass as a loyal Ionian among the Ionians, and a loyal subject with Darius. But Herodotus has no doubts. The Ionian Revolt was an ill-advised venture, and its instigators, Histiaeus and Aristagoras, were not merely typical of the self-serving Greeks who made themselves useful to the Persians, but they thoughtlessly began a chain of calamities that culminated in the expedition of Xerxes. Their lust for power brought upon Greece the vengeance of the Persians.[10]

The immediate catastrophe was the defeat in 494 B.C. off Lade, which has now been covered by silt from the Maeander River, but was then an offshore island of Miletus. Herodotus tells a story of how the Ionians chose as admiral Dionysius of Phocaea, who promised them victory if they would train hard, but when he attempted to impose his regimen, the soft, foolish Ionians mutinied. So the Samians, disgusted with the lack of discipline, listened to overtures from the son of their old tyrant, and during the battle, they deserted and started the rout. But some stayed and fought, notably the Chiots, and Dionysius himself sailed off, first to raid Phoenicia, and then to live the life of a pirate around Sicily, plundering Carthaginian and Etruscan shipping.

Miletus fell soon after, and the Persians took terrible vengeance. Herodotus writes, with some exaggeration, about massacres of the men, and enslavement and deportation of the women and children; in fact, Miletus was not wiped out, though it never quite recovered.[11] In Athens, where the tragic poet Phrynichus staged a play on the fall of Miletus, the audience wept, and Phrynichus was fined for reminding the Athenians of the calamity. But Sybaris did not mourn, Herodotus remarks, with strange acerbity, for as a citizen of Thurii, which was a refoundation of Sybaris, he was, in a sense, an adoptive Sybarite himself. So ended the revolt, and the Ionians were reduced to slavery for the third time: twice to Persia and once to Croesus of Lydia (6.32).

Chapter Seven
Miltiades and Marathon
Preliminaries

After the fall of Miletus, the Phoenician fleet sailed north to the Chersonese, the long peninsula that flanks the European side of the Hellespont. The tyrant of the cities there was Miltiades, son of Cimon, whom Herodotus first introduced at the Danube bridge, some two decades earlier. Herodotus now digresses at length to tell how Miltiades' family secured power in the Chersonese. The story bristles with difficulties. The first Miltiades went to the Chersonese at the invitation of a local Thracian tribe known as the Dolonci. Herodotus here reproduces an oral tradition that belonged to Miltiades' clan, the Philaids, who traced their descent to the Homeric hero, Aias. Miltiades the elder was happy to go, for he wanted to escape the tyranny of Pisistratus in Athens. Yet, a few sentences later, we learn that Miltiades was a friend of Croesus, and that once, when he made war on Lampsacus and fell into the hands of the Lampsacenes, Croesus secured his release. Philaid tradition tried too hard to make Miltiades an enemy of Pisistratus, for Croesus fell about the same time as Pisistratus established his tyranny, and probably Miltiades went to the Chersonese before there was a Pisistratid tyranny for him to dislike.[1]

Stesagoras, the nephew of Miltiades, succeeded him, and when he, in turn, died during another war with Lampsacus, the Pisisitratids dispatched his brother, Miltiades, son of Cimon, to take over. Once he arrived there, the chief men of the Chersonese came to offer their condolences on Stesagoras's death, whereupon Miltiades put them in chains. The *coup d'état* had Pisistratid backing; yet Philaid tradition insisted that there was no love lost between the Pisistratids and Miltiades. The Pisistratids had secretly murdered Miltiades' father; Herodotus will tell the story later.

For the moment, he continues with the vicissitudes of Miltiades in some of the most obscure Greek that he ever penned (6.40). He was expelled by the Scyths, who struck back after Darius's Scythian expedition; we know nothing of this raid, but after Darius's debacle in Scythia, there were revolts in Byzantium and Chalcedon, and perhaps the Scythian raiders were taking advantage of Persian preoccupation elsewhere. At some point during Miltiades' rule in the Chersonese, he took Lemnos and gave it to Athens, which was to be a point in his favor in the trial that he faced at the end of his life. When did all this occur? Herodotus's prose is too difficult for certainty, but it is likely that Miltiades was forced out of the Chersonese shortly after Darius's Scythian expedition, by the Scyths rather than the Persians, although the Persians showed no interest in defending him, and that he returned during the Ionian Revolt, when the Persians were too busy to stop him.[2] But his turn came at last. When he learned that the Persian fleet was approaching, he loaded what he could on five triremes, and fled for Athens. Four ships got away, but the Persians captured one, commanded by Miltiades' son, Metiochus. Darius received Metiochus gladly, and gave him a Persian wife, by whom he begot children.

Meanwhile, Artaphrenes reorganized Ionia. He forced the cities to settle their disputes by peaceful means, which was reminiscent of Athens's policy later within her own empire, and he measured the land and assessed tribute, which continued "up to my time as it was assessed by Artaphrenes" (6.42.2)"; presumably what Herodotus meant was that Artaphrenes' survey was so thorough that it did not need redoing, and continued to serve as the basis for the Athenian assessment of tribute, since in Herodotus's day Ionia was part of the Athenian Empire.[3] The following year there was a more surprising development. Mardonius, Darius's son-in-law, who replaced Artaphrenes, deposed the quisling tyrants in the Ionian cities and set up democratic governments in their stead. What became of this reform is a mystery. Tyrannies were to be found later in at least some of these cities.[4] Perhaps the point here, too, is the comparison with imperial Athens, for she too favored democracies in his subject cities, although in practice she was anything but doctrinaire.

But Mardonius's goal was Athens and Eretria. He mustered naval and land forces at the Hellespont and moved westward along the coast. All went well: Thasos fell, and Macedon bowed again to Persian

suzerainty. But at Mt. Athos, the fleet was battered by a storm, and
the Brygi, a Thracian tribe, mauled the army and wounded Mardonius
himself. Mardonius withdrew, but not before conquering the Brygi.
That detail may lead us to suspect that he had gained his objective,
which was to reestablish Persian domination in the north Aegean, and
ready the scenario for the next campaign. It was not long in coming.

Marathon

Herodotus proceeds, with due deliberation, to the Battle of Marathon, which was to mark the climax of Persia's imperial advance.
There, for the first, Greeks had the courage not merely to stand and
fight the Persians, but even charge them on the run (6.112.3). Before,
it had been a fearful thing "even to hear the name of the Medes." But
preliminaries were necessary, and in structure they parallel those
before the Ionian Revolt. Darius sent heralds to Greece to demand
earth and water, and at the same time ordered a fleet mustered. Much
of Greece was ready to surrender. Many of the cities on the mainland
gave earth and water, and all the islands. Particularly Aegina.

Thus the ancient feud between Athens and Aegina, which had been
a parergon to the digression preceding the Ionian Revolt (5.80–88),
now becomes central to the preface to Marathon. When Aegina gave
earth and water, the Athenians assumed that she planned to attack
them with Persian aid. Their envoys hurried to Sparta and accused
Aegina of betraying Greece. Thus, in a roundabout way, the concept
first emerges of Hellas: free Greece, whose member states owe it
loyalty against Persian aggression.

King Cleomenes was roused to action. He went to Aegina to arrest
the pro-Persian leaders, but he found them well-organized under a
prominent Aeginetan, Crius. What authority did Cleomenes have, he
wanted to know. Where was his fellow king, Demaratus? Cleomenes
vowed revenge, but for the moment, he had to depart, frustrated.

The story switches to Sparta, and background material. Herodotus
gives the official Spartan tradition of how Sparta got two royal
families, and tells what the royal prerogatives were; then he proceeds
to relate how Cleomenes' co-king, Demaratus, refused to support
Cleomenes on Aegina. Demaratus's motive is hard to discover.
Probably he was neither defeatist nor, at this point, pro-Persian,[5]

though later he joined the Persians and became a wise advisor at Xerxes' court. Herodotus says he was moved by spite. Cleomenes, who was probably not above a little spite himself, determined that this potential traitor must go. The Achilles' Heel of Demaratus was his ancestry, for there was reasonable doubt if he was the legitimate son of the previous king, Ariston. Cleomenes induced Leutychides, who belonged to a collateral line, to impeach Demaratus; the quarrel was referred to Delphi, and the Pythia was bribed to give the requisite answer. Demaratus was deposed, Leutychides became king, and shortly after, Demaratus, wounded by a jibe from Leutychides, fled to Persia. But Herodotus treated his memory kindly, whereas he noted that Leutychides' chicanery did not go unpunished, for he was convicted of taking a bribe sometime later, during a campaign in Thessaly after Xerxes' defeat, and banished from Sparta (6.72).

Cleomenes had his way. He and Leutychides went to Aegina, where they arrested ten wealthy Aeginetans of good families and deposited them in Athens as hostages. But then requital fell upon Cleomenes, and his end had a degree of mystery. The plot against Demaratus was uncovered. Cleomenes retired from Sparta, out of fear of the Spartiates, who soon brought him back, for they suspected him of intrigues across the border in Arcadia. But he became insane, very conveniently it seems, and in a fit of madness killed himself. His death was divine retribution, Greece decided, but various cities disagreed over what sacrilege it was for which the gods exacted the penalty. Herodotus describes one in some detail: Cleomenes, helped by Aegina and Sicyon, attacked Argos, defeated her at Sepeia (494 B.C.), and burned the fugitives in a sacred grove. The Spartans themselves attributed Cleomenes' insanity to dipsomania. We moderns, not untypically, tend to suspect *raisons d'état*.

Aegina waited until Cleomenes was dead (that says something for the old king's influence) before she sent envoys to demand justice. Sparta offered to hand over Leutychides to Aegina, but the Aeginetans hesitated; they preferred to take him with them to Athens to ask for the return of their hostages. Athens refused, and the bitter feud with Aegina continued.

Aegina seized a sacred ship of Athens that was bound for a festival held at Sounion on the east tip of Attica. To settle accounts, the

Athenians supported a *putsch* by an Aeginetan exile, Nikodromos, directed against the rich landowners who controlled Aegina. But the plan miscarried, and the oligarchs massacred seven hundred of the revolutionaries, though Nikodromos and some supporters got away, and Athens gave them a home at Sounion. The Athenians got the worst of the fighting, and lost four ships.

Not all of this can be compressed into the brief period between the arrival of Darius's heralds and the Battle of Marathon the next year, in 490 B.C. Nikodromos's *putsch* took place some three or four years afterward. But what is remarkable is the disparity of power between Athens and Sparta. Aegina might disregard the former, but she had to submit to Sparta even though she probably had no formal alliance with her. King Cleomenes simply assumed the role of protector of free Greece when he suppressed the pro-Persians on Aegina. But the next year, when Persia attacked, Cleomenes had already succumbed to dipsomania, or perhaps death.

The Battle

Meanwhile, as Herodotus put it, the Persian "did his own thing." Darius ordered an army mustered and put two commanders in charge, a Mede, Datis, and his own nephew, Artaphrenes, son of the Artaphrenes who had suppressed the Ionian Revolt. The fleet sailed from Samos to Naxos, which was taken, and on to the holy island of Delos, which the Delians evacuated in fright. But Datis sent them a reassuring message; Persian policy toward the cults of their subjects was conciliatory under Darius, though under his son it was to become harsher. After the fleet left, an earthquake shook Delos; Herodotus (6.98) cites the Delians for the tradition, though later Thucydides (2.8.3), who probably got his information from Athens rather than Delos, was to claim that the first earthquake there took place on the eve of the Peloponnesian War. What Heaven meant by the quake was to mark the beginning of an age of troubles, for, remarked Herodotus with deep pessimism, in the reigns of Darius, Xerxes, and Artaxerxes, "more evils befell Greece than in the twenty generations before Darius" (6.98.2). Herodotus penned this not long before the death of Artaxerxes at the close of the year 424 B.C., and it is the old historian's judgment on the age through which he lived.

The fleet sailed on to Eretria, which appealed to Athens for help, and Athens ordered the four thousand cleruchs whom she had settled on the land of Chalcis after she defeated her in 506 B.C. to go to Eretria's aid. But they hurried back to Athens, claiming that an Eretrian friend had warned them of a fifth column in the city. In fact, Eretria did stand siege for a week before the betrayal took place. The Eretrians were deported to Cissia in the salt desert of interior Iran, which even then produced oil, though not all were taken (their descendants, who still lived in Cissia seven centuries later, believed that there were seven hundred and eighty captives),[6] for Eretria could still muster a force ten years later to resist Xerxes (8.46).

Then the Persians sailed to Marathon, and the Athenians marched out to meet them. The battle is overlaid with legend. The Athenian generals dispatched a "day-runner," Philippides, to Sparta, and on the way, he encountered Pan, who promised his aid; the Spartans, however, could not help until the moon was full. Scholars assume that this taboo applied to the month of the Carnean festival in Sparta, and use this assumption to help date the battle, but Herodotus is silent about the festival.[7] The Athenians received the news without surprise, but it is sensible to think that they now aimed to delay battle until the Spartans could arrive.

With the Persians was an expert on Greek religion, who no doubt knew the reason for the Spartan delay: Hippias, Athens's ex-tyrant, who had guided the invaders to Marathon. He was now an old man, and the night before the landing, he dreamed that he slept in his mother's arms. He took this to mean that he would die on his native soil and be buried there. But as he disembarked, he sneezed and lost a tooth, and when he could not find it, he realized that only the tooth would rest in his native soil. The deceitful dream merely underscored man's weakness before destiny.[8]

Thus the Athenians wanted to delay battle until the Spartans came, while the Persians knew that they should force a quick decision, and it was the latter who had their way. But the tradition that Herodotus relates claimed that the Athenians chose the time for battle. Leading them were ten generals, "of whom the tenth was Miltiades" (6.103.1), and five were for attack, five for a defensive posture.[9] Then Miltiades approached the polemarch Callimachus, who had an eleventh vote, and put the question to him: "It lies in your power, Callimachus, to enslave Athens or set her free" (6.109.3). Great choices go with great deeds; there was to be a similar alternative put to the admiral Eurybiades before the Battle of Salamis. Callimachus chose to fight. The generals who had supported Miltiades ceded him their days of command (Herodotus believed that they took turns), but Miltiades waited for his own day.

Then he drew up his battleline. Herodotus knew that Callimachus, rather than Miltiades, led the right wing, the traditional post of a Greek commander, but he explained simply: "For the Athenians had a custom then, that the polemarch was responsible for the right wing." On the left was a contingent from Athens's little ally, Plataea. To prevent the Persians from outflanking him, Miltiades stretched his hoplite line to the same length as the Persian front by thinning his center, but this meant that his line was weakest at the point where the Persians posted their best men. He was attempting a dangerous and desperate maneuver. The Athenians would crash into the Persian line, and while their weak center tried to hold the crack Persian troops opposite them, the stronger Athenian wings would rout the Persian wings, and wheel round against the flanks of the Persian center.

The battle was a near thing. The Greeks charged on the run, over some eight stades—4,854 English feet—between the two lines. Herodotus (6.112.3) remarks that no Greek army had charged before, and it must have been a hard run for hoplites in full armor; impossible, in fact, unless they increased their speed very gradually over the course.[10] The Greeks broke in the center, but they routed the Persian wings, and then closed on the flanks of the Persian center and defeated it. The Persians fled for their ships, with the Greeks at their heels. At the ships, there was a sharp struggle that Herodotus describes with overtones borrowed from the *Iliad*; most of them got away, and sailed round Cape Sounion to take Athens from the south. They did this, rumor said, because the Alkmaeonids gave them a signal with a shield. But the Athenians got back to Athens before the ships reached Phaleron, and forestalled, the Persians sailed home. Their dead at Marathon numbered 6,400, and Athens lost only 192.

The account is brief and unsatisfactory, and almost every point has provoked scholarly argument. Marathon had already become both a symbol and a legend by the time Herodotus wrote. Miltiades was the architect of victory; he put the choice of freedom or slavery to the polemarch, and it was on his day of command that the Athenians attacked. They charged the Persians, unafraid, over a distance of "no less than eight stades," for like Homeric heroes, these warriors were endowed with no ordinary endurance and courage. Marathon marked the point when the *terribiltà* of Persia began to wane.

The Spartans arrived after the battle was over. They inspected the field, complimented the Athenians, and went home.

The Aftermath

Two digressions follow Marathon. One is a remarkable defense of the Alkmaeonid clan that has given grounds for suspicion that Herodotus had a special relationship with it.[11] The second is more coda than digression, for it relates the end of Miltiades, and just as Histiaeus's death concluded the Ionian Revolt, so does that of Miltiades conclude Marathon.

Herodotus (6.115) mentioned in passing the shield signal at Marathon and the suspicion of treason that rested on the Alkmaeonids. Now he recapitulates: he cannot think that the Alkmaeonids would want Athens subject to Persia, and Hippias as tyrant, and he repeats the unhistorical Alkmaeonid tradition[12] that the clan had *always* opposed tyranny. Nor would the Alkmaeonids have betrayed Athens out of pique, for the Athenians had always esteemed them. But there was a shield signal; that was a fact, but beyond that, all was unreliable rumor.

The Alkmaeonids

Now Herodotus launches into an excursus on Alkmaeonid legends. Their chronology is beyond repair: Alkmaeon, the founder of the family fortune, was a coeval of Croesus (6.125), but his son, Megacles, married Agariste, daughter of Cleisthenes of Sicyon, who was dead before Croesus began his reign.[13] Among Agariste's suitors was a son of the early tyrant of Argos, Pheidon, and Herodotus is the only ancient author who dates Pheidon so late.[14] The courtship of Agariste had become a folktale, and folktale chronology lacks logical order. But a fine story it is. The tyrant of Sicyon preferred the two Athenian suitors, but his favorite, Hippokleides, disgraced himself at the final banquet by getting drunk and dancing a jig while standing on his head on a table. So Megacles won Agariste, and their son was Cleisthenes, who "set up the tribes and the democracy" (6.131.1) in Athens. This Cleisthenes had a niece, also called Agariste, who married Xanthippus, and just before she bore a son she dreamed that she gave birth to a lion. The child was Pericles (6.131.2).

Only here does Herodotus mention the great architect of Athenian imperialism. Pericles' name concludes the digression on the Alkmaeonids, and represents the acme of Alkmaeonid renown. But there is a hint of ambiguity. Pericles a lion? For the Greeks, lions symbolized ferocity as well as courage, and if it is fair to wrest a value judgment out of a few words, Herodotus saw Pericles as a man who brought glory to his clan, but whose qualities were those of a tyrant. An oracle foretelling the birth of a lion had preceded the birth of Cypselus, and he had become tyrant of Corinth! (5.92β).

The End of Miltiades

Leaving the Alkmaeonids, Herodotus turns with his next breath to the fall of Miltiades, and it may be significant that Miltiades' family, the Philaids, were rivals of the Alkmaeonids and that Pericles' father helped bring down the old victor of Marathon. For Miltiades persuaded the Athenians to entrust him with seventy ships against an enemy he would not name, and with them, he attacked Paros, ostensibly because the Parians had helped the Persians, but Herodotus knew of a private motive that he preferred. The attack failed, and Miltiades returned to Athens, wounded in the thigh, and without the booty he had promised. His enemies (Pericles' father was most vehement, and the Alkmaeonids may have won some of their pro-Persian reputation from this dispute) brought him to trial, and Miltiades, whose wound was suppurating, had to leave his defense to friends. But the Athenians fined him an enormous sum, which his son Cimon was to pay later, after Miltiades was dead.

So ended Miltiades. He had given Athens Lemnos, and had settled an ancient grudge with the Pelasgians, but the Athenians declined to take this into account when they fined him. Herodotus digresses briefly on how the Pelasgians were driven from Attica and came to Lemnos, and how Miltiades captured the island. This is the coda to Marathon, and to the career of its hero.

Chapter Eight
The Campaign of Xerxes

The last three books of the *History* have a single theme: the expedition of Xerxes and its defeat. Darius shuffles quickly off the stage. Marathon had angered him, and he planned revenge, but first a revolt in Egypt and then his own death interrupted him in mid-course. But before he died, he proclaimed as his heir Xerxes, not his eldest son, but the child of Atossa, Cyrus's daughter, whose marriage to Darius lent him a degree of legitimacy. Herodotus relates a tale—a family legend, perhaps—that the exiled king of Sparta, Demaratus, gave Xerxes a debating point to support his case for the throne, but it was apocryphal, for Xerxes had been designated crown prince and viceroy of Babylon long before Demaratus came to Persia,[1] and what Darius did in the year before he died was to proclaim Xerxes king, thereby nipping in the bud any dispute over the succession. Darius died in November, 486, and Xerxes ruled on alone until his murder in 465 B.C.

The Mission of Xerxes

The character of Xerxes had already taken shape in Greek literature by the time Herodotus wrote. He was a feckless prince, in sharp contrast to his father, and an archetypal Oriental despot, generous at one moment and vengeful the next, but always unable to recognize the limits to his power. Herodotus thought his throne name meant "warrior" (in fact, it means something like "hero among rulers") but the Xerxes of the *History* is more of a tragic king who is humbled in the midst of his pride.[2]

Herodotus tells how Xerxes resolved to invade Greece. At first he was reluctant, but his cousin Mardonius was a "hawk," and he was seconded by the Pisistratids from Athens, and the Aleuads, whom

Herodotus (7.6.2) denominates "kings of Thessaly," and he was eventually persuaded. First, he summoned a council of nobles to announce his intentions and learn their opinions. He told them that he was not introducing any new *nomos* (the word means both "custom" and "law") but obeying one he had inherited, for conquest had always been a Persian custom, and Heaven approved of it. He could not be outdone by his predecessors; he, too, had to add to Persian power. Then he announced the expedition, and the reasons for it. One was vengeance, which is a leitmotiv of the *History*, but the second was vainglorious imperialism: Xerxes would make his empire coterminous with Heaven. Yet, the reference to the Persian *nomos* of expansionism must strike the reader with peculiar force. Imperialism, for Herodotus, was a custom—unlike Thucydides, who saw it a natural state—and this custom, which the Persians had adopted, had made them great since the time of Cyrus.

Then the debate began. Mardonius spoke for the expedition, and made a speech of the sort an intelligent Greek might have made if he were a Persian imperialist. Persia's power was so vast that Xerxes need expect no resistance. In addition, the Greeks were disunited and unskilled in war. "Since they have the same tongue, they ought to use heralds and messengers or any other means to settle their disputes rather than fighting" (7.9.β.2). The criticism was meant for Herodotus's contemporaries, and it was a palpable hit.

Then Xerxes' uncle, Artabanus, took up the role of wise adviser and spoke against the invasion. He referred back to the Scythian campaign of Darius, which Xerxes' campaign paralleled on a larger scale. "But you, O King, intend to make war on men who are far better than the Scyths and are said to be valiant, whether on land or sea" (7.10.2–3). Xerxes had spoken of Heaven's approval; Artabanus pointed out that Heaven loved to cut down the high and mighty. He condemned Mardonius for deriding Greek customs, and concluded with words that fitted a Greek patriot better than a Persian. Persia, he thought, would be defeated.

Xerxes angrily rejected Artabanus's advice, but later, in bed, he reflected, and decided that Artabanus was right. Then he slept and had a dream: a man appeared to him, and told him that he was wrong to change his mind. The expedition should go ahead.

But the king paid no heed, and next day countermanded the expedition. That night, the same dream reappeared. "Know this well," the strange man said, "if you do not invade forthwith, this will be the result. As you became great and mighty in a short while, so will you speedily be brought low again" (7.14).

Frightened, Xerxes turned to Artabanus, who advised him not to fear dreams; there was a rational explanation for them. But explanation or not, Artabanus agreed to put on the king's clothes, and sleep in the king's bed, where the apparition came to him, too. It knew him, and threatened him for influencing Xerxes against the invasion. "Neither in time to come, nor now, will you escape the penalty for trying to turn aside what must be" (7.17.2). Artabanus told Xerxes what had happened, and he was now willing to recognize that the expedition had divine sanction.

The dream was part of Xerxes' tragic destiny; he could not control his fate.[3] But there was another factor, too, that set the path that Xerxes had to follow. It was the *nomos* of the Persians to expand, and Xerxes could not be a less successful imperialist than his ancestors. The dream was explicit: if Xerxes failed to advance, he would be speedily reduced to low estate. There is more than a little irony to the fact that later (9.41), before the final defeat of Persia at Plataea in 479 B.C., Mardonius was to urge his officers to follow the same Persian *nomos*, join battle, and not retreat.[4]

Xerxes was a prisoner of his mission, but on the whole, he was a happy prisoner. As he readied his expedition, he had a third dream: he saw himself crowned with olive that spread all over the earth, and then it vanished. The olive was sacred to Athens, and its disappearance could only have signified Xerxes' defeat. But he misunderstood the warning. The *magi* told him that his dream meant he would be master of the whole world, and he happily accepted their word (7.19).

The Preparations

The tale of how Xerxes resolved to invade Greece borrowed a theme from Homer and elaborated upon it. In the *Iliad* (2.6–34), Zeus sent a deceitful dream to Agamemnon to tell him he would take Troy if he attacked at once. In the sequel, Agamemnon suffered a notable humbling of his pride. The story of Xerxes' preparations

expands upon another loan from the *Iliad*, the Catalog of Ships
(2.484–877), but develops it into an exposition of Oriental pride and
vainglory, with the insistent suggestion of coming disaster in the
background.

Xerxes spent four years making preparations. He had a canal dug
through the peninsula of Athos at its narrowest point, now known as
the Vale of Provlaka. The canal was intended as a monument to the
king's power, Herodotus conjectured, for if he had wished, he could
easily have had his ships dragged across the Vale. He had the
Hellespont bridged, and when a storm broke down the first span, he
reacted angrily, ordering the Hellespont scourged and put in chains:
that is, fetters were thrown into the sea. "Bitter water," the Persians
intoned over the strait, "our despot lays this punishment on you, for
you did him wrong, though he had done you none. King Xerxes will
cross you, whether you will or no" (7.35). Xerxes had joined figures
from myth like Salmoneus and Ixion, who had impiously claimed
godhead.

Finally, the bridges were ready. There were two of them, designed
to shield each other from the force of the prevailing winds, and held
in place by great hawsers that, in Herodotus's day, hung in the Stoa of
the Athenians at Delphi.[5] Then the army set out from Sardis, led by
Xerxes in a chariot drawn by sacred white Nesaean horses (he also
had a carriage where he could rest when he chose). At Troy, he
paused for sacrifice, and at Abydos, at the eastern end of the bridges,
he sat on a stone seat made upon a hill at his command, and reviewed
his army and fleet mustered beneath. It took seven days and nights for
the army to cross the bridges: a statistic sanctioned by folktale, if
nothing else.

At Doriscus, on the European side, Xerxes counted his army.
Herodotus catalogs the subject peoples of the empire, much as they
must have appeared in the New Year's Festival at Persepolis, when
they gathered to pay tribute. The statistics Herodotus gives are like the
millions and billions that modern journalists cite: they convey the
impression of enormous size and power. There were 1,207 triremes
(7.89.1), 80,000 horsemen (7.87.1), and a total land army of
1,700,000 (7.60.1). Through this vast host, Xerxes made his way in
a chariot, asking what each nation was, as he came to it, and then he

reviewed the fleet in like manner, sitting under a golden canopy on the deck of a Sidonian ship. A panorama of pomp and circumstance.

But in the midst of it all was the hint of impending disaster. As the army left Sardis (7.37); there was an eclipse of the sun (the story has probably combined two eclipses, one visible at Susa in 481 B.C., and the other at Sardis in the fall of 480) and Xerxes, disturbed, asked the *magi* for an interpretation. They assured him that the eclipse portended the destruction of Greece. But one Pythius, a rich Lydian who had entertained Xerxes lavishly, was fearful, and dared ask the king to release his eldest son from the army. Xerxes had the son's body split in two, and set up, one half on either side of the road along which his army marched.

Then too, at Abydos, Xerxes and Artabanus have their last conversation. Xerxes wept at the sight of his army, for the thought struck him that man's life was short and filled with misfortunes he could not escape. Artabanus replied with his customary pessimism; he foresaw the difficulties that Xerxes would face as he marched into a hostile land, where there was no harbor large enough for his fleet, and where, every day he advanced, he would stretch his supply line further. Xerxes did not dispute the point, but he would have none of his uncle's pessimism. Men must risk greatly to win greatly. Then Artabanus suggested a specific precaution; let the king dismiss the Ionians, for either they would enslave Athens, their mother-city, in which case they would be contemptible, or they would try to help her, and thus harm Xerxes. (An unkind cut, this, for in fact, the Ionians remembered their kinship with Greece only after the Persians were in retreat.) Xerxes remained resolutely blind. The Ionians would be true to him, and with that, he sent Artabanus and his pessimism back to Persia, to govern in his absence.

Finally, the section on the preparations concludes with a conversation between Xerxes and Demaratus, who now assumes Artabanus's role as wise advisor to the king. The exchange is a gem of irony. Xerxes, at the height of his vainglory, asked if the Greeks would dare lift a hand against him, and laughed when Demaratus replied that they would indeed resist. He could not understand that free men, without a despot to impose discipline on them, might unite to defend themselves. But Demaratus assured him that the Greeks did, in fact, have a despot. "For being free, they are not free in all things, but law is over them for master, which they dread in their hearts more than your people fear you" (7.104.4). Xerxes was uncomprehending and amused, but he dismissed Demaratus kindly.

Thus the king set forth. He was not an unattractive man, but he had little understanding or wisdom, and he was blinded by his own vainglory. And yet he was well warned of the dangers ahead.

The March Through Thrace

Though Herodotus describes the advance of the Persians as if there were a single army following a single route, they advanced in three columns, one, commanded by Mardonius and Masistes, marching along the coast, the second, under Tritantaechmes and Gergis, following an inland route, and the third, which escorted Xerxes, marching between the other two, under the command of Megabyzus and Smerdomenes. The Thracians in the area left the path still uncultivated in Herodotus's day, and it must be on this that his detailed knowledge of Xerxes' route is based. We can follow it on a modern road map, for it does not deviate greatly from the National Highway that runs today from the Turkish border to Thessaloniki, ancient Therma.[6]

Doriscus, a Persian fort built on a hill some twenty-three kilometers east of modern Alexandroupolis, was strong enough that the Greeks never succeeded in taking it, even after they had driven the Persians out of every other foothold in Europe (7.106). The route west to Neapolis (Kavala) passed "the Samothracian fortresses," one of which was probably at Alexandroupolis. The army drained the river Lisos (the Filiouri?) and reached Stryme, today Pagouria, south of the modern highway. The route then swung north of Lake Vistonis, crossed the river Nestos, and near Pistyrus the army found a brackish lake which the pack-animals drained dry. Pistyrus is probably modern Pontolivadon, a village some eighteen kilometers east of Kavala.[7] Thence the route went south of Mt. Pangaeus to the river Strymon, where the Persians had a fort at Eion under the command of Boges, who was later to defend himself to the death when he was beseiged in 477–476 B.C. by an army of the Delian League led by Miltiades' son, Cimon. There, though Herodotus does not say so, probably most of the army took the shortest route to Therma, which would follow the present highway south of lakes Volvi and Koronia. But Xerxes, averred Herodotus, marched past Stageiros, and thence to Akanthos, whose remains are on a hill overlooking Ierissos, a fishing village nowadays, but it was there that the fleet mustered prior to passing through the Athos canal.

Xerxes' army marched along three separate routes, but what Herodotus traced years later was the path recognized by local tradition. Which of the three routes did this path follow? We learn later (8.115.4) that during his march, Xerxes deposited the holy chariot of Ahura-Mazda—Zeus, Herodotus called him (7.40.4)—at Siris, modern Sere, which lies north of the path that Herodotus has mapped. It may have been on the route of the inland column. From Akanthos to Therma, Xerxes probably went by the shortest path that followed the modern highway from Mt. Athos to Thessaloniki, through the Holoman Pass. But the route that Herodotus describes would have him retrace his steps in part and loop into Thessaloniki from the northeast.[8] It does not seem possible.

However, Xerxes did pass through wild country, where there still roamed Asiatic lions and aurochs, the latter now extinct, and the former reduced to one small herd in northwest India. The climatic pattern of Thrace and Macedonia is that of central Europe rather than the Mediterranean, and the rivers flow year round. As the great army moved south, it would encounter streams reduced to trickles in the summer, and if it exhausted the lakes and rivers in the north, what degrees of thirst would it suffer as it pushed on into Greece?

At Thessaloniki (Therma), Xerxes paused, and his army stretched for almost forty kilometers along the shore from Thessaloniki to the mouths of the Loudies and Aliakmon rivers. Before Xerxes left Sardis, he had sent heralds to the Greek states, Athens and Sparta excepted, to demand earth and water, and now we hear of their return, though when they reached Xerxes, he was already in Pieria, south of the Aliakmon. Some states had given the symbols of surrender, and Herodotus (7.132) lists their names. The loyalist Greeks struck back, swearing to "tithe" any city that gave itself up to Persia without being forced into it; that is, they would destroy the city and dedicate a tenth to Apollo. Thus, almost parenthetically, at the first contact between

Xerxes' host and the defenders of Greece, Herodotus introduces the
story of Greek preparations.

The Greek Preparations

It is the fact of surrender that Herodotus records. The Greeks that
gave earth and water were the Thessalians, Dolopes, Enienes, Perrhaebians, Locrians, Magnesians, Malians, Achaeans of Phthia, and all
Boeotia except Thespiae and Plataea. Why they surrendered does not
interest Herodotus. But it transpires that the reason was not only
precaution: pro-Persian turncoats had also been at work. In Thessaly,
the Aleuad clan, hereditary chiefs of Larissa, supported the Persians,
but the majority of Thessalians did not follow its lead, and were
prepared to resist (7.172). The Opuntian Locrians were to fight at
Thermopylae, and so perhaps it was only the Ozolian Locrians who
surrendered. In the major city of Boeotia, Thebes, there were divided
counsels,[10] though Herodotus passes over that fact, and later Xerxes
had to be assured by the king of Macedonia that Boeotia was really on
his side before he spared it (8.34). Nor does Herodotus note the time
factor. The heralds bearing earth and water reached Xerxes while he
was in the region of Pieria, just north of the Olympus-Ossa range; by
then, the Greeks had decided to abandon all northern Greece. It was
a moment of panic.

The Greek-preparations digression follows a familiar pattern. First
a Spartan story; then an Athenian one. The Greeks "who were of the
better way of thinking" (7.145.1) had already formed an alliance
before the Persian army reached Sardis, but the details did not interest
Herodotus. It is only from scattered references that we can put together
a coherent picture. When Xerxes resolved on his invasion, Demaratus
got word to Sparta (7.239). The loyalist Greeks sent *probouloi*
("deputies") to the Isthmus of Corinth to deliberate, and there they
met a delegation from Thessaly urging them to make a stand at Mt.
Olympus (7.172). Whereupon they sent ten thousand hoplites,
reinforced by a contingent of Thessalian cavalry, to the Vale of Tempe
where the Peneios flows between Olympus and Ossa, but withdrew
when Alexander I, king of Macedon, told them how vast the Persian
forces were. All this happened before Xerxes crossed the Hellespont
(7.173).

Herodotus himself thought the Greeks withdrew from Tempe because they learned there was another pass through the mountains (there are, in fact, three),[11] and that they need not have been surprised at the numbers of the invaders, for they had already sent three spies to Sardis, whom the Persians captured, and then freed on Xerxes' orders, so that they could report how invincible his army was (7.146–47). But in any case, the expeditionary force retired from Tempe to the Isthmus, where the *probouloi* debated again what to do, and decided to defend the pass of Thermopylae. Meanwhile, the Persians had advanced as far as Pieria, the region round about the modern city of Katerini, where Xerxes received earth and water from the fainthearted Greeks. Probably it was then that the *probouloi* swore to "tithe" those cities that surrendered voluntarily.[12] It was a moment of crisis and the oath may have been their last act. Word came to them that Xerxes was in Pieria, Herodotus (7.177) reports, and "breaking off their session at the Isthmus, they set out, some on foot to Thermopylae and some by sea to Artemisium." We do not hear of them again.

Upon all this, Herodotus imposes his usual story pattern. Xerxes sent no heralds to Sparta or Athens, because the heralds that Darius had sent before Marathon had been put to death at both cities (7.133). That was sacrilege, and though Athens suffered no retribution so far as Herodotus knew, the Spartans were denied auspicious omens whenever they sacrificed, until they sent two Spartiates, Sperthias and Bulis, to Xerxes to offer their own lives in atonement. Xerxes, "from high-mindedness," let them go, and the curse troubled Sparta no more—but years later (it was 430 B.C., the second year of the Peloponnesian War) the sons of Sperthias and Bulis fell into Athenian hands while on a mission to Persia, and were put to death.

Then follows the parallel story that tells how Athens prepared for the invasion. It touches only what Herodotus considered the highlights. First, he pays tribute to Athenian courage. Athens saved Greece, for the outcome of the war hung on the choice she made, either to surrender or remain steadfast, and, forced to choose, Athens chose the loyalist side (7.139). It was Athenian naval power that tipped the balance, and the tribute to Athens as savior of Greece is also a tribute to the Athenian fleet, and as well, a preface to the stage entrance of that Athenian who persuaded his city to build it.

It was perhaps early in 480 B.C., just after the Delphic oracle reopened in the spring, that Athens consulted it, and received a response that told them to flee before the Persian onslaught. The Athenian envoys were dismayed, and one Timon, a "notable man" at Delphi and no doubt the Athenian *proxenos*, urged them to approach the Pythia again, this time as suppliants bearing olive-branches. The second oracle they received was hardly more reassuring, but it referred to a wooden wall that would survive, and aid "you and your children" and concluded with a cryptic reference to "holy Salamis" that would destroy the "offspring of women at the time of sowing or harvest." It was small comfort. Clearly Delphi put its trust in the big battalions. The envoys accepted the oracle and took it home, where the Athenians interpreted it variously,[13] but there were two favorite explications. One was that the "wooden wall" referred to an old wattled palisade that once fenced the Acropolis, and the other, which had the support of the soothsayers, made the "wooden wall" the fleet and Salamis the site of its defeat.

Against this background of despair and bewilderment, Herodotus introduces Themistocles. "There was a certain Athenian, who had recently become one of the leading men, and his name was Themistocles, but he was called the son Neocles" (7.143.1).[14] The entrance is dramatic, and Herodotus may perhaps have sacrificed a degree of accuracy to heighten the drama, for Themistocles, who had been archon in 493–492 B.C.[15] was not a recent arrival to Athenian politics. But he had not been born into a great ruling family; he had won his own way into the political elite without the backing of a powerful gossiprede, and had risen to top rank in the decade after Marathon which was marked by political struggle and ostracisms. Ostracism, whereby a politician might be exiled by referendum for ten years, was a weapon traditionally instituted by Cleisthenes, but never used until someone in the early 480s rediscovered it. The "someone" may not have been Themistocles himself, but he used the weapon with skill and daring.[16] Herodotus says none of this. Themistocles, he tells us, who had recently arrived within the political elite—a backhanded reference, perhaps, to the ostracism of his rival, Aristides, in 482 B.C.—offered his own interpretation of the "wooden wall" oracle.

The fleet was the wall, as the soothsayers claimed, but the reference to Salamis was hopeful, for the god called the island "holy," not "abominable," which would have been more fitting if Athens was to perish there. It was a straw for the desperate to grasp, but as it happened, Themistocles had already persuaded Athens to build a fleet. The silver mines at Laurium had provided the treasury with a windfall profit, and Themistocles had prevailed upon the Athenians to use it to build two hundred warships "for the war—he meant the war against Aegina" (7.144.2).[17] This war had dragged on, and was settled only in 481, when all the loyalist states composed their differences and joined in the defense of Greece. But the Aeginetan war saved Greece, Herodotus remarks, for it forced the Athenians to become skilled seamen.

The scene shifts to the meeting of the Greek allies. The league resolved to seek help from Argos, Syracuse in Sicily, Corcyra, and Crete, for they intended to see if "all Greece might be one, and if they would all put their hearts in it . . ." (7.145.2). The embassies set forth, and Herodotus describes their adventures with a trace of *parti pris*.

Argos sent no help. The Argives told Herodotus that Delphi had advised them to be neutral: they had suffered terribly at Sparta's hands only thirteen years earlier. However, they did not refuse the alliance outright; instead they proposed terms that Sparta was bound to reject. There was a story elsewhere in Greece that Argos made a separate peace with Xerxes. Herodotus tells it with a *caveat*: "I am bound to report what is said, but I am not at all bound to believe it" (7.152.3). His judgment on the Argives is lenient. If men were to bring their faults to market to exchange them, they would gladly take their own home again, once they had inspected their neighbors'.

A mission went to the tyrant of Syracuse, Gelon, who together with his ally, Theron of Akragas, controlled most of Greek Sicily, and the spokesman for Sparta made the appeal. Let Gelon help the allied Greeks, for their danger was his: if Xerxes overran Greece, he would attack Sicily next. Gelon replied by pointing out that the common good, as the Spartans and their ilk saw it, had never included the defense of Sicily. But no matter. He would provide an enormous force and feed the whole Greek army, provided that he could be commander-in-chief.

The Spartan replied briefly that Sparta provided the commanders. Gelon then offered to settle for command of the navy. Thereupon the Athenian envoy broke in to say that, though Athens might yield the naval command to Sparta, she would yield it to no one else. So Gelon dismissed the envoys in disgust. Herodotus (7.162.1) borrows a phrase from a speech of Pericles and puts it in Gelon's mouth: "Tell Greece that the spring is taken out of the year."[18]

In fact, Gelon was in danger himself. The tyrant of Himera on the north coast of Sicily had been expelled by Theron in 483, and had gone for help to Carthage, where he was the guest-friend of the Magonid king, Hamilcar. Thus in 480, as Xerxes advanced into Greece, an army under Hamilcar landed at modern Palermo and marched east to Himera, where Gelon and Theron routed him. It was a close thing: Herodotus reports that Gelon had an embassy waiting to give the Persians earth and water if they won at Salamis. As it turned out, Salamis and Himera were won at the same time—on the same day, the Sicilian Greeks claimed (7.163–68). Gelon lived only two more years, but he left a lasting memorial: the temple of Athena that was built with booty from Himera still stands, and, fitted out with a baroque facade, serves as the cathedral of modern Siracosa.

Gelon had a valid excuse for not helping to defend Greece. But for Corcyra, Herodotus had no sympathy. They promised help, and they did man sixty ships, which waited off the south coast of the Peloponnesus to see how the war would go. When the Greeks won, the Corcyraeans averred that they had been delayed by unfavorable winds.

Crete sent no help because Delphi advised against it in no unmistakable terms. Herodotus had either heard nothing of the tradition that Cretan archers fought at Salamis, or he chose to ignore it as a fabrication,[19] but he neither excuses nor blames the Cretans.

Tempe to Thermopylae

Herodotus had left Xerxes in Pieria, north of the Olympus-Ossa range. The pass through the Vale of Tempe was open, for the ten thousand hoplites sent to hold it, under the Spartan polemarch Euaenetus, had retreated. But Xerxes did not use the Tempe pass; instead he advanced through another pass which he learned was safer

(7.128.1), that went through upper Macedonia "through the land of the Perrhaebians, down to the city of Gonnos" (7.173.4). There are two possible routes: one runs southwest from Katerini, through the Petra pass, and loops south and east back to Gonnos, while the other goes directly over a shoulder of Mt. Olympus, past the village of Kalipefki, and then descends by an indifferent road to Gonnos.[20] Yet, the direct route through Tempe was unguarded! Probably the truth is that the Persian army marched in three divisions, as it did in Thrace, and used more than one pass. Consequently, local tradition reported, correctly, that the Persian army had marched through the land of the Perrhaebians, but forgot that it had also used Tempe, which Xerxes himself cautiously avoided. There is a parallel later, equally curious: the Persians fight hard to win the pass of Thermopylae, and then, apparently, do not use it (8.32–34).

The modern traveler who visits the pass of Thermopylae nowadays gets little hint of its appearance in 480, for silt from the Spercheios River has advanced the shoreline of the Malian Gulf by nearly three miles, but when Herodotus knew it, the coast road along the south edge of the gulf ran for almost four miles between the sea and the precipitous side of Mt. Kallidromos, and at either end, the defile was so narrow that there was room for only a single cart. To the east, across the Malian Gulf, lay Euboea, and if the Persian fleet wanted contact with the land force engaged at Thermopylae, it would have to control the Trikeri channel to the north of the island, and the even narrower channel of Oreon, before it got to the Malian Gulf. The *probouloi* at the Isthmus of Corinth had decided to send a modest force to hold Thermopylae, and at the same time, station a fleet at Cape Artemisium on the north tip of Euboea, close enough to Thermopylae to keep in touch with the army (7.175.2; 8.21.1). They did not know, Herodotus noted (7.206.2)—and there is no reason to disbelieve him, for reconnaissance was poor and topographical maps nonexistent[21]—that there was a path which outflanked Thermopylae, and hence the Greeks were to be caught off guard by the speed with which Xerxes captured the pass.

The Persian force that approached Thermopylae had now reached great size, for it was swollen by contingents from Thrace and northern Greece that had now surrendered. Herodotus pauses again to number them, and reaches a grand total of 5,283,220 men, noncombatants included.[22] The triremes in the fleet numbered 1,207, each with crews of two hundred, plus thirty marines, and there were three thousand galleys of fifty oars in addition. For the camp followers, pack animals, and dogs, Herodotus had no statistics, but he marveled how such a host could be fed and watered. Well he might.[23]

As the Greeks prepared to defend Thermopylae, the Delphians themselves sought an oracle from Apollo, and were told to pray to the winds (7.178). The Athenians too had received an oracle bidding them to pray to the North Wind, Boreas (7.189). Scholars have taken Delphic policy as pro-Persian, and with some justice, but Delphi had a concern we do not entirely appreciate: oracles that thrive must appear to be right, and at this point in time, it was reasonable to suppose that the Persians would win. Fortunately, it was also reasonable to suppose that the north wind—still called the *Vora*—would blow, for in summer, it can cause sudden storms in the north Aegean.[24] Artabanus had warned Xerxes that he should take care: lightning from Heaven struck the tallest buildings or trees (7.10.ε). Now what was only a storm metaphor for Artabanus would become reality, and Boreas would strike the vast Persian fleet.

The Storm

As the Persian navy left the Thermaic Gulf, a squadron of ten ships sailed ahead to mark a reef in the channel between the island of Skiathos and the tip of the Magnesian peninsula, met three Greek ships off Skiathos, and gave chase. Two were captured, but one, from Athens, kept ahead of its pursuers for some sixty miles, all the way to the mouth of the Peneios river, where the crew beached their vessel and escaped. Greek scouts on the heights of Skiathos witnessed all this, and signaled to the fleet at Artemisium, which promptly withdrew behind Euboea—Herodotus claims that it went as far south as Chalcis, where Euboea is separated from the mainland by a narrow strait known as the Euripus. Then the Persian armada arrived, straggling along under sail with supply ships in the rear, and anchored in eight rows on the open beach of the Magnesian peninsula, between Kasthanie (near modern Keramidion) and Sepias (Pourion).[25] It was an exposed anchorage. A short voyage further on would have brought the ships to the safety of the Pagasite Gulf, but the Persian admirals must have believed that the Greek fleet was still at Cape Artemisium, where it could attack them as they emerged from the narrow Skiathos channel that they had to navigate before they reached the gulf. So they chose to pause and spend the night on the open coast of Magnesia. It was a disastrous decision.

In the early morning, the wind arose, and blew a gale for three days. On the second day, scouts on Euboea got word to the Greek fleet lying off Chalcis, and it hastened back to Artemisium.[26] However, when the gale blew itself out early on the fourth day, the Persian fleet moved promptly around the cape of Magnesia and into the safety of the Pagasite Gulf. The Greeks at Artemisium watched it sail past without challenging it; they did, however, capture fifteen stragglers and interrogated their crews (7.193–95). But now Herodotus shifts attention to the battle at Thermopylae.

The Saga of Thermopylae

Thermopylae was legend by the time Herodotus wrote. Specifically Spartan legend. Three hundred Spartiates fought and died in the pass, true to their traditions to the end, and leading them was their king, Leonidas, who had learned from an oracle that if Sparta was to be saved, a king must die. Herodotus treads on hallowed ground here, and he betrays a particular concern for exactitude. He examined the terrain: he saw, on the hill where the Greeks made their last stand, the stone lion that commemorated Leonidas, and he describes the Anopaea path, by which the Persians outflanked Leonidas's position, with enough detail to suggest that he walked over it himself.[27] Legends could not be treated carelessly.

The structure is equally careful. First we have Xerxes' advance to Thermopylae through Thessaly and Achaea; we are told later, almost casually, that before he left Thessaly, he knew that Leonidas's little army was waiting for him at Thermopylae (7.208). Herodotus describes the terrain around the Malian Gulf and Thermopylae itself as a traveler coming from the north would see it. Finally, Xerxes reached the pass: the *Gates*, as the local people called it. To the north, Xerxes possessed everything; to the south, Greece was free.[28]

Then the Greek forces. Herodotus catalogs them: thirty-one

hundred from the Peloponnesus, four hundred from Thebes, and seven hundred from Thespiae. A call went out for volunteers from the Thermopylae area: all the Opuntian Locrians came who could bear arms, and one thousand men from Phocis. The commander was Leonidas: Herodotus introduces him with a flourish, and gives his lineage back to Heracles. He brought with him the royal bodyguard of three hundred Spartiates, and if he had other Lacedaemonians as well (there were certainly helots: 8.25.1), Spartan tradition overlooked them. It was a small force. The Spartans had sent these men in advance to stiffen resistance, Herodotus explained, but they wanted to keep the Carnean festival before they marched out in force. The rest of Greece was celebrating the Olympic Games (7.206). Thermopylae seemed to be a strong position, and the Spartans at home were confident.

But Leonidas's little force was not, and Herodotus starts the preliminaries of the battle by describing the panic as Xerxes approached. The Peloponnesians wanted to go home, but the Phocians and Locrians objected strenuously, and Leonidas sided with them. But he sent for reinforcements. Evidently, it was only when the Peloponnesians reached Thermopylae, that they learned of the Anopaea path that the Persians were to use to outflank them, and they wanted to retreat, for as far as they were concerned, the Isthmus was the final line of defense. But Leonidas would have none of it. He sent for help and prepared for battle.

The scene shifts to Xerxes' camp. Xerxes sent a mounted scout to reconnoiter, and he reported that he saw some Spartans taking exercise, and others combing their long hair. Ridiculous behavior, Xerxes thought, and summoned Demaratus to explain. Demaratus's reply to Xerxes sums up Sparta's claim to be the savior of Greece: if Xerxes could overcome the Spartiates, the rest of Greece would fall. But Xerxes was unconvinced, and waited four days before he joined battle, thinking that the Greeks would seize the chance to retreat. Later (8.15.1), we are to discover that the engagements at Artemisium and Thermopylae coincided, and hence Xerxes was waiting for his fleet, delayed by the gale, to take up position. But here Herodotus attributes Xerxes' delay to his incomprehension.

For two days, the Greeks fought off all attacks. Then, when Xerxes was at a loss what to do, Ephialtes of Malis played the traitor, and informed him of the Anopaea path. Delighted, Xerxes sent his best troops, the ten thousand "Immortals," with Ephialtes as guide, under orders to traverse the path during the night, and fall on the Greek rear the next day.

Leonidas had detached the thousand men from Phocis to guard the Anopaea path, for they had volunteered, and with some reason. They knew the path as a route used by the Thessalians to raid Phocis, bypassing the wall that the Phocians had built to block the pass of Thermopylae (7.215; 7.176.3–5). By daybreak, the Immortals had climbed the path to the fork where one branch veered into Phocis and the other led downhill to the rear of Leonidas's position. There they encountered the Phocians, who had time only to put on their armor before a shower of arrows routed them. They rallied, however, and prepared to defend the path into Phocis. But the Persians were not going to Phocis, as the Phocians imagined; instead they hurried on their way along the other path.

The scene shifts to Leonidas's force in the pass. During the night, the seer Megistias had prophesied death in the morning, and deserters also brought word. But full comprehension did not come until scouts arrived after dawn. There was more than one story of what happened next, but Herodotus thought that Leonidas, seeing his allies fearful, sent them home, but considered it unseemly for himself and his Spartans to retreat. The Thespians and the Thebans also stayed, the latter under duress, Herodotus insists, for he was unwilling to believe there was such a thing as a patriotic Theban. He was unfair, for in this desperate situation, Leonidas could hardly have wanted four hundred potential quislings in his force, and we have other evidence that there was a loyalist party in Thebes, and the four hundred belonged to it.[29] Leonidas was realistic: he wanted his Peloponnesian allies to get home safely to fight again at the Isthmus if need be. But hoplites could not retreat in good order with an enemy force at their heels and so Leonidas stayed, and held the pass until his allies could get away.

Now the final struggle. Later writers would embroider it, but Herodotus is brief. The Greeks determined to sell their lives dearly, but after Leonidas had fallen, and they were surrounded by the Immortals in the rear and the main army in front, the Lacedaemonians and Thespians withdrew behind the Phocian wall on a hill and held out as long as they could. The Thebans surrendered.

So ended the battle. Various *gestes* follow: how the Spartiate Dieneces was told that the cloud of Persian arrows would block the sun, and replied that then the Greeks would fight in the shade, and how two Spartiates, afflicted with eye disease acted differently: one rushed, sightless, into the fight and died gloriously, while the other went home and met contempt. Once more Herodotus harps on Theban treachery: in utter contrast to the Spartans and Thespians, they abjectly gave themselves up. And now, in the final scene, Demaratus comes on stage.

Demaratus had warned Xerxes before the battle, and Xerxes had not believed him. Now he admitted his error and asked with new respect how many Spartans there were. Eight thousand Spartiates, Demaratus replied, plus other Lacedaemonians who were not first-rate, but good men nonetheless. How then, Xerxes demanded, could the Persians overcome them? Demaratus's suggestion was that he seize Cythera, and use it as a base against Lacedaemon. Athens was to use this tactic more than a half-century later, during the Peloponnesian War, but it is an anachronism here. Xerxes' brother, Achaemenes, spoke against it, and Demaratus's futuristic advice came to nothing.

Artemisium Concluded

On the morning of the first day of battle at Thermopylae the storm at sea had ceased, and the Persian fleet left its exposed roadstead and sailed for Aphetae in the Pagasite Gulf, first, however, detaching a squadron of two hundred ships to sail round Euboea and take the Greeks from the rear. It reached Aphetae by early afternoon, still in fighting trim, to the disappointment of the Greeks, who had hoped that the gale had done more damage. Herodotus now introduces the contingents of the Greek fleet; Athens had the largest: one hundred and twenty-seven ships, which she manned with help from Plataea, and in addition, she lent twenty hulls to Chalcis. But the admiral was the Spartan, Eurybiades, for the other allies refused to have an Athenian as leader, and Athens shrewdly bided her time (8.3).

The first engagement at sea took place in the late afternoon of that same day. Herodotus tells an incredible tale of how the Greeks were so unnerved when they saw the Persian fleet that they planned another retreat, but the Euboeans, desperate for time to evacuate dependents, gave Themistocles an enormous bribe of thirty talents, of which he distributed eight to Eurybiades and the Corinthian commander, Adeimantos, and pocketed the rest. Who were these "Euboeans" and how could they have raised so great a sum in a few hours? The story is part of the libel with which Themistocles's enemies mauled his reputation in the years after Xerxes' defeat, and we need not believe it. The mission of the Greek fleet was to prevent the Persian ships from cooperating with Xerxes' army at Thermopylae, and to do that, it had to defend the north Euboic Gulf. It could not retreat.

Meanwhile, word came of the Persian squadron circumnavigating Euboea. Now the Greeks had reason to be unnerved; nevertheless, in late afternoon, they put out to offer battle, and fought until darkness fell. That night, there was a violent thunderstorm, and it caught the squadron sailing around Euboea off "The Hollows," where the Aegean shore of the island curves inward between Cape Othonia to the north and Cape Kaphereus (Kavo Doro) at the southeast tip.[30] The main Persian fleet at Aphetae was unharmed, but the storm did nothing for morale, and when day came, it was content to remain at anchor.

The Greeks, however, were elated, for an Athenian squadron of fifty-three ships arrived with news of the Persian wreck off "The Hollows." In the late afternoon, they offered battle again, but the Persians showed no interest in another engagement that would end with nightfall. The Greeks captured a few stragglers and returned to Artemisium.

But on the third day, while Leonidas was making his last stand at Thermopylae, the Persian fleet put to sea about noon, and advanced in crescent formation toward Artemisium. This time, the battle was fierce and evenly fought. The Persians suffered more than the Greeks (8.18), but Greek losses were heavy, and half the Athenian fleet was damaged, although it reappears with undiminished strength at Salamis. Unable to fight again without some repairs, the Greeks decided to pull back; then word came of the fall of Thermopylae, and they retreated forthwith in good order, with the Corinthian squadron leading and the Athenians bringing up the rear. They were making for Salamis (8.40.1).

The Thermopylae-Artemisium battle—for it was a combined operation—concludes with a strange charade. Xerxes invited the sailors of the fleet to view the field of Thermopylae, which he ordered carefully prepared: of the twenty thousand Persian dead, he had all but one thousand concealed, but all four thousand Greek corpses were on display. The sailors, however, were not deceived. An Ionian tale, perhaps, for Ionians served in Xerxes' fleet. At any rate, it smacks of folk tradition.

Thermopylae to Salamis

To Xerxes, the Greeks remained incomprehensible, but some of his entourage now had a glimmering of understanding. A few deserters from Arcadia came to the Persian camp, and Xerxes asked them about Greek preparations. They told him that the Olympic Games were being held, for which the prize was an olive crown. Then the son of Artabanus, Tigranes, marveled aloud at these Greeks who strove, not for money, but simply for excellence. But to Xerxes' mind, Tigranes' words were a mark of timidity (8.26).

Now that the pass of Thermopylae was won, we must believe that a Persian detachment took possession of it, but Herodotus indicates that the main army advanced by a route that must have passed between Mount Oite and Mount Kallidromos to join what is roughly the modern highway between Lamia and Levadhia. It was the Thessalians who guided the Persians that way, for they wanted revenge on their enemies, the Phocians.[31] Herodotus names the cities burned, and records that they caught some Phocians and raped and killed the women. But most of the Phocians got away in time.

Xerxes advanced, pillaging and ravaging as he went, through the pass of Belessi to Panopea (Aghios Vlassios), three kilometers west of the modern highway, where he divided his forces. He himself, with the main army made for Athens, going by way of Thespiae and Plataea, and burning them both. At the same time, a detachment skirted Mt. Parnassos and took the road to Delphi, for Xerxes knew about the treasures there "better than those he had left in his own palaces" (8.35.2). The Delphians fled, except for the prophet of Apollo and sixty men. But the god defended himself. As the Persians approached the sanctuary of Athena Pronaia at the entrance to Delphi, lightning flashed, and a landslide roared down Parnassos upon them. From the temple of Athena issued a war cry. The surviving Persians fled, and the Delphians caught a number and slew them. A Delphian story, no doubt fitted out with sacred embroidery, but the temple of Athena Pronaia *was* damaged about this time,[32] for the repairs can still be seen, and a landslide at Delphi, perhaps encouraged by human hands, need not strain our credulity. At any rate, the treasures of Delphi remained safe for another century.

The Fall of Athens

The Greeks retired from Artemisium to Salamis, except for the Plataeans who had helped man the Athenian triremes; they disembarked opposite Chalcis and hurried home to evacute their city. It seems that the Athenians were faced with a *fait accompli*. They had understood that Leonidas's little force at Thermopylae was the advance guard of the main allied army that would march north after the Carnean festival in Sparta, and hence they expected that it would be already in Boeotia (8.40). They now discovered that the Peloponnesians had been slow to move; they had got no further than the pass known as the Kaki Scala, where the legendary highwayman Skiron once hurled travelers into the sea, and were building a wall across the Isthmus of Corinth. The Athenians could only beg the fleet to put in at Salamis so that they could evacuate their households.

Had the Athenians been deceived? By the time Herodotus wrote, Leonidas's last stand was already a legend, that was to blossom into a tale of self-sacrifice, whereby the patriot king laid down his life in accordance with an oracle that Sparta must lose either a king or her liberty.[33] But the Greeks at Thermopylae had proclaimed that they were only an advance guard (7.203), and Herodotus noted that the speed with which the pass fell caught the allies by surprise (7.206). If this is true, then it seems that the *probouloi* had planned a strategy whereby Leonidas would hold Thermopylae only until the main army was ready to come up, while the battle fleet stood off the Persians at sea. Meanwhile, a reserve fleet gathered at Pogon, the port of Troezen (8.42.1), to protect the Isthmus if necessary, for to the Peloponnesian mind the Isthmus was the final line of defense, and perhaps the only feasible one. The main army moved slowly and was now only at the

Isthmus; it is an open question whether it had ever intended to go
further.

So the Athenians, led by Themistocles—though Herodotus leaves
his name unsaid at this juncture—docked at the Peiraeus and
proclaimed the evacuation. Most of the refugees went to Troezen, but
some went to Aegina and the island of Salamis. They moved quickly,
for the oracle (7.141.1) had told them not to await the Persian
onslaught; moreover, the sacred snake on the Acropolis disappeared,
which was taken as a sign that Athena had left her city, and the
Athenians were to do likewise. There is no hint of prior planning, but
only an orderly reaction to imminent danger that was not expected so
soon. A garrison was left on the Acropolis, but it was made up of
comptrollers of the treasury, men whose poverty had prevented them
from going to Salamis, and some, too, who felt they knew the true
meaning of the oracle's reference to "wooden walls" (8.51.2). They
barricaded the Acropolis with wooden palisades and stood seige.

Herodotus's account is cursory, but the general tenor is clear.
Surprised by the swift fall of Thermopylae, the allies were left without
clear contingency plans, except that the Peloponnesians wanted to
defend themselves by making a stand at the Isthmus. The fleet at
Salamis did not know what to do. The commanders deliberated, as the
Athenian generals had done before Marathon, and the Ionian
commanders before the battle of Lade. The pattern that emerged
before Marathon emerges here too: it was the Spartan admiral,
Eurybiades, a shadowy figure like the polemarch Callimachus at
Marathon, who made the choice to fight, and by that deliberate act,
saved Greece. These were frail vessels to change the course of history.
Yet, as Herodotus put it, "Thus, after this conflict of words, the men
at Salamis prepared to fight a battle there, for Eurybiades would have
it so" (8.64.1).

But has Herodotus imposed his own preferred historical pattern on
the tradition? Plutarch (*Them.*, 10) reports that when the "Wooden
Wall" oracle was received from Delphi, Themistocles persuaded the
Athenians that their ships were the wooden walls, as Herodotus
relates, and adds that he carried a decree "to entrust the city to
Athena, the guardians of the Athenians, and that men of military age
should embark on their triremes and save their children, wives and

slaves as best they could"; and in 1959, Michael Jameson discovered at Damala, ancient Troezen, an inscription purporting to be this decree.[34] It dates to the third century B.C., and is at best a copy of a reconstruction of the decree that Themistocles proposed. Yet, it seems to represent a tradition that does not quite follow Herodotus's reconstruction of the pattern of events leading up to Salamis.

According to this alternative tradition, something like this happened. The Athenians consulted Delphi in the spring of 480 and received the "Wooden Wall" oracle. An anxious debate ensued about its meaning. During much of this, Themistocles was absent, for he commanded the Athenians in the contingent that went to the Vale of Tempe before Xerxes crossed into Europe, and when that force retired to the Isthmus, he probably went with it, and took some part in the deliberations of the *probouloi* there. It was perhaps only after they had made plans to defend Thermopylae that Themistocles could return to Athens, where he found a city anxious and uncertain what to do. He realized at once that there was an interpretation of the oracle that would fit the allied tactics very well. The "wooden wall" was the fleet, and the oracle was bidding the Athenians to man their ships and evacuate the city. Of course, if Leonidas did hold Thermopylae, and if the Peloponnesian main army moved up to support him, the evacuation might be unnecessary, but the best plans could fail, and Themistocles preferred to be ready for the worst contingency.

Modern scholars often forget that Themistocles was a man of his times, and no doubt believed in oracles as much as the average Athenian. If Apollo commanded the Athenians to retreat before the Persians, then he looked forward to the possibility that Thermopylae might fall, and Athens be taken. Thus Themistocles carried a decree that provided not only for mustering the fleet, but also for the evacuation of Athens: all this just before Leonidas set forth to Thermopylae. The decree found at Troezen reconstructs the ordinance. The women and children were to go to Troezen, the old men and slaves to Salamis, and the treasurers and priestesses of the temple were to stay on the Acropolis to guard the goddess' property. All other Athenians and resident aliens were to man two hundred triremes, which should be taken as a round number rather than a statistic. Each ship was to have ten marines and four archers; Herodotus says nothing of these, but since each Persian ship carried thirty marines (7.184.2), it is reasonable to suppose that the Athenians had some as well. Half the fleet was to proceed to Artemisium and the other half was to "station itself around Salamis and the rest of Attica to guard the land." Ostracized citizens were to go to Salamis and wait there for the people to make a decision about them. The decree breaks off in the midst of a provision dealing with citizens who had been deprived of rights.[35]

The Athenian fleet retreated from Artemisium to the Peiraeus and proclaimed an evacuation that had already been planned in advance, while the rest of the fleet waited behind Salamis. Herodotus (8.42) mentions now, for the first, the reserve fleet mustered at Pogon, which joined the ships at Salamis. In Athens, the garrison fortified the Acropolis with wooden barricades as best it could, for the old Mycenaean walls that once protected it were by now partially demolished. But a group of attackers scaled the cliff on the north side, by the shrine of Aglauros, where no one had anticipated danger, and the Acropolis fell. The defenders took refuge in the temple of Athena, but the Persians slew them nonetheless, and burned the Acropolis. How much plunder they found is hard to guess, for no doubt the Athenians had removed as much as they could, including the *xoanon* or wooden statue of Athena Polias that was the city's most sacred cult image.

Herodotus (8.51.2) represents these defenders of the Acropolis as indigent, but strong-minded men who acted on their own initiative. But when the fleet learned that the Acropolis had fallen, it reacted with panic (8.56). What had the admirals expected? To be sure, panic need have no rational cause, but we may suspect that the defense of the Acropolis was an intentional part of the Greek strategy, designed to give the navy a breathing space.[36] It failed.

As Herodotus saw it, Salamis was a crisis point where the decision of one man, Eurybiades, decided the course of history. Themistocles' contributions were two: he found Athens irresolute and divided over the "Wooden Wall" oracle, offered a clever interpretation, and thus made the victory at Salamis possible, and second, he faced the crisis squarely, and forced Eurybiades to make the choice, whether to fight or not. It was not the "Themistocles Decree" that was his great achievement. For Herodotus, history was not a matter of documents.

The Preliminaries to Salamis

Once again, Herodotus (8.43–48) enumerates the fleet, noting the size of each contingent. The triremes totaled three hundred and seventy-eight, he assures us, although the sum of the contingents is only three hundred and sixty-six. But the bulk of the section on the preliminaries to Salamis describes the councils of the commanders in both camps: the Greeks quarrelsome and outspoken, while the Persian council was orderly and undemocratic. The Greek captains panicked when news came of the sack of Athens, and some left the council for their ships, determined to leave immediately. But the rest stayed for the decision. They would fight at the Isthmus. Night, which could cover the retreat, had already fallen.

Themistocles returned to his ship. There he met his gossip, Mnesiphilos,[37] who learned what the decision was, and warned Themistocles that if the allies retreated from Salamis, the fleet would disperse, no matter how much Eurybiades might try to prevent it. It was a dramatic encounter, with Mnesiphilos acting the wise-advisor role. Modern readers[38] have felt that Herodotus has denigrated Themistocles by giving Mnesiphilos credit for the victory at Salamis, but Herodotus was not the man to let concern for Themistocles' reputation stand in the way of a literary topos, and in any case, his contemporaries would not have thought it strange that a man's sponsor and gossip should encourage him to see his duty and perform it in a moment of crisis.[39] Themistocles received the advice gladly, returned to Eurybiades' ship, and persuaded him to call another council.

When the commanders gathered, Themistocles burst into earnest entreaty, urging them to stay and fight. The Corinthian general, Adeimantos, spoke against him, but Themistocles would not be drawn into an argument; instead he turned to Eurybiades and put the choice to him. "It is in your power to save Greece . . ." (8.60α). The Greek ships, fewer and heavier than the Persians, would acquit themselves better in restricted waters, and, if the Greeks won, the Persian army would not dare advance to the Isthmus. Megara, Aegina, and Salamis would be saved.

Adeimantos attacked again, and now Themistocles upbraided him bitterly. Then he spoke again to Eurybiades, more bluntly. If he stayed, he would be a "good man": an *aner agathos*, an example of the moral and physical courage on which a Spartiate prided himself. The clinching argument came last; if the fleet did not stay and fight, the Athenians would take their wives and children, and sail away to the west to find a new home in Italy. Eurybiades was won over, and Herodotus thought it was the last argument that did it. The die was cast.

Meanwhile, the Persian fleet had reached Phaleron, and Xerxes, too, called a council. Here there were no quarrels or vehement speeches. The subject tyrants and princes who provided ships took their seats in order of rank, beginning with the king of Sidon, and Mardonius put the question to each of them and collected their replies. Only one warned against battle: Artemisia from Halicarnassus, whose contingent was esteemed second only to that of Sidon, and she was (in the view of a native son) the king's best counselor (7.99). Artemisia's advice betrays the lucubrations of a couple generations of arm-chair strategists after the Persian defeat. She plays a Cassandra-role, while Xerxes is the magnanimous despot who disbelieves her but takes no offense. So the Persian fleet put out to sea. Night intervened, during which Xerxes' army commenced its march to the Isthmus.

Herodotus now interrupts to give the roll of the Greeks who came to defend the Isthmus. The Carnea at Sparta and the Olympic Games were both over, but not all the Peloponnesians rallied. Herodotus's judgment is harsher now than hitherto: "If I may speak freely, those who remained neutral helped the Persians" (8.73.3).

The scene shifts to the Greeks on the night before battle. The mutterings of the Peloponnesians against Eurybiades' decision to fight had broken into open insubordination. There was a last council, and Themistocles, seeing the debate going against him, slipped out and sent a trusted retainer, Sicinnus, to Xerxes with the message that the Greeks were panic-stricken and divided; now was the moment to attack. The Persians had already decided to give battle, but Sicinnus's message did affect their tactics. They landed a force on Psyttaleia

(Lipsokoutali)[40] in the channel between Salamis and the mainland, and moved their ships forward to block the strait and prevent escape. They spent the night on these maneuvers, while in the Greek camp there continued a "great joust of words" (8.78).

Then Aristides appeared, a statesman whom Herodotus's informants regarded as the paragon of civic virtue—and no friend of Themistocles. Herodotus is too succinct: he tells us that Aristides had been ostracized, and had just returned from Aegina where he had spent his exile; the implication, wrong or not, is that he was only now returning. He took Themistocles aside and told him that he had seen the Persian maneuvers: the Greeks were already surrounded. Themistocles asked him to tell that to the other Greeks, for he himself could not hope to convince, but even Aristides could not end the wrangling. Finally a Tenian trireme arrived that had deserted from the Persians, and confirmed Aristides' report. Morning came and the generals addressed their men. Themistocles' speech was outstanding, for he spoke of the antithesis of human nature and character, and of how men should make a choice for greatness. At Salamis, the choice had been made.

Salamis

Herodotus limns an impressionistic picture. The Persians attacked and the Greeks rowed astern—and then started to fight, though Herodotus has three stories of how it happened. As for the battle itself, he notes individual exploits. The Ionians in the Persian fleet faced the Lacedaemonians, and fought well for their overlords. Artemisia escaped an Athenian pursuer by sinking a ship of Xerxes' fleet, and passing herself off as a patriotic Greek; fortunately, Xerxes, who witnessed the sinking, took her victim for an enemy, and thought all the more of her. The Great King watched it all, and noted the names of the successful captains. But his navy was put to flight, and as it withdrew from the strait, the Aeginetan ships wrecked havoc on it. It was, in fact, the Aeginetan squadron that got the most credit in the battle.

Herodotus tells an unflattering story of the Corinthians that he learned in Athens. Adeimantos fled, making for the Megarian channel with his squadron, until, just past the temple of Athena at Sciros, he was met by a mysterious vessel that reported the victory. So the

Corinthians turned round. The story was exclusively Athenian; the rest of Greece said that the Corinthians fought well, and so, no doubt, they did (8.94.4).[41]

The final action belonged to Aristides: he led a group of Athenian hoplites on to Psyttaleia and slaughtered the Persians there. In Aeschylus's *Persians*, produced eight years later, the exploit on Psyttaleia is treated as a major disaster that redounded to Aristides' credit, but Herodotus is noticeably brief. He exercised independent judgment on what did and did not deserve emphasis. He does not find space to describe Persian raids on Sounion and Rhamnous, and though the Persian army was advancing toward the Isthmus while the battle was fought at sea, we hear nothing of it. Instead, he concludes with an oracle. The Greeks, who thought the Persians would try again, towed such disabled ships as they could to the town of Salamis on Cape Varvara (Kynosoura), but the wind drove a great deal of wreckage up on Cape Colias, thereby fulfilling a prophecy of Bacis that had not been understood before: "The women of Colias shall cook with oars," for the women had shattered oars as firewood. Thus Herodotus moves on to Xerxes' retreat.

Xerxes' Retreat

The king weighed the consequences of the defeat, and decided to pull back, but he was reluctant to reveal his decision. Therefore he started a causeway to Salamis from the mainland that Herodotus believed was intended to mask his intention, and he may have been right, but it is possible that Xerxes contemplated beseiging the Athenians on Salamis, and not until some days had passed did he realize how badly his fleet was hurt, and how difficult it would be to stay where he was, now that he had lost command of the sea. Herodotus pictures Mardonius giving welcome advice: let Xerxes retreat with most of the army while he himself remained with thirty thousand men to subjugate Greece. Xerxes summoned the estimable Artemisia for a second opinion, and she produced a masterpiece of *realpolitik*. If Mardonius stayed and was successful, all credit would redound to the king; if he failed and lost his life, it would be no matter. What was important for the integrity of the Persian Empire was that the dynasty remain safe. In any case, Xerxes could claim to have achieved his objective: he had burned Athens.

Artemisia's advice was what Xerxes wanted to hear, and the narrative of the retreat proceeds with various short digressions. Xerxes sent Artemisia to Ephesus with some bastard sons of his, and along with them went their pedagogue, a Carian eunuch whose revenge on the slave dealer who castrated him makes a nice tale. The fleet slipped away for the Hellespont under cover of night; when the Greeks discovered their retreat they gave chase, but failed to catch even a straggler. When they reached Andros, they landed to discuss their next move. Themistocles wanted to continue up to the Hellespont and destroy the bridges there, but Eurybiades argued that the Greeks should do nothing to cut off the retreat of the Persian army; otherwise it might stay in Greece, and his Peloponnesian allies were not hard to convince. The Peloponnesian army under Cleombrotus that was building a wall across the Isthmus was equally cautious; an eclipse of the sun (October 2) was enough to send it home, leaving the wall unfinished (9.10.3). Themistocles made the best he could of the situation, and attempted to persuade the Athenians that Sparta's prudent policy was the better one, after all.

Now, in the hour of Themistocles' triumph—for Herodotus grants him as much credit for Salamis as he gives Miltiades for Marathon—he appears deceitful and shrewd beyond the limit that the Greeks considered admirable.[42] First, he reconciled the Athenians to the council's decision and told them to go home, repair their houses, and sow their crops. Then he sent Sicinnus again to Xerxes to say that he had prevailed on the Greeks not to destroy the Hellespontine bridges, and thus the retreat was secure. Next, he demanded an indemnity from Andros, and when he got a refusal, laid siege to it. Thereupon some of the other cities and islands that had helped Xerxes perforce hurried to pay Themistocles indemnities. Herodotus knew that Carystus and Paros paid, and suspected there were others. Themistocles made a profit for himself, and Herodotus implies that was his sole motive, but we should remember that Athens was facing a hard winter and needed the wherewithal to survive it. Moreover, the parallel with Miltiades is intriguing: he too had followed up his victory with a similar attack on Paros.

Herodotus deals swiftly with the difficulties of the Persians on their retreat. The pick of the army went with Mardonius into winter camp in Thessaly, while Artabazus escorted Xerxes to the Hellespont with a detachment of sixty thousand men. The rest seem to have been expendable. They lived off the land, and when the land could not provide, they died of famine, plague, and dysentery. A storm had already broken down the Hellespont bridges, but the fleet was there to provide transportation, and with the remnant of his army that survived, Xerxes reached Sardis. Herodotus heard a story that had Xerxes go by ship from the mouth of the Strymon to Asia, but he disbelieved it, and so may we.

Now that the battle was over, the Greek commanders met at the Isthmus to award the prize of valor. Themistocles was the unanimous second choice, but each man's first choice was himself. So the prize remained unawarded, but Themistocles was greatly honored, particularly at Sparta, which gave him an olive-crown and a fine chariot, and escorted him with a royal guard of honor to the border. Herodotus relates that one of his enemies in Athens, Timodemus of Aphidnae, wild with envy, made a point of reminding him that the distinctions Sparta conferred on him were the due of Athens, and not merely himself, until Themistocles replied that it was true enough that Sparta would not have honored him had he come from Belbina (an islet off Sounion) nor, he added with venom, would they have honored Timodemus even though he belonged to Athens! With that, Herodotus leaves Themistocles. The next year did not belong to him, and he gets only passing mention.

Chapter Nine

The End of the Expedition: Plataea and Mycale

The Interval

Artabazus, who escorted Xerxes to the Hellespont with a detachment from Mardonius's army, was already a notable man, Herodotus remarks, and became all the more so after the battle of Plataea. He and his descendants were to become virtually feudal satraps of *Katpatuka* in northern Asia Minor, with their seat at Dascylium.[1] At Plataea, however, he distinguished himself chiefly by the expedition with which he retreated. After the king was safely in Asia, he rejoined Mardonius, but he was in no hurry, and the rest of the campaign is marked by the rivalry of these two commanders. On his return journey, Artabazus paused to take Olynthus and massacre its inhabitants, and then to besiege its neighbor, Potidaea. But the siege turned out badly, and after suffering heavy casualties in an attempt to storm the city, he abandoned it and went off to Mardonius's camp.

The Persian fleet wintered in Ionia, most of it at Cyme, and in the spring it mustered at Samos. But the command of the sea was lost for good. The fleet numbered only three hundred ships, and its mission was merely to prevent revolt in Ionia. No one imagined that the Greeks would venture to cross the Aegean. Mardonius was carrying on the campaign, and the Persians still expected victory.

Their assessment was not entirely foolish. The allied navy mustered at Aegina: a mere one hundred and ten ships this year, for the main effort had to be made on land. But the admiral was Leutychidas, a Spartan king: evidence of the new prestige of the naval arm in Spartan eyes, for Eurybiades had been a mere Spartiate. The commander of the Athenian contingent was Xanthippus, the father of Pericles. At Aegina, the Greeks met six fugitives from Chios, who had plotted to kill the Chiot tyrant, but one of their fellow conspirators had betrayed them, and now they had come to Aegina to urge the Greeks to advance to Ionia. But the fleet did not dare. It sailed as far as Delos, but would go no further. Herodotus put it succinctly: fear guarded the space between Delos and the Asia Minor coast.

The scene switches to Mardonius in Thessaly, still in winter camp. He first consulted the oracles, and then sent Alexander I of Macedon as his emissary to Athens to propose a separate peace. Alexander's visit provides a forum for political statements that must have held a certain irony for readers in the early years of the Peloponnesian War. Alexander transmitted Mardonius's offer, and then, speaking as a friend, urged Athens to accept it. Then the Spartan envoys spoke in opposition, for the Spartans had learned of Alexander's mission, and sent spokesmen to dissuade Athens from accepting Mardonius's offer. Athens, of all cities, should not make a separate peace, they said, for she had been the cause of the invasion (it was conventional wisdom in Sparta that Athens's intervention in the Ionian Revolt had brought on the Persian attack), and anyway, she was the champion of liberty. Sparta and her allies would contribute to Athens's immediate needs. She should not let Alexander's smooth talk win her over.

Then the Athenians answered, and their reply was magnificent. As long as an Athenian was left alive, Athens would never make a separate peace. They would not betray Greece, bound together, as it was, by common blood, language, way of life, and common gods whose temples the Persians had desecrated. They would endure without Spartan help. Only let the Spartans come and fight with them in Boeotia against Mardonius, for when he learned that Athens had rejected his overture, he would surely invade again.

The Spartans left, reassured, and Athens waited.

Preliminary to Plataea

Ten months after Xerxes took Athens, it was in Persian hands again. As soon as Mardonius learned that Athens had rejected his offer, he moved south quickly, for he wanted to capture Athens a second time, partly because he was impetuous, and partly because he wanted to send word to Xerxes, who was still in Sardis, that Athens was taken. The Athenians waited for help from the Peloponnesus, but the Spartans were busy with the festival of Hyakinthos at Amyklae.

When Mardonius reached Boeotia, the Athenians could wait no longer, and left for Salamis once again.

But their determination to fight was more sharply honed than ever. Mardonius sent a Hellespontine Greek, Murychides, to Salamis to repeat his offer of peace, and when he appeared before the Council of Five Hundred, one councillor, Lycidas, suggested that the offer should be transmitted to the assembly. His colleagues stoned him to death, and the Athenian women did the same for his wife and children. Meanwhile, Sparta delayed.

During the Hyakinthian festival, it was customary for all Spartiates from Amyklae to return home, even when they were on campaign, for the paean to Apollo Hyakinthos.[2] Moreover, they could afford to be dilatory, for their wall across the Isthmus was nearly complete, and they were safe. The Athenian representatives in Sparta pressed hard, and envoys from Megara and Plataea seconded their efforts, but the ephors put them off for ten days. Herodotus implies that they might have refused help in the end, had not a man from Tegea, whose influence with them was great, reminded them that if Athens went over to Persia, no wall across the Isthmus could save the Peloponnesus. The story is hardly credible, for the ephors needed no Tegean now to tell them the value of the Athenian navy, and there was a cause for delay that Herodotus fails to mention: it was important to harvest the crops before conscripting great numbers of helots into the army.[3] But the story is a dramatic one, typecasting the Spartans as reluctant warriors, thinking only of their own interests, and by Herodotus's day, it was part of the mythology of Plataea that was believed in Athens, at least.

The ephors acted swiftly. Without a word to the envoys they dispatched an army of five thousand Spartiates, each attended by seven helots, and another five thousand Lacedaemonians, who must have been *perioikoi* (9.10.1; 9.28.2). The commander was Pausanias, regent for Leonidas's young son, Pleistarchus, and his colleague was his cousin, Euryanax, whose role in the story Herodotus tells is minimal. Next day, the envoys approached the ephors and told them that since Sparta was breaking faith, Athens would make her own peace with Persia. The ephors replied that their army was already on the march. The offensive had begun.

Herodotus was indulgent with Argive medism, but it was the Argives who sent a runner to Mardonius to tell him that the Spartans were advancing, and that neither could they stop them nor would they try. Mardonius put Athens to the torch and moved toward the Isthmus, hoping, perhaps, to catch Pausanias unprepared. Years later, the Greeks were to point to a rock by the road from Megara to Pagae and claim that the Persians had shot it full of arrows one night.[4] It marked the furthest point of Persian conquest. On hearing that Pausanias's army was at the Isthmus, Mardonius fell back to Thebes and built a fortified camp near Skolos,[5] denuding Theban territory of timber to do it, allies though the Thebans were.

Herodotus concludes with two stories. The first is full of foreboding. While the Persians were preparing their camp, a Theban, Attaginus, gave a banquet for the Persian and Theban leaders. It was a balanced invitation list: fifty Persians and fifty Thebans, along with Mardonius and Herodotus's informant, Thersander of Orchomenos. In a moment of clairvoyance, the Persian who shared Thersander's couch prophesied that in a little while, few of the Persian host would be alive, and he wept. Thersander asked why he did not say this to Mardonius. The Persian replied like a voice from Greek tragedy, "What must be by God's decree, man is powerless to turn aside" (9.16.4). Thersander may have embroidered the story, but he probably did not fabricate it, and it shows how far defeatism had already infected Mardonius's forces.

The second story tells of the ordeal of the Phocians. Phocis was now conquered, and one thousand Phocians appeared in Mardonius's camp as unwilling allies. Mardonius sent his cavalry against them as if to massacre them, but they stood their ground as the Persian horse wheeled about, and then withdrew. Mardonius sent them his compliments; they had more hardihood than he had thought (their enemies, the Thessalians had been denigrating them) and he bade them fight well for Persia.

The Battle of Plataea

Plataea was "the most splendid victory of all we know" (9.64.1), and Herodotus distributes praise and blame judiciously. Sparta's allies followed her lead; the Athenians crossed from Salamis to rendezvous at Eleusis, and the army moved through the Cithaeron range and took up position on the lower slopes, facing the Persians along the river Asopus on the plain below. The story proceeds, incident by incident.

The First Exploit

The Athenians drew first blood. Since the Greeks would not venture into the plain, Mardonius attacked with his cavalry, which was led by Masistius, armed like a cataphract from head to toe. The Megarians bore the brunt of it, and they sent word that they could not hold. Thereupon Pausanias asked for a contingent to take the Megarian post, and when all the rest held back, the Athenians volunteered, and three hundred picked men supported by bowmen and led by one, Olympiodorus, took up position at Erythrae in advance of the Greek line. As the Persians skirmished, an arrow struck Masistius's mount, and it reared and threw its rider. The three hundred closed in, caught the horse, and killed Masistius. The cavalry charged *en masse*, to recover the body, but now reinforcements came to help the Athenians, and the Persians were beaten off. Masistius's corpse was paraded in a cart along the line for the Greeks to admire, but more important was the realization that the Persian cavalry was not invincible. Thus the Greeks decided to descend the slopes to a better water supply. Their new position was near the spring of Gargaphia and the precinct of Androkrates. The Spartans took up their position there, and the line stretched generally eastward for not much less than five kilometers, fronting on the Asopus river.

Debate: Tegea against Athens

When the Greeks drew up their line, Sparta held the command post on the right wing, but both the Athenians and the Tegeans claimed the left wing. Herodotus reports a debate between them. The Tegeans claimed an ancestral right to high honor, for one of their ancient kings had slain Heracles' eldest son, Hyllus, when the Heraclids made their first attempt to return to the Peloponnesus. As for the Athenians, they had no claim to honor for past or present deeds.

The Athenians were more conciliatory, though they too had myths of valor that flattered them. But they had one patent proof of their courage: the victory at Marathon. Marathon was already a powerful charter myth. Yet, the Athenians would accept whatever post the Spartans prescribed, and the Spartans forthwith shouted that they merited the left wing. There is a subtle twist to this. When Herodotus wrote, Athens was no longer conciliatory, and Sparta no longer so generous.

The Battle Formation

Then the Greeks drew up their battle line. On the right, the Lacedaemonians, and next to them, the Tegeans. They did not hold the left wing, but they had an honorable post next to the Spartans. Then Corinth, flanked by a small contingent from her colony, Potidaea. And so on to the left wing, where eight thousand Athenians were ranged "last and also first" (9.28.6), with Aristides in command. Alongside the hoplites, who numbered 38,700, there fought 110,000 light-armed troops, among them eighteen hundred from Thespiae that had lost all its hoplites at Thermopylae the previous year.

Then the enemy array. Mardonius posted his Persians facing the Spartans, then the Medes, Bactrians, Indians, and Sakai. Opposite the allied left he put the medizing Greeks, whose exact number Herodotus did not know, but he put it at fifty thousand. Thus both sides were ranged for battle, and made sacrifices to the gods.

The Sacrifices

Both Pausanias and Mardonius had Greek advisers who came from Elis, which was famous for its soothsayers.[6] Herodotus interrupts the narrative of battle to describe their backgrounds. Tisamenos, Pausanias's diviner, belonged to the family of the Iamidae that traced its descent from a byblow of Apollo, and the Spartans had paid well for his services, for they gave Spartan citizenship to both him and his brother—reluctantly, to be sure, but the Persian invasion was impending, and they needed his services. On the Persian side was a scion of another Elean family, Hegesistratos, who was Sparta's bitter enemy. The Spartans had once intended to execute him for the mischief he had done them, but while he was in fetters, he cut off half his foot and escaped. Now he was in Mardonius's employ. But the omens he took indicated that the Persians should stay on the defensive. Thus for eight days the armies faced each other.

The Persian Move

Meanwhile, men and supplies kept flowing in for Pausanias over Mt. Cithaeron by the Dryos Kephalai pass,[7] until one of the quisling Thebans advised Mardonius to cut the route. The Persian cavalry rode by night to the end of the pass and intercepted a convey of teams that was hauling food to the Greeks. Two more days passed; the cavalry continued to harass, but neither side would join battle.

On the eleventh day, an anxious Mardonius convened a council, where Herodotus pits him against Artabazus. The latter, prudent and farsighted, urged the Persians to withdraw to Thebes and use its wealth to purchase allies among the Greeks, whereas Mardonius was for attack. The Persians should ignore the ill omens of Hegesistratos, he said, and instead rely on the custom of the Persians always to take the offensive. Mardonius was still the embodiment of Persian aggression,[8] but his foil, Artabazus, had already acquired a degree of wisdom. But the council was drama without result. Mardonius ordered battle at dawn, but nothing happened.

There was, however, one consequence of Mardonius's apparent decision to attack. Under cover of night, the king of Macedon, Alexander, rode to the Athenian lines, identified himself as a patriot Greek, and told the Athenians of Mardonius's decision. The Athenian generals hurried to Pausanias with the news. Pausanias panicked and asked the Athenians to take the right wing, opposite the Persians, while he took the left against the medizing Greeks. The Athenians agreed, and at dawn, began the exchange. But Mardonius noticed it and moved his Persians over to face the Spartans in their new position, whereupon the Spartans resumed their former post. The strange narrative ends with Mardonius taunting the Spartans with cowardice.

All three parts of this curious tale are dubious, but they cohere. Mardonius's war council resulted in Alexander's night journey to the Athenian lines, and his mission in turn led to the unflattering story of Pausanias's loss of nerve. If the war council did not occur as Herodotus describes it, then neither did its sequels. As it turned out, Mardonius forgot his determination to join battle at dawn, if he had ever felt it. Instead, the cavalry pressed its attacks, until it managed to foul the spring, Gargaphia, the only source of water for the Greeks, since they did not dare approach the Asopus river. Mardonius's tactics had succeeded; the Greeks rapidly found themselves without food or water.

The Withdrawal

It was the twelfth day, and the Persians still declined battle. Pausanias, unable to wait longer, decided to try to retire under cover of night. His new position was to be the "Island," ten stades distant from the Asopus and Gargaphia (its site has never been identified to everyone's satisfaction),[9] but a battle line close to five kilometers long does not shift position easily. When daylight failed, the center pulled back to the temple of Hera outside the walls of Plataea. Herodotus called it flight, but the flight halted in orderly fashion at the Heraeum outside Plataea, where the men grounded their arms and rested. They had carried out orders as they understood them.[10]

But Pausanias faced a problem with one of his Spartiates, Amompharetos, commander of the Pitanate regiment, who would not disgrace Sparta by fleeing before the Persians. He had not known of the plan to retreat, and he would have none of it, no matter how much Pausanias and Euryanax cursed and entreated. The argument went on, and the Lacedaemonian contingent waited.

Meanwhile, the Athenians had not moved. Herodotus believed that they distrusted the Spartans, but actually they were trying to synchronize their retreat on the left with Sparta's on the right, for they sent a herald to Pausanias to ask instructions. The herald found the altercation with Amompharetos in full cry, and Pausanias could only ask the Athenians to close up and follow the Spartan lead. The herald departed, and Pausanias decided at last to retreat, leaving Amompharetos and his men behind. As he hoped, common sense overcame Amompharetos to the extent that he slowly followed the main Lacedaemonian army as it withdrew. Pausanias reached a point called Argiopion where a temple of Eleusinian Demeter stood, and there he halted and awaited for Amompharetos's contingent to catch up. Hardly had it done so when the Persian cavalry was on him.

The Battle

When news of the Greek retreat reached Mardonius, it confirmed his overconfidence and, with his final speech, Herodotus adds a last touch to his persona. He summoned the Aleuads and taunted them: so much for their tales of Spartan courage! And immediately he led the Persians in hot pursuit of the Lacedaemonians and Tegeans, who were the only Greeks he could see. His army took no time to form up, for were not the Greeks running away?

Pausanias sent a desperate message to the Athenians, asking them to close up, but the Athenians were under attack themselves from the medizing Greeks. So the Lacedaemonians and Tegeans were left alone as the Persian foot came up, grounded their large, rectangular, wickerwork shields to form a barricade, and from behind them, loosed a barrage of arrows. It was a dramatic moment. Pausanias, with his sacrifices returning ill omens, and his men distressed by Persian fire, turned toward the Heraeum and prayed to Hera for help. Then the Tegeans charged, the omens shifted, and Pausanias, ending his prayer, led his Lacedaemonians forward.

The Persians fought bravely, but once their shield barricade broke, the superiority of the Greek hoplite panoply carried the day. Twice (9.62.3; 9.63.2) Herodotus remarks that what defeated the Persians was their lack of body armor, for they matched the Greeks in courage and physique. The thousand picked men who surrounded Mardonius on his white horse fought hard as long as Mardonius was still alive, but after he was killed the whole army gave way before the Greeks and fled helter-skelter to the fortified camp near Skolos. Thus, Herodotus concluded, the Spartans took vengeance on Mardonius for Leonidas's death at Thermopylae, and Pausanias won "the fairest victory of all those we know."

A final word about Artabazus. When the battle began he led his forty thousand men forward at a prudent pace, but when he saw Mardonius's army in flight he hurried off forthwith, not for the fortified camp, but for home. Later (9.89), Herodotus returns to the story. Artabazus reached Phocis and Thessaly before news of the defeat, and rushed on through Macedonia and Thrace, abandoning men overcome by fatigue and hunger. Thus at last he reached Asia safely.

The medizing Greeks fought poorly, except for the Boeotians. Herodotus pointedly remarks on the resolution with which the Thebans opposed the Athenians. But at last they too gave way and fled, not to the Persian camp, but to Thebes itself. As for the Greek center that had retreated during the night to the Heraeum, it hurried foward in some confusion to join the battle, and a contingent from Megara and Phlius was caught and dispersed by a squadron of Theban cavalry. Meanwhile, the last phase of the battle was being fought at the Persian fort. When the Athenians joined the Spartans and Tegeans, they breached the wall, poured in, and then it was a massacre. Herodotus (9.70.5) claimed that a mere three thousand barbarians survived, whereas the Lacedaemonian, Tegean, and Athenian fallen combined numbered only one hundred and fifty-nine.

Conclusion: Aristeia, *Dedications*

No formal *aristeia* or meeds of valor were voted after the battle of Plataea, unlike Artemisium, Salamis, and Mycale. But Herodotus gives his own opinion. In Xerxes' army, the Persian infantry were the best, and the Sakan horse, and of the Greeks, the best were the Lacedaemonians. Herodotus thought that the bravest Lacedaemonian of all was Aristodemos the Runaway, who had survived Thermopylae the year before, and suffered disgrace for it,[11] but the Spartans attributed his courage to a death wish, and judged another braver. But the man who won the most glory of any Greek at Plataea was Pausanias, son of Cleombrotus.

Herodotus has three stories to relate about him. In the first, he is all chivalry. During the battle a Greek slave woman, who had been the concubine of Darius's nephew, appealed to him as a suppliant, and he accepted her with the magnanimity of a true king. In the second, he is the right-thinking Greek opposed to barbarism in the modern sense of the word. An Aeginetan named Lampon proposed that he should mutilate Mardonius's corpse in retaliation for Leonidas's mutilation after Thermopylae, but he would have none of it. Such acts were for barbarians; the Persian dead at Plataea were requital enough for Leonidas. The third story contrasts the sensible, moderate Pausanias with the foolish, covetous Persian king. Filled with wonder at the magnificence of Mardonius's tent, he ordered Mardonius's cooks to prepare him a Persian meal, which he set beside a Spartan one. Then he summoned the Greek generals and pointed out the moral; Xerxes, whose wealth was so enormous, had attacked poverty-stricken Greece to take the little she possessed. *Nothing in excess.*

Once the battle was over, the allies marched on Thebes, besieged it for nineteen days and forced the Thebans to surrender the leading collaborators, particularly Timagenidas and Attaginus. Attaginus, however, escaped, and though Pausanias captured his children, he refused to visit their father's sins upon them. The rest of the medizers he put to death. But he was moderate, if firm; the oath taken by the allies two years before to "tithe" those Greeks who medized voluntarily was quietly forgotten. Vindictiveness would have been counterproductive.

Here Herodotus leaves Pausanias, still chivalrous and admirable. Later sources that deal with his subsequent history have little good to say of him, but Herodotus lets him leave the stage, untarnished.

The Battle of Mycale

Mycale took place on the same day as Plataea, and the association of the two battles lent it greater glory, which redounded to the Athenians whose victory it was, for the Spartans were late in joining battle, though what delayed them was the rough terrain over which they had to advance, rather than dilatory behavior. It also marked the end of a segment of history that began with the Ionian Revolt, for at Mycale the Ionians turned on their Persian overlords. "Thus, for the second time," Herodotus (9.104) wrote, "Ionia revolted from Persia."

The Greek fleet under Leutychides lay at Delos, and there three Samians met them. Their leader, Hegesistratos, spoke with Ionian prolixity, urging the allies to cross the Aegean, for the Ionians were ready to revolt as soon as the fleet appeared. Leutychides interrupted; what was the speaker's name, he demanded. "Hegesistratos" ("army-leader"), was the reply, and Leutychides took it as a good omen. He accepted the Samian pledges and prepared to act.

The fleet made for Samos, but the Persians, who had been alerted, had no intention of fighting at sea. They withdrew to the mainland, beached their ships, and built a stockade around them. The armada of the previous year had shrunk to a poor remnant. The best part, the Phoenician squadron, had been sent home, and there remained only the Egyptian and Ionian fleets, the latter of dubious loyalty. However, the commander of the Persian forces in Ionia, the Achaemenid Tigranes, "the handsomest and tallest of the Persians" (9.96.2), came down to defend the fleet. Herodotus assigns him sixty thousand men, perhaps an exaggeration.[12]

The allies disembarked and advanced against the Persians, who grounded their shields to form a barricade. The Athenians, Corinthians, and Sicyonians on the Greek left reached the line of shields first, forced them down, and routed the Persian army after a brief fight. The pursuit was so hot that when the barbarians fled inside their stockade, the Greeks followed on their heels. Meanwhile, the Samians, whom the Persians had disarmed as a precaution, did what they could to help the allies, and the other Ionians followed their lead. The Milesians, who had been ordered to guard the lines of retreat, slaughtered the fugitives mercilessly.

Herodotus did not hide his disapproval of the first Ionian Revolt, but of this second one he has little to say, except to indicate that it produced a split among the allies. For when they gathered at Samos to hold a council, the Peloponnesians, led by Sparta, favored resettling the Ionians in Greece, on land that could be taken from the medizing Greeks, but Athens objected. She would not hear of such a plan; the Ionian cities were *her* colonies, and the Peloponnesians had no right to decide their fate. Athens was already grasping the policy that would make her the mistress of the Aegean within a few years. The Peloponnesians yielded; Samos, Chios, and Lesbos were admitted to the alliance, and the fleet set sail for the Hellespont to destroy the pontoon bridges that the Greeks imagined were still intact.

The Conclusion

The conclusion is unexpected, for it is composed of four tales, two brief, and enclosing two that are longer. The first of the brief stories came from Herodotus's native city, for it tells how a Halicarnassian saved Xerxes' brother, Masistes, from a murderous attack by the admiral of the Persian fleet, Artayntes, who was maddened by

Masistes' taunts. The Halicarnassian was rewarded with Cilicia to govern.

The last story is a cautionary tale about Cyrus, the founder of the Persian Empire. One Artembares, whose descendant the Athenians, as almost the last act of 479 B.C., were to crucify on the shore where Xerxes' bridge over the Hellespont had touched Europe, suggested to Cyrus that the Persians move from their rugged homeland to some more comfortable area of their empire, and Cyrus agreed that the suggestion was attractive. But soft lands bred soft men, he warned, and if the Persians chose luxury, they must expect to be subjects rather than rulers. The Persians understood, and stayed where they were. This is the story that concludes the *History,* and it should be read beside the tale of how Pausanias contrasted Persian luxury with Spartan poverty. Aging empires grew soft, and Artembares' descendant was to pay with his life for the decay of Persia under a ruler less wise than Cyrus.

The two central stories are one Persian, one Athenian. The first tells how Xerxes lusted for, first, the wife of his brother, Masistes, and then her daughter, and thus drove Masistes to attempt revolt. Xerxes leaves the *History,* not with the character of an evil man, but rather as a despot governed by whims and lusts who brought destruction on those around him. Masistes' wife died horribly as a result of Xerxes' affair, and Masistes and his sons were cut down as they rode to Bactria to raise a revolt.

The other tale describes the last Athenian action of 479, the siege of Sestos. The Peloponnesians had gone home, but the Athenians under Xanthippos invested Sestos on the Chersonese. The Persian commander Artayktes was an unscrupulous man who had, by deceit, got Xerxes' permission to plunder the shrine of a native deity whom the Greeks identified with Protesilaus, the first Greek to die in the Trojan War. Protesilaus had his revenge. For Sestos fell, Artayktes was caught trying to escape, and Xanthippus crucified him and stoned his son to death before his eyes. Then the Athenians, guilty of atrocity as they make their exit, returned home.

Thus the year 479 ended, and the *History* of Herodotus along with it. The invasion of Xerxes had worked itself out.

Chapter Ten

The Sources

The Evidence for Written Sources

Some four centuries after Herodotus, another historian from Halicarnassus, Dionysius, briefly described the beginnings of historical research: "Before the Peloponnesian War [431–404 B.C.] there were many early historians in many places. Among them were Eugeon of Samos, Deiochus of Proconnesus, Eudemos of Paros, Democles of Phygele, Hecataeus of Miletus, Acusilaus of Argos, Charon of Lampsacus, and Amelesagoras of Chalcedon. A second group was born a little before the Peloponnesian War and were Thucydides' early contemporaries; these were Hellanicus of Lesbos, Damastes of Sigeum, Xenomedes of Ceos, Xanthus of Lydia, and many others." All of these wrote histories of individual tribes or cities, using records from temples or secular archives, and telling myths and folktales which, remarked Dionysius, who lived in the society that produced the emperor Augustus, "seem silly to present-day men." Herodotus, however, enlarged the historian's scope. "He chose not to write down the history of a single city or nation, but to put together many, varied events of Europe and Asia in a single comprehensive work."[1]

This is a well-worn passage. Taken at face value, it indicates that before Herodotus there was a clutch of shadowy writers who wrote local histories. Herodotus himself mentions only one of them, Hecataeus of Miletus, who wrote a work in two books on historical geography (*Periegesis*), accompanied by a map that showed the world as a disc edged by Ocean, and another work on genealogies. He lived through the Ionian Revolt, and twice gave the rebels advice that they rejected (5.36.2; 5.125). Herodotus says nothing pejorative about him, though once (2.143) he tells a tale that has been taken as ridicule. In Egypt, Hecataeus gave the priests of Amon his own pedigree, beginning with a god and descending through sixteen generations, whereupon the priests showed him the series of statues of their high-priests, three hundred and forty-five in all, each representing a generation of men. The story illustrated the antiquity of Egypt, and it is not clear that Herodotus meant it as a joke at Hecataeus's expense, as some commentators have thought. In any case, the tale probably derived from Hecataeus's own *Periegesis,* and the joke, if joke it is, was told by the victim himself.[2]

Herodotus had absorbed what Hecataeus wrote about Egypt, but too little survives to be sure how dependent Herodotus was. The description of the phoenix, the hippopotamus, and the hunting of the crocodile had parallels in Hecataeus.[3] Hecataeus called Egypt "the gift of the Nile," and Herodotus (2.5.1) approves of the description without mentioning its source. At Buto, Herodotus viewed the floating island of Chemmis, reported that he saw no sign that it floated, and was skeptical about floating islands in any case. However, a fragment of Hecataeus states that Chemmis, which he spelled "Chembis," floated.[4]

All this indicates familiarity with Hecataeus but not dependence. Outside Egypt, Herodotus quotes Hecataeus only once, for a variant version of how Athens expelled the aborigine Pelasgians from Attica (6.137). Perhaps he found in Hecataeus his list of Persian satrapies (3.88–97)[5] and the myth of Scythian descent from a union between Heracles and a woman who was half snake (4.8–10).[6] His disapproval of the Ionian Revolt may have come in part from him, for Hecataeus thought it was foolish, and so did Herodotus. But Hecataeus was a friend of Artaphrenes, the satrap at Sardis during the revolt, and his attitude can have been no secret. For that matter Hecataeus and Herodotus belonged to the same social class, and may have had more in common than an interest in historical geography. But Herodotus had progressive ideas about cartography, and was contemptuous of maps that showed the earth circular, with a Europe and Asia of equal size and all surrounded by Ocean. Hecataeus's famous map shared this disdain but not alone, for he was part of an Ionian tradition of cartography, and the concept of the circumambient Ocean went back to Homer.[7]

Hecataeus is the most solid of Herodotus's predecessors, although evidence is lacking to substantiate theories of widespread borrowing.[8]

There is less to say about the other writers mentioned by Dionysius (and some he did not mention), and they are harder to date. Charon of Lampsacus is credited with a number of works, including one on Persia, two on Lampsacus, and a chronicle of the kings and ephors of the Lacedaemonians, based on Spartan sources. We cannot show that Herodotus read him, but it is at least possible, for though Jacoby,[9] a generation ago, dated him to the last decades of the fifth century, too late for Herodotus, more recent scholarship is inclined to make him earlier. His *Persika* [On Persia] took up only two books; other than that, we can say only that it included an account of Mardonius's expedition into northern Greece in 492 B.C. Charon's scope was narrower than that of Herodotus.

Xanthus of Lydia wrote a work *On Lydia* which Herodotus may have used; in the next century, the historian Ephorus claimed that Herodotus got his "starting-points" (*aphormai*) from him, but his meaning is obscure.[10] The *History* does begin with Lydia, and in that sense Xanthus may have provided Herodotus with a starting point. But surviving fragments show no parallels with Herodotus. He borrowed nothing from Xanthus that we can identify.

Even more shadowy is Dionysius of Miletus, who wrote a work on Persia down to Darius's death, and then followed it with a sequel.[11] The one morsel of information that we know about his works reveals that he described the revolt of the *magi,* and named Smerdis's brother Panxouthes rather than Patizeithes, as Herodotus does. Dionysius of Halicarnassus overlooks him, which is a tribute to his obscurity. However, the king lists of Lydia and of Media in Herodotus do not synchronize, which has given grounds for suspecting that he took his lists from two separate sources, and *faute de mieux,* Dionysius of Miletus is a candidate for one of them.[12] As for Acusilaos of Argos, a fragment has turned up in an Oxyrhynchus papyrus;[13] it gives a straightforward account of the myth of the Lapith king Caeneus who was changed from a man into a woman. It reads like an entry in a mythology handbook: the sort of material purveyed by the *logioi,* or prosewriters, whose imaginary debate on the causes of the Persian War begins the *History.* Herodotus's researches were a different sort of thing.

Hellanicus of Lesbos was a prolific writer who was still working in

the last decade of the fifth century, but a *Persika* by him could have
antedated the *History,* although we cannot show that Herodotus used
it.[14] However, he demonstrates the availability of chronological
sources, for three of his works betray a fascination with dates. One
was a local history of Athens dated by archon years. A second was on
the victors at the Carnean Festival in Sparta, and the third was on
priestesses of Hera in Argos, who held office for life; Hellanicus
reckoned their tenure by years, thus producing a chronological
framework. Another writer whom Herodotus may have used was
Pherekydes of Athens, who wrote a work containing much information
about the Philaids, the family to which Miltiades belonged,[15] but
what Herodotus has to say about Miltiades' ancestors might as well
have been obtained from any well-informed member of the clan. We
are far from being able to demonstrate Herodotus's dependence.
Moreover, his failure to mention any prose writer except Hecataeus is
remarkable, for he frequently cites poets, not merely Homer and
Hesiod, but even one as *récherché* as Aristeas of Proconnesus, the
author of the *Arimaspeia.* In part, this is because familiarity with the
poets was the mark of an educated Greek, but that cannot be the
whole reason. Herodotus, it is clear, regarded himself as an independent researcher whose analysis of the Persian War was an original
achievement.

What is evident is that Herodotus did not conduct his researches in
a vacuum. The fifth century was a period when records and genealogies
were being ferreted out, and what may have been left to memory in
the past was put in writing. Herodotus maintained the persona of an
oral historian working with oral sources.[16] He put down the stories
that people told him, even when he did not accept their truth
(2.123.1; 7.152), and he would not impose his own critical judgment
so far as to suppress variant versions—as Hecataeus did, for in his
proem he made a claim for accuracy. All versions were evidence for
Herodotus, and he would not neglect evidence in his research.

The Sources Cited

Halfway through the Egyptian *logos* (2.99.1), Herodotus announces
that what he has written so far is based on observation (*opsis*),
judgment (*gnome*), and interrogation (*historie*), but from that point

on he will relate stories of Egypt, some told by the Egyptians themselves, and some by other nations about Egypt (2.147.1). Elsewhere, he prefaces various reports with phrases such as "the Greeks say," "the Lacedaemonians say," "the people living around Thermopylae say," to give only a few examples.[17] Not infrequently he contrasts the reliability of these sources: the priests of Ptah in Egypt told how Psammetichus discovered that the Phrygians were the world's most ancient people; the Greeks, he adds, related silly stories about his experiment (2.2–3). Or at times he is precise about his limitations: he describes the golden statue of Marduk-Ba'al at Babylon, but he had not seen it himself, for Xerxes had removed it; he could only tell what the Chaldaeans said (1.183). Four times[18] only he mentions informants by name, but all of these gave him private information. The sources designated as "Greeks," "Carians," "Scythians," and the like seem to purvey information which, if not official, was shared widely among the peoples named. It was part of the body of tradition that they preserved.

Can we take this view seriously? When Herodotus says of the Nile Delta that "the Ionians say" it is Egypt, and that its coast stretches from the so-called watchtower of Perseus to the salt marshes of Pelusium (2.15.1), can we believe that this was an oral tradition widespread in Ionia? It may be argued that behind many of these references to oral traditions there lies a literary source: Hecataeus took Egypt as the Delta, and so we can read "the Ionians say" as "Hecataeus writes." But Hecataeus's geographical notions, like his map, belonged to a school of Ionian *savants*. Herodotus was strictly accurate when he wrote "the Ionians say."

Or was the persona of an oral historian purely conventional, in which case we must treat these interjections as literary fictions?[19] This is not to accuse Herodotus of dishonesty, but simply to suggest that he was not merely the father of history, but also of the literary conventions that affect historiography. Herodotus was capable of literary convention. But before we weigh his claim to be an oral historian, we must look at what oral history consists of.

The nature of oral tradition

The boundary between a literate and a nonliterate culture is notoriously difficult to define, and if it would be incorrect to denominate the Greece of Herodotus as nonliterate, neither would it be right to think that the elements of oral culture were dead.[20] Oral history is transmitted by what we may visualize as a long series of interlocking conversations continuing from generation to generation, and each generation makes its own adjustments to the tradition. What is of social relevance is remembered and subjected to interpretation; what ceases to be relevant is forgotten.

Let us look first at problems of chronology. In Africa south of the Sahara, where the elements of oral culture are still alive, the sources of history for the precolonial period are generally professional storytellers and official keepers of state traditions, and usually they have at best a hazy notion of absolute chronology.[21] However, they can, by means of genealogy, establish an area of time within which an event took place. In nearly every state headed by kings or chiefs, the custodians of traditions possess king lists, in what is supposed to be chronological order, and when these states came into contact with writing, such lists were often the first morsels of history to be written down. In them, kings generally appear as consecutive rulers, even when their reigns in fact overlapped. The Behistun inscription provides an example of this, for there Darius names nine ancestors who were kings before him, without indicating that, in part, they ruled in parallel lines of the Achaemenid house.[22] The same sort of distortion affects Herodotus's dating of the fall of Media and the rise of Cyrus, for by his reckoning Cyrus became king in 558 B.C., and the act by which he secured the throne was the overthrow of the king of Media, Astyages, whose fall, therefore, belonged to the same year. The two are made to rule consecutively. In fact, Cyrus first succeeded his father, Cambyses I, as vassal king of Anshan, and only later, in 550, did he unseat Astyages.

However, some regnal lists can assign a sum of years to a reign with great accuracy, for statistics of that sort could be preserved with great care, sometimes by means of mnemonic devices.[23] It follows that when we find a reign measured precisely in oral tradition, we should pay attention, for the statistic may depend on a reliable method of time reckoning. Herodotus (5.65.3) provides an example: he assigns thirty-six years to the Pisistratid tyranny before its expulsion from Athens. If Herodotus knew the date of the expulsion—Thucydides (6.59.4) gives 510 B.C.—then he knew that Pisistratus routed his opponents at Pallene and became tyrant in 546: a troublesome date, for Herodotus puts Cyrus's first conquest, his overthrow of Croesus, just after Pallene. Yet we must not discard the thirty-six years, for oral tradition tends to be exact about such things.

At the same time, genealogies are subject to adjustment, sometimes due to social considerations, sometimes from structural amnesia, a process that streamlines tradition by forgetting irrelevant details.[24] Generations tend to lengthen with time, and genealogies preserved in oral traditions now, may list no more names than they did a century ago, though there are a hundred more years to account for. Herodotus's rule of thumb for a generation was three to a century (2.142.2), but when he listed the pedigrees of the two Spartan royal houses (7.204; 8.131.2), he traced both back to Heracles, whom he placed nine hundred years before his time, and at three generations to a century the pedigrees cannot stretch so far. Consequently these generations must be calculated at forty years. Structural amnesia, combined with a determination to make Heracles the progenitor of the Spartan kings, has resulted in a generation too long to be probable. [25]

It must ultimately have been the Spartans themselves—specifically the Spartan kings—who stretched these generations, for the royal houses derived prestige from descent from Heracles. Herodotus probably got these pedigrees in Sparta, for, as Plato[26] noted, the Spartans had an extraordinary appetite for genealogies. There is no compelling reason to think that he got them through an intermediary, such as Hecataeus. But there is no such thing as a standard generation in Herodotus.[27] His three generations to a century is a rule of thumb, and usually he follows the practice of the oral historian who deals with areas of time rather than precise years.

The methods of transmission

Oral traditions found in African states generally fall into two categories: official and private. The first category represents the "truth" about the past as the state recognizes it, and it is common to find professionals charged with its preservation.[28] The Yoruba town of Ketu in Nigeria, for instance, had an hereditary official known as the *baba elegum* who knew the town history by heart. Rwanda, a kingdom until 1961, had an assortment of officials: genealogists who remembered pedigrees, memorialists who knew the important events of reigns, rhapsodists who preserved panegyrics on the kings, and the *abiiru* who kept the secrets of the dynasty. There are exceptions: Burundi, which ceased to be a monarchy in 1966, had no official traditions as such, but history was transmitted by songs, tales, and proverbs. But, in general, organized states had both official traditions and specialists who were charged with preserving them.

Private traditions are those transmitted by individual groups, such as families and clans, which may have a official status within the clan, but as far as the outside world is concerned, they are private, and are handed down with less care, though at the same time there is less motive to distort. However, oral traditions are never transmitted purely for the love of objective knowledge. Private traditions may be put to political and social uses less blatantly than official ones, but there is still the wish to put the clan's ancestors in a good light.

When Herodotus cites ethnic groups as sources, such as "the Carians" or "the Spartans," *inter alia,* the implication is that he is giving their official traditions.[29] Thus the Cretans could say that the Carians once inhabited islands under Minoan suzerainty, but Carian tradition differed (1.171), and Sparta, Thera, and Cyrene all had traditions about the founding of Thera and Cyrene (4.150–51; 4.154.1). More than once Herodotus notes the Spartan version of a morsel of Spartan history differed from that held by the rest of Greece.[30] He saw himself as a reporter of traditions such as these, but he declined to vouch for their accuracy.[31] Yet, the question arises: if Herodotus could draw on oral traditions, were there specialists in archaic Greece who preserved them, as there have been, and are, in other parts of the world?

The evidence is meager, but tantalizing. Aristotle[32] names among the officials necessary for a city various registrars called "temple-remembrancers, archive keepers, and remembrances." The "remembrancer" (*mnemon*) was a registrar of property, but the name seems to indicate an official who relied simply on his memory at one time, before literacy became common. From Crete we have an inscription that sets forth the rights of one Spensithios, who was to be *poinikastes* (specialist in Phoenician letters) and *mnemon* of a Cretan city, and his descendants after him.[33] Slight as it is, the evidence suggests that Herodotus found keepers of tradition in various cities and temples, and that these specialists could expound history. At Delphi, a *hieromnemon* could have told him of Croesus's dedications and other memorials— the *erga* ("works") of famous men—and would give official answers to queries about oracles that Delphi had given, although this need not imply that the oracles were kept on file.[34] Temple memorialists could elucidate difficult inscriptions or describe important mementoes; one in the Theban temple of Ismenian Apollo may have given Herodotus a hand with "Cadmean letters" he found on some tripods dedicated there (5.59), and another at the Samian Heraeum may have expounded upon the picture of the bridge built by the engineer Mandrocles over the Bosphorus, and dedicated to Hera by Mandrocles himself (4.48).

In one instance we find Herodotus interviewing an official such as this. At Sais, in Egypt, he approached the temple of Neith to inquire about the source of the Nile. His interlocutor was the temple scribe, and if we may infer from evidence for Egyptian temples in the Hellenistic period, he was the keeper of traditions. The scribe of Neith purveyed myth, but he was performing his proper function of expounding priestly wisdom.[35]

He was, however, a scribe rather than a "sacred remembrancer" (*hieromemnon*), for Egypt had long used writing, and literacy was a qualification for the priesthood. In contemporary Greece, too, many memorialists must have used writing, but they still acted as spokesmen for an undifferentiated group, such as the priests of Dodona (2.52), whose spokesman told Herodotus that the Pelasgians had no names for their gods until they got them from Egypt. Only occasionally did he single out an individual as a source, because his information was unique, or because—as in the case of the scribe of Neith—Herodotus did not believe him.

There were also private family traditions, usually favorable to the family in the sense that forgetfulness obscured what cast aspersions on its past, but less prone to official bias. The family status was what concerned such traditions. Thus, when Herodotus indicates that both the great political families of Athens of the fifth century, the Philaids and the Alkmaeonids, had been hostile to the Pisistratid tyrants, he is reflecting the traditions of the two families, which forgot that they had ever cooperated with the tyrants. Yet, family traditions could not be distorted outrageously without provoking disbelief; they had to compete with other family traditions, and with official tradition as well, which it was difficult to impose upon. Alkmaeonid and Philaid tradition notwithstanding, the archon list that was inscribed and set up in the marketplace of Athens about 425 B.C. bore evidence that both families had cooperated with the tyrants.[36] A better case is the competition between the two versions of how Athens was freed from her tyranny. The story with a degree of official sanction gave credit to the tyrannicides, Harmodius and Aristogeiton: a statue-group of the pair was erected in the *agora*, and their descendants received special honors. The competing tradition, for which both Herodotus and Thucydides vouched, claimed that the tyrannicides were motivated by a private quarrel, that they killed the wrong man, and that Athens was delivered from the tyrant four years later through the efforts of the Alkmaeonids. We may safely assign this tradition to the Alkmaeonid family. Yet, in spite of this family's prominence, and the authority of Herodotus and Thucydides, it did not displace the official version, for the descendants of the tyrannicides continued to receive honors into the fourth century.

There are a number of instances in the *History* where Herodotus has clearly drawn upon family traditions. He knew what the Gephyraean clan, to which the tyrannicides belonged, said about its antecedents (5.57.1), and his defense of the Alkmaeonids against the charge of medism at the battle of Marathon belonged to Alkmaeonid tradition. His slighting references to king Cleomenes of Sparta must derive from the traditions of the house to which he belonged, for Cleomenes' heirs belonged to another branch that had no reason to cherish his memory. He may have dealt kindly with Artabazus, who fled ingloriously from Plataea, because one of his sources was Artabazus's family. The descendants of Demaratus, who governed three towns in the Caicus valley as Persian vassals,[37] were probably the source for the tale of Demaratus's friend, Dicaeus, who had seen a foreboding vision prior to Salamis (8.65). The grandson of Zopyrus who won Babylon for Darius came to Athens as an exile (3.160) and may have had tales to tell there. Family traditions were kept with less

care than their official counterparts and faded badly after three
generations, but they probably had much color, some of it political,
and they were strong on genealogy.

Finally there were the legends of storytellers. Who knows what
Herodotus learned at Halicarnassus, where the Oriental world
marched with the Greek? As we have seen, he may have heard there
about the turncoat Phanes, and the story of the Magian Revolt could
have been based on one of the versions of the Behistun inscription that
reached Ionia; fragments of an Aramaic version have turned up in
Egypt.[38] Herodotus made a point of disdaining idle tales, but a
discriminating listener must have found a good many that were not
idle.

Archives

In 403 B.C., Athens organized a central archive in the Metroon, the
temple of the Mother of the Gods. Before that time, our information
about her archives is scanty, though a late source states that they date
back to the sixth century B.C.[39] Outside Athens, our evidence is even
scantier, but no doubt temples kept archives: inventories, for the most
part, including lists of priests,[40] but perhaps secular records too. A fair
amount of archival material was preserved.

How accessible these records would be to the curious researcher,
however, is another question. Unless a document was published,
Herodotus would have been at the mercy of *mnemones* and *hieromnemones,* and as we suspect, many of these were still working within
an oral tradition. Publication meant inscribing a document and setting
it up in a public place. Herodotus cites twenty-four inscriptions, half of
them Greek, and half non-Greek. Some he copied, for he gives the
texts, but one at least, an inscription on the Great Pyramid at Gizeh
(2.125.6), he paraphrased from memory. On the whole, he does not
seem to have valued documentary evidence highly, though the reason
may have been, not that it was unavailable, but that it was inaccessible.

Conclusion

We must conjecture, but we can be brief. Herodotus was gathering
his source material at a time when a minor explosion of historical
research was taking place, but he was in the vanguard. It is likely that

he was widely read; he was not isolated from the intellectual milieu of his time, but we can *prove* that he read only one predecessor, Hecataeus, and we cannot demonstrate real dependence even on him. It is futile to conjure up shadowy predecessors whose works he may have copied.

Yet, he lived at a time when oral traditions were still preserved with care, and he probably gleaned much of his information from oral sources: from *mnemones, hieromnemones,* family traditions, and individuals with tales to tell. Even without the structures intended to preserve oral traditions, memories can remain fairly green for three generations. The Persian Wars were still within the three-generation span when Herodotus did his research, and indeed, there were still men alive who had witnessed the great invasion firsthand. The persona of an oral historian that Herodotus assumed must be taken seriously.

Chapter Eleven
The Characters of the History

Characterization betrays not merely an historian's bias, but his values too, and though there is a guarded, ambiguous quality to Herodotus, his characters and the roles he assigns them serve to indicate his outlook. There are no heroes. Leonidas at Thermopylae comes close, for legend had it that he knew an oracle which said that the Spartans must lose either a king or their state, and so he sought death for himself. Herodotus mentions the legend, and appears to suspend judgment. Miltiades is near heroic stature at Marathon, but immediately thereafter he dies a squalid death. The Ionian Revolt has no heroes at all. Histiaeus and Aristagoras are mere irresponsible adventurers.

On the Oriental side, Cyrus, Darius, and Xerxes are all embodiments of Persian imperialism. Cambyses was mad, and his madness took the form of an exaggerated persona: both his despotism and his expansionism were out of bounds. But the first Oriental despot to inflict wrong on the Greeks was none of these; he was Croesus of Lydia, with whom Herodotus begins. He was the first of his type whom Herodotus presents, and his story, which introduces the *History*, is a tale of imperialism in microcosm.

Croesus

The Lydian empire reached its height under Croesus, and its court attracted nearly all the Greek sages, including Solon, who is presented as a spokesman for the pessimistic folk wisdom that Herodotus clearly approved. Croesus put his favorite query to Solon: who was the happiest of men? Solon replied with two stories of men who had lived and died well, and when Croesus, irritated, wanted to know what Solon thought of his grandeur, he replied with the wisdom that concludes Sophocles' *Oedipus*: we should suspend judgment about men until they are dead. One should always look at the end. Croesus dismissed the advice as stupid. Yet, he belonged to a dynasty that began with Gyges, who had overthrown his king, Candaules, and married his wife; and Candaules' dynasty was destined to be avenged in five generations.

Then Croesus suffered two disasters, both of which he triggered himself. First, he lost his son and only heir, Atys, for though he had another son, he was dumb and could not inherit. Croesus mourned his son for two years, but when he learned of the rise of Cyrus, his old appetite for imperialism reawakened, and he planned a preventive war.

The rest is well-known. Sardis fell, and Cyrus put Croesus on the pyre. There, in his affliction, Croesus remembered Solon, and called him three times by name. Cyrus heard, asked why, and on learning the reason, comprehended the frailty of human fortunes, and realized that he himself could suffer a fate like Croesus's. And so he ordered the fire quenched, but that was beyond his power, and Croesus would have perished had not Apollo sent rain.

There is a note of irony in the conclusion. When Atys died, Croesus was left with no heir, and the dynasty could not continue. But in the sack of Sardis, Croesus's other son, who was dumb, found his voice. The dynasty got an heir just as Croesus's empire came to an end.

The Croesus-myth lends itself well to Claude Levi-Strauss's structural analysis. The main theme is the mutability of fortune. The binary oppositions are happiness and its reverse, life and death, lust for empire and its nullity, human overconfidence and human gullibility that lets men mistake the indications of what the future holds. Croesus combines the contradictions of his character-type: he is a tyrant who wrongs the Greeks and attacks Cyrus, but at the same time, he is a generous man who acquired wisdom and whom Apollo loves. He is a great king, and also a vulnerable human being. The mediating figure is Solon, with his cautious pessimism. Two disasters smote Croesus: the first doomed his dynasty, and the second his empire, and as his empire perished, the dynasty found an heir again. The two opponents, Croesus and Cyrus, discovered common ground in the wisdom of Solon, though it had no practical effect on the course of Persian imperialism. Croesus has tragic elements in his makeup; yet, Herodotus eschews a tragic ending: Croesus lives on as a wise advisor to Cyrus and Cambyses.

Croesus provides an analogy with all imperialists in the *History*. He was an Oriental despot with a lust for empire, but he was not an evil man. He was merely blinded by his own greatness, and he had no inkling, until too late, of the mutability of human life. Once he has fallen, the Persian kings take over his persona, including not only his blindness but his luxury. The Persians had been a poor people with neither good food nor wine before they conquered Croesus (1.70), but by the time of Xerxes, their luxury could amaze the Greeks (9.82).

Xerxes

The greatest Oriental despot of all was Xerxes, and Herodotus creates for him a persona with overtones from Sophoclean tragedy. He establishes his character early in two dialogues with Artabanus, a wise advisor whose wisdom consists of the same cautious pessimism as Solon's did. In the first (7.8–18), he announces his intention of invading Greece, and Artabanus incurs his wrath when he had the hardihood to oppose him. But than another side of Xerxes' character emerged. His temper cooled; he reflected on Artabanus's advice and decided it was sound. But, as it turned out, his position demanded that he play the role of an imperialist.

At the Hellespont, Xerxes and Artabanus have their second dialogue. Xerxes weeps for the brevity of life (7.45–56), and Artabanus, in a speech full of dramatic irony, outlines the perils the Persians had to face as they advanced into Greece. But in vain. Xerxes could not comprehend the possibility of defeat.

On the balance, he is not unattractive. His caprices were no worse than those of Greek tyrants.[1] The same man who wept for the brevity of human life could also react cruelly when Pythius the Lydian asked that his eldest son be released from army service (7.45–46). His physical beauty and stature outmatched that of any man in his realm (7.187). Herodotus has given him some of the charisma of the Persian kings implicit in the handful of old Persian texts that have survived, where the Achaemenids are the chosen of Ahura-Mazda, but essentially he conceived him in Greek terms, as a man whose pride and overconfidence blinded him to reality.

His greatness insulated him from understanding. He could tell his nobles that Persian custom (*nomos*), sanctioned their imperialism (7.8), but he could not comprehend that other people might be equally determined to follow their *nomoi*, and when Demaratus explained to him that the Greeks would resist because their *nomos* compelled them (7.102), he dismissed him as a fool. Yet, afterward, he could praise Demaratus for his sound advice, and ask for more, which again he declined to take (7.234–37). Before Salamis, he is pleased to have the outspoken advice of Artemisia, but he will not follow it (8.68–69). After his defeat, he does comprehend his danger, and is glad to take Mardonius's offer to stay behind in Greece while he himself retreated to Asia. But did he learn much? He exits from the *History* with the story of Masistes' wife that tells how Xerxes' passions brought disaster on his brother and his brother's wife. Xerxes is a qualified tragic figure; his greatness suffered a reverse rather than a fall, and he learned little from it. He is a mixture of generosity, cruelty, magnanimity, and tyranny, whose actions cause greater suffering to others than himself. He had a great role to play, but to the end, he failed to know himself.

Themistocles

Themistocles' entry into the *History* requires explanation. Athens had received the Wooden Wall oracle from Delphi, and opinion was divided as to its meaning. "There was," wrote Herodotus, "a certain man of the Athenians who had recently come to the fore; his name was Themistocles, and men called him the son of Neocles" (7.143.1).[2] Faint praise, and a trifle inaccurate. Themistocles, who had been archon in 493–492 B.C., was not a newcomer to politics, but I suspect that what Herodotus had in mind was that Themistocles had recently become a man with political "clout," and that he had done this by worsting Aristides in the fight for the navy. Yet, there is subtle denigration of sorts, too. Homer had used the formula in the *Iliad* (10.314) to introduce an incompetent spy, Dolon, and the Greeks knew their Homer.

The portrait of Themistocles is drawn with care, but there is about it some of the ambiguity that we also find in fifth-century treatments of Odysseus's character.[3] It was his *gnōmē* (the word denotes both good judgment and political cunning) that made Athens a naval power, but he had claimed that the fleet was to fight Aegina, and hence it was the war with Aegina that saved Greece. His strategy led to the victory at Salamis, though at a key moment, when the fleet panicked at the news that Athens had fallen, it was the dramatic intervention of his gossip Mnesiphilus that steadied him (8.57). In Sparta, he received honors such as had been conferred on no one else. Envy prevented him from receiving the prize of valor, for each Greek commander voted to confer the prize on himself, but Themistocles was the choice for second place (8.124). We may take this as praise for Themistocles. Herodotus wastes little time on compliments, and by his standards the praise is more than tepid.

Yet, Themistocles had a sharp eye for his own personal advantage. When he failed to persuade the Greeks to break down the bridges over the Hellespont after the victory at Salamis, he promptly became an advocate of the opposite policy, and as a final touch, sent a message to Xerxes to claim credit for safeguarding his retreat (8.109–10). Earlier, at Artemisium, he bribed Eurybiades and Adeimantus to stay and fight, using money that he got from the Euboeans; most of it, however, stayed in his own pocket (8.4–5). Herodotus can approve of shrewdness: witness his admiration for Artemisia, who was chased by an Athenian warship at the battle of Salamis, and, unable to escape, rammed a ship of the Persian fleet, and thus the Athenians mistook her for a friend and let her go (8.87–88). But the shrewdness of Themistocles is excessive.

Athens herself is treated with an ambivalence comparable to that of Themistocles. Herodotus praises her staunchness and concurred with the view—which was Athens's own—that it saved Greece,[4] but he also believed that the docility with which she accepted Spartan leadership was assumed, and that her ambition for empire was part of her character, although it was revealed only later (8.2–3). Athens, like Themistocles, knew where her own advantage lay, and if her cunning policy had any single architect, it was Themistocles. The crowning touch of Themistocles' characterization was that he prepared for his ostracism and exile in Persia while at the same time bringing about Xerxes' defeat. No matter what the eventuality, Themistocles intended to thrive.

Pausanias, the son of Cleombrotus

Herodotus would not lionize Pausanias any more than Themistocles. On the one hand, he won Plataea, the "most glorious victory known to us" (9.64), and in its immediate aftermath he displayed chivalry and high character. He would not impale Mardonius's corpse when an Aeginetan suggested it as revenge for Leonidas (9.78–79), and when a woman of Cos, who had been made a Persian concubine, appealed to him, he responded with gallantry (9.76). On the other hand, his qualities of leadership in the battle itself are not immediately apparent, and at one point, on receiving word that Mardonius would attack at dawn, he reacted with trepidtion (9.46).

Pausanias's arrogant behavior after Plataea, and his attempt to betray Greece to Persia was an important component of the propaganda that justified the Athenian Empire. Thucydides (1.128–29) gives the Athenian view: he quotes a letter that Pausanias wrote to Xerxes asking for Xerxes' daughter in marriage in return for Greece, and Xerxes' reply. Pausanias so alienated the Ionians that they approached Athens to take over, and thus hegemony was thrust upon the Athenians. This must have been the quasi-official Athenian view of Pausanias about the time that Herodotus was completing his *History*. Yet, Herodotus will have none of it. He refers to Pausanias's ambition to be tyrant of Greece with an expression of doubt (5.32), but it was not Xerxes' daughter, but the daughter of Megabates, the king's cousin, to whom he was betrothed. By implication, he rejected Thucydides' letters, and along with them, a part of Athenian justification of her imperialism.

Themistocles' characterization is colored by his subsequent medism. Not so Pausanias. After his victory, he pointed out to the Greek commanders the senseless lust for empire that affected Xerxes, by making the contrast between a Spartan meal and a Persian banquet. He exits from the *History* a wise, moderate man, and if Herodotus does not make him a hero, he is far closer to heroic stature than Themistocles.

Conclusion

Some salient points emerge. Oriental and Greek are characterized with a difference: barbarians such as Croesus and Xerxes have roles in history to play that partly submerge their individuality. Both are empire-builders whose pride is humbled, though Croesus achieved a wisdom that Xerxes did not. The Greeks are limned with hard realism. But among them, we should note that it is the complex, not quite admirable characters that interest Herodotus. He might regard Aristides as the most upright man in Athens, but he assigns him only a slight part in the victory at Salamis. Themistocles was a cunning self-seeker, but he was also a courageous, shrewd politician who made things happen, and Herodotus recognized his importance. There are few black-and-white characters. Aristagoras, who was a mere mischief-maker, is close to being an exception, but he suffers from Herodotus's judgment on the Ionian Revolt. Yet, he had an important part to play in the making of history.

The prejudices of Herodotus are not easy either to assess or explain, though they were probably shaped in part by the political context of Greece in the 430s. His treatment of Thebes is a pointed contradiction of that city's later official "history" that her medism was the work of pro-Persian oligarchs without popular support,[5] his disdain of the Ionians may have been fashionable, and his lenience toward Argive medism may stem from some antipathy toward the Peloponnesian League. Yet, between Athens and Sparta, it is hard to choose. Plataea, which the Spartan hoplites won, was the most glorious victory (9.64), but it was the Athenian fleet that saved Greece (7.144). But such heroes as Herodotus has among the Greeks are Spartans. Leonidas dies at Thermopylae loyal to his *nomoi*, and Pausanias contrasts sharply with Themistocles: the former was an admirable victor and the latter a clever rogue who rose to the occasion. As for the tales of Pausanias's later arrogance and medism, which were "charter myths" of the Athenian Empire, Herodotus treats them with a mixture of skepticism and silence.

Finally, the characterizations incorporate literary motifs. Xerxes is a great king brought low, Themistocles an Odysseus-figure, Pausanias the gallant victor who represents the virtue of moderation, and Aristagoras a mischief-making self-seeker. The need for dramatic presentation also makes demands: the tactic by which Cyrus defeats the Lydian cavalry of Croesus is suggested by Harpagus the Mede (1.80), and the necessity of Salamis is pressed upon Themistocles by

Mnesiphilus (8.57). In both instances, the victors lose some credit, but is this an intentional slight, or dramatic presentation? We should remember that the exigencies of the storyteller could conflict with the principles of objective history, and that they might win.

Chapter Twelve
The Aftermath

Herodotus's reputation was to be ambivalent. Four centuries after the *History* appeared, Cicero summed it all up in the opening scene of his *Laws* (1.5). Cicero, his brother Quintus, and his friend Atticus, were discussing the merits of Cicero's poem on Marius, and Atticus raised the question of accuracy. Cicero demurred; accuracy, he suggested, was the business of the historian, not the poet.

> "I understand, brother," said Quintus, "that you think one set of rules should be observed in history and another in poetry?"
> "Yes," agreed Cicero, "for in history, everything is meant to lead to the truth, but in poetry, a great deal is intended for pleasure—although in Herodotus, the father of history, and in Theopompus, there are a countless number of legends."[1]

Cicero's judgment was entirely conventional. Herodotus was recognized as a pioneer. His denomination of his work as an *histories apodexis* ("publication of research") defined a field of intellectual endeavor, and he was the first to use *historia* to mean "history" in the modern sense (7.96.1). Moreover, his work was consistently admired for its literary style. Aristotle (*Rhetoric*, 3.9.2) quotes it as an example of old-fashioned *lexis eiromene* ("running style"); Cicero and Quintilian compliment it, and the Greek writers of the Roman Empire paid it tribute.[2] The unknown author of *On the Sublime* (13.2) called it "most Homeric." He helped to form the style of the secular historians of the Byzantine Empire, such as Procopius and his continuator, Agathias, and the school that followed them down to the eclipse of Byzantium. But it was his style and not his content that excited admiration; thus, Agathias was to prefer Herodotus's critic, the untrustworthy Ctesias of Cnidus, to him as a source.[3]

For the business of the historian was to tell the truth. That sentiment, repeated over and over again, became hackneyed, but it was nonetheless a credo. It was also Herodotus's weak point. He acquired the reputation of being unreliable, biased, parsimonious in his praise for the heroes who repelled the Persian onslaught, and downright mendacious.

Probably it was Thucydides who struck the first blow. Thucydides never mentions Herodotus by name, but when he sets forth his own credo as an historian, by implication he reproves his predecessor. "The absence of an element of romance in my account of what happened, may well make it less attractive to hear, but all who want to attain a clear view of the past, and also of like or nearly like events which, human nature being what it is, will probably occur in the future—if these people consider my work useful, I shall be content. It is written to be a possession of lasting value, not a work competing for an immediate hearing" (1.22.4). The judgment of antiquity was that here, Thucydides was contrasting his work with that of Herodotus, and claiming for himself a serious purpose that was absent in the *History*.[4] But Herodotus was equally unfortunate in his spiritual descendant. Thucydides' successors were writers like Xenophon, Polybius, Sallust, and Procopius: serious historians who preferred contemporary events, whereas Herodotus had Ctesias of Cnidus, a fraudulent romancer, who borrowed Herodotus's style, used him as a source, and repaid him by blackening his reputation.

For the history of Ctesias[5] we are almost completely dependent on a summary by Photius, patriarch of Constantinople in the ninth century. He was an Asclepiad from Cnidus who in the late fifth and early fourth centuries B.C., became court physician to Artaxerxes II, and, after leaving Persia, wrote a *Persica* and an *Indica* that might have been classified as historical novels, except that the genre was not yet invented. Nothing that remains of his work inspires trust. But two points should be made about him.

First, he claimed to have used sources that sound like official Persian documents: royal records written on leather.[6] He claimed "inside knowledge" and used it to expose Herodotus. His pretensions were probably no more genuine than those of "Dictys of Crete," another ancient novelist of sorts, who pretended to have been a war correspondent at Troy, but even when Ctesias's "facts" were exposed, faith in Herodotus was not necessarily restored. Second, he was pro-Spartan: *philolakón* (Lacedaemonian-lover), Plutarch (*Artaxerxes*, 13) was to call him, and he made the Persian Wars into a "charter myth" for the Spartan empire of the early fourth century. His account of Thermopylae treated Leonidas and his little band as legendary heroes, withstanding first a Persian force of ten thousand led by "Artapanos" (Xerxes' uncle, Artabanus?), then a force of twenty thousand, and then fifty thousand. Salamis, for which Athens claimed the credit, became a mere pendant to the war. It came after Plataea, and Athens had a mere one hundred and ten ships.[7]

In part, the problem was that the Persian War rapidly became a legend with political overtones. After Xerxes' defeat, Sparta was to face a challenge to her leadership in the Peloponnesus, a helot revolt, and the growing menace of imperial Athens that was to result in war in 431 B.C. Thermopylae became the example of Sparta's dedication to Greek freedom and proof of her valor. For Athens, her claim to be Greece's savior rested on the same war, particularly the victories of Marathon and Salamis. In the next century, the Persian War became the symbol of Greek patriotism. "When we [the Athenians] had endured in the face of every danger, we were straightway awarded the meed of valor, and not much later, we got the sovereignty of the sea, given by the other Greeks . . ." wrote Isocrates (*Paneg.* 72) about 380 B.C., and his pupil, Ephorus, who wrote a *Universal History* in thirty books, treated the war in the spirit of his master, though he used Herodotus as a source. Years later, when Greece was only a province of the Roman Empire, the Greeks were to look back on the war as proof of their worth. Herodotus was an unsatisfactory encomiast, and he was open to criticism from every patriot.

His other flank was open to another kind of critic who questioned his reports of foreign countries on the basis of superior knowledge. Alexander the Great's conquests opened up the east, and countries such as Persia and Egypt were suddenly better-known. Herodotus was popular and much used in the Hellenistic period, but unfortunately it also became a convention for historians to attack their predecessors for inaccuracy, with unfortunate results for his reputation. Manetho, an Egyptian high priest from Heliopolis who wrote a history of Egypt in

Greek, also produced an essay pointing out Herodotus's lapses.[8] We have the titles of a number of similar pamphlets directed against Herodotus down to the end of the Roman Empire, all lost but one. The sole survivor is Plutarch's *On the Malignity of Herodotus*.

The inaccuracies that Plutarch claims are generally ill-founded, although he scores a point when he argues that Herodotus was ungenerous in his treatment of Thebes. But the general tenor of his complaints betrays an attitude that harks back to Isocrates. Herodotus was mean-spirited, and preferred what was discreditable to the Greeks. His diffusionist model, that led him to ascribe an Egyptian origin to Greek religion, had gone out of style, and Plutarch accused him of being a barbarian-lover because he found barbarian roots in everything Greek. He besmirched the Spartans, the Thebans, and the Corinthians, diminishing the glory of an heroic epoch that should have been left undefiled, and to make matters worse, he wrote so well that people read him!

The Renaissance inherited Herodotus's ambivalent reputation. He was fairly popular: there were forty-four editions or translations in Europe between 1450 and 1700, compared with forty-one of Thucydides.[9] But along with the popularity went disbelief, and it was particularly Herodotus's accounts of foreign countries that excited skepticism. His rehabilitation was a slow business. Momigliano has dated its beginning to 1566, when Henri Estienne brought out an edition of Lorenzo Valla's Latin translation of Herodotus, and prefaced it with his own *Apologia pro Herodoto*. But Herodotus's reputation remained an open question in the eighteenth century, and I suspect that Napoleon's expedition to Egypt did as much for it as academic battles. We have come a long way by 1800, when we reach James Rennell's *The Geographical System of Herodotus examined by a comparison with Other Ancient Authors, and with Modern Geography*. "We may add," wrote Rennell, "that superstition made him credulous in *believing* many improbable stories, but love of truth prevented him from asserting falsehoods." Herodotus was honest, but naive.

The nineteenth century attacked Herodotus with better weapons. As the archaeology of Egypt, Persia, and Assyria became better known, it grew clear that Herodotus's marvellous tales were not imaginary. Our own century has developed a lively respect for him as a reporter. Another group of scholars turned their attention to his sources. Did he plagiarize Hecataeus on Egypt, or Dionysius of Miletus on the Persian invasion? It is unlikely that we shall ever have enough evidence to end this controversy, but Herodotus has emerged from it with a heightened reputation as a researcher.

His charm is undeniable, and it tends to obscure the serious purpose behind the *History*. Herodotus was searching for the *aitia* of the war, and the *aitia* was the moral cause: who or what was to blame? He sought his answer in the attack and counterattack of Greek and barbarian, and he centered on the rise of Persian imperialism and made it his leitmotiv. The *History* ends at the turning point of Persian imperialism, when the Persian custom of expanding reached its watershed and could not continue longer. There Herodotus stops. But his *History* was published just as Athenian imperialism reached its crisis point. Herodotus draws no analogies, but analogy was a mode of thought in the ancient world.

Notes and References

Abbreviations used are those of the *American Journal of Archaeology* 74 (1970): 3–8, supplemented from *Transactions of the American Philological Association* 107 (1977): v–vi, and *Oxford Classical Dictionary*, 2d ed. (1970).

AAA: *Athens Annals of Archaeology*

ActaAntiqAcadScientHungaricae: *Acta Antiqua Academiae Scientiarum Hungaricae*

AJAH: *American Journal of Ancient History*

AJP: *American Journal of Philology*

AntCl: *L'Antiquité classique*

ANET: *Ancient Near Eastern Texts relating to the Old Testament*, ed. J. B. Pritchard, 2d ed., Princeton, Princeton University Press, 1955.

ANSMN: *American Numismatic Society, Museum Notes*

AntJ: *Antiquaries Journal*

ATL: Benjamin Dean Meritt, H. T. Wade-Gery, and M. F. McGregor, *The Athenian Tribute Lists*. Cambridge: Harvard University Press, 1939–53.

BCH: *Bulletin de correspondence hellénique*

BIFAO: *Bulletin de l'Institut français d'archéologie orientale*

BZ: *Byzantinische Zeitschrift*

CAH: *Cambridge Ancient History*

CJ: *Classical Journal*

CP: *Classical Philology*

CQ: *Classical Quarterly*

CR: *Classical Review*

CSCA: *California Studies in Classical Antiquity*

FGrH: Felix Jacoby, *Fragmente der Griechischer Historiker*, Leiden: Brill, 1923–30; Berlin: Weidmann, 1940–.

GRBS: *Greek, Roman, and Byzantine Studies*

HSCP: *Harvard Studies in Classical Philology*

JEA: *Journal of Egyptian Archaeology*

JHS: *Journal of Hellenic Studies*
JNES: *Journal of Near Eastern Studies*
PCPhS: *Proceedings of the Cambridge Philological Society*
PP: *La Parola del Passato*
RE: *Pauly-Wissowa, Real-encyclopädie der Klassischen Altertums-wissenschaft,* Stuttgart: J. B. Metzler, 1894–.
RFIC: *Rivista di Filologia et d'Istruzione Classica*
SIG: Wilhelm Dittenberger: *Sylloge Inscriptionum Graecarum,* Hildesheim: G. Olms, 1960.
YCS: *Yale Classical Studies*
ZPE: *Zeitschrift für papyrologie und epigrafik*

Chapter One

1. W. Schadewaldt, *Die Antike* 10 (1934): 168.

2. Hdt. 2.123.1; 7.152.3.

3. Russell Meiggs and David Lewis, *A Selection of Greek Historical Inscriptions to the End of the Fifth Century B.C.* (Oxford: Clarendon Press, 1969) no. 32 (hereafter Meiggs-Lewis).

4. Dion, Hal., *de Thuc.* 5. Aulus Gellius (15.23) dates his birth to 484 B.C., but it is unlikely that he had exact information; cf. J. Enoch Powell, *The History of Herodotus* (Cambridge: University Press, 1939), p. 84; F. Jacoby, *RE,* supp. 2, p. 230; Alden A. Mosshammer, "The Apollodoran *Akmai* of Hellanicus and Herodotus," *GRBS* 14 (1973): 5–13.

5. Cf. Hdt. 1. 171.

6. Victor J. Matthews, *Panyassis of Halicarnassus,* text and commentary (Leiden: Brill, 1974), p. 28.

7. *SIG,* p. 608.

8. Hdt. 9.11.3; 9.55.2. The term was also applied to non-Spartan Greeks: cf. 5.51.2.

9. *ATL,* 3: 149–54; Wallace McLeod, "Studies in Panyassis—A Heroic Poet of the Fifth Century," *Phoenix* 20 (1966): 97.

10. Ph.-E. Legrand, *Hérodote,* vol. 1 (Paris: Société d'Édition: "Les Belles Lettres," 1955), pp. 12–16; Jacoby, *RE,* supp. 2, pp. 242–46. For the foundation of Thurii, see Diod. Sic. 12.9–11; D. Kagan, *The Outbreak of the Peloponnesian War* (Ithaca, Cornell University Press, 1969), pp. 154–69; N. K. Rutter, "Diodorus and the Foundation of Thurii," *Historia* 22 (1973): 155–76.

11. Jacoby; V. Ehrenberg, "The Foundation of Thurii," *Polis und*

Imperium: Beiträge zur alten Geschichte, ed. K. F. Stroheker, and A. J. Graham (Zurich: Artemis Verlag, 1965), pp. 298–315.

12. Diod. Sic. 12.35.1–3.

13. Diog. Laert. 9.50.

14. August Meineke, ed., *Stephan von Byzanz* (1848; reprint ed., Graz, 1958), p. 315.

15. Kurt von Fritz, *Die Griechische Geschichtsschreibung.* vol. I. Von den (Berlin, de Gruyter, 1967), pp. 128–57; (hereafter *GG*); W. W. How and J. Wells, *A Commentary on Herodotus*, vol. 1 (Oxford, 1912), pp. 16–20, (hereafter *HW*); Legrand, 1:24–29; John L. Myres, *Herodotus, Father of History* (Oxford, 1953), pp. 4–9; Jacoby, pp. 247–67.

16. J. Wells, "Herodotus and Athens," *CP* 23 (1928): 317–31.

17. *Herod or Aet.* 1–2.

18. Plut. *Mor.* 862 A–B (*de mal. Her.*); cf. Jacoby, pp. 226–29; cf. E. Badian, *Antichthon* 5 (1971): 23, n. 59, who rejects the story.

19. Plutarch, *Mor.* 864 D (= Aristophanes of Boeotia, *FGrHist.* iii B no. 379, F5).

20. Pl. *Hp. Ma.* 282 D–E; 285 B.

21. Jacoby, p. 262; Powell, p. 27.

22. 1.104; 109–10; 112.3; cf. Alan B. Lloyd, *Herodotus, Book II: Introduction* (Leiden: Brill, 1975), pp. 38–49 (hereafter Lloyd).

23. Meiggs-Lewis, no. 34.

24. Powell, p. 29, suggests two trips, one before 461 and the other possibly after 448.

25. A. H. Sayce, "The Season and Extent of the Travels of Herodotus in Egypt," *JP* .14 (1885): 257–86, esp. 258–60; Camille Sourdille, *Sur La Durée et L'Etendue du Voyage d'Hérodote en Egypte* (Paris; Leroux, 1910), pp. 5–28. For trenchant but overly severe criticism of Sourdille, see Lloyd, 1:68–72.

26. John Ball, *Contributions to the Geography of Egypt* (Cairo: Government Press, 1939), pp. 199–201.

27. Cf. O. E. Ravn, *Herodotus' Description of Babylon* (Copenhagen: Nyt Nordisk Forlag, 1942). pp. 93–96.

28. Hdt. 4. 75. 1; cf. Tamara Talbot Rice, *The Scythians* (London: Thames and Hudson, 1957), p. 90.

29. Hdt. 4. 53.4; 4. 71–72; Rice, pp. 87–90; cf. *GG*, 1:130

30. Hdt. 1. 171–72.

31. Hdt. 2. 143.4; cf. P. Montet, *Eternal Egypt* (Mentor, N.Y., 1968), p. 326.

32. Hdt. 2. 69. 3; cf. Lloyd, 2:309–10.

33. Hdt. 4. 27; cf. J. D. P. Bolton, *Aristeas of Proconnesus* (Oxford: Clarendon Press, 1962), p. 198, n. 15.

34. Cf. Hdt. 8. 85. 3; 9.110.2. Both *orosangai* and *tykta* derived from Persian: *HW*.

35. cf. Legrand, 1:75; D. Hegyi, "Historical Authenticity in Herodotus," *ActaAntiqAcad ScientHungaricae* 21 (1973): 73–87.

36. K. von Fritz, "Herodotus and the Growth of Greek Historiography," *TAPA* 67 (1936): 315–40.

37. Meiggs-Lewis, no. 57.

38. *Mor.* 785 B; cf. T. Gomperz, "Hérodote et Sophocle," in *Mélanges Henri Weil* (Paris: Thorin et fils, 1898), pp. 141–46; Karl-August Riemann, *Das Herodoteisches Geschichtswerk in den Antike* (Munich: Diss. München, 1967), pp. 2–3.

39. R. Pischl, "Zu Sophokles' Antigone, 909–912," *Hermes* 28 (1893): 465–68. J. Th. Kakridis, *Homeric Researches* (Lund: C.W.K. Gleerup, 1949), pp. 152–64, cites parallels from modern Greek folksongs, but they are much less exact.

40. See note 18; cf. Myres, p. 12.

41. H. Eiteljorg, "New finds concerning the entrance to the Athenian Acropolis," *AAA* 8 (1975): p. 94–95.

42. Tönnes Kleberg, *Büchhandel und Verlagswesen in der Antike* (Darmstadt: Wissenschaftliche Buchgesellschaft, 1967), pp. 4–6.

43. Pl., *Ap.* 26, d–e; cf. N. Lewis, *Papyrus in Classical Antiquity* (Oxford: Clarendon Press, 1974), p. 74. For the orchestra, see *The Athenian Agora: A Guide to the Excavations and Museum* (Athens: American School of Classical Studies, 1976), pp. 90–93.

44. Jacoby, *RE*, supp. 2, p. 233; *HW*, 1:9. For the view that Herodotus outlived the Archidamian War, see O. J. Todd, "On the date of Herodotus' Death," *CQ* 16 (1922): 35–36; J. Wells, in *Studies in Herodotus* (Oxford, 1923), pp. 169–82; C. W. Fornara, *JHS* 91 (1971): 25–34.

45. Thuc. 2.27; 4.56–57.

46. Cf. R. Lattimore, "The composition of the Histories of Herodotus," *CP* 53 (1958): 9–21.

47. For the argument that the Assyrian *logoi* dropped out of the text, see G. Huxley, *GRBS* 6 (1965): 201–12; J. G. MacQueen, *CQ* 28 (1978): 284–91; R. Drews, *AJP* 91 (1970): 181–91, who argues that the references are a later addition by Herodotus himself.

Chapter Two

1. Herodotus is identified as Halicarnassian in all manuscripts, but Aristotle (Rh. iii.9 p. 1409a, 29) who quotes the first five words of the introduction, calls him Herodotus of Thurii, indicating that that was the reading of the copy he knew, and perhaps the original reading. Our first firm example of the use of the term "of Halicarnassus" comes from an inscription on a round marble statue base from the library of king Eumenes (197–159 B.C.) of Pergamon: Max Frankel, ed., *Altertümer von Pergamon*, 8:1: *Die Inschriften von Pergamon* (Berlin, 1890), no. 199; Jacoby, *RE*, supp. 2, pp. 205–13; Legrand, 1:5–7.

2. Cf. Henry Immerwahr, "*Ergon*: History as a Monument in Herodotus and Thucydides," *AJP* 81 (1960): 261–90; Robert Drews, *The Greek Accounts of Eastern History* (Cambridge: Harvard University Press, 1973), p. 87. The "works of men" included both deeds and physical monuments.

3. Cf. Hdt. 8.144.2; G. Pugliese Carratelli, "Europa ed Asia nella Storia del Mondo Antico," *PP* 40 (1955): 5–19.

4. J. A. K. Thomson, *The Art of the Logos* (London: Allen and Unwin, 1935), pp. 18–20.

5. Diod. Sic. 2.37.6 attests it first.

6. Cf. S. Cagnazzi, "Tavola dei 28 *Logoi* di Erodoto," *Hermes* 103 (1975): 385–423.

7. Cf. F. Hampl, *GB* 4 (1975): 116–71; B. Shimron, *Eranos* 71 (1973): 45–51.

8. 1.6.2; cf. A. Maddelena, *Interpretazioni Erodotee* (Padua, 1942), pp. 1–16; G. de Sanctis, *RFIC* 15 (1936): 2–3.

9. Frg. 22 (J. M. Edmonds, *Elegy and Iambus*, vol. 1, *LCL*, p. 205); cf. R. Drews, p. 7; M. E. White, "Herodotus' Starting Point," *Phoenix* 23 (1969): 39–48.

10. A. L. Oppenheim, in *ANET*, 2d ed., p. 306; cf. J. A. S. Evans, "What Happened to Croesus," *CJ* 74 (1978): 34–40.

11. Possibly a Greek dynasty established itself at Sardis in the restless period after the Trojan War: G. M. A. Hanfman, *Letters from Sardis* (Cambridge: Harvard University Press, 1972), p. 192; J. G. Pedley, *Sardis in the Age of Croesus* (Norman: University of Oklahoma Press, 1968), pp. 4–5, 25–30.

12. Meiggs-Lewis, no. 6; cf. M. F. McGregor, "Solon's Archonship: The Epigraphic Evidence," *Polis and Imperium: Studies in Honour of Edward Togo Salmon*, ed. J. A. S. Evans (Toronto: Hakkert, 1974), pp. 31–34.

13. J. A. K. Thomson, pp. 78–84.

14. Cf. Heinrich Bischoff, "Die Warner bei Herodot," in *Herodot*, ed. W. Marg (Munich: Berk, 1962), pp. 302–19; R. Lattimore, "The Wise Advisor in Herodotus," *CP* 34 (1939): 24–35. For clever advisors in folktale, see Stith Thompson, *The Folktale* (1946; reprint ed., Berkeley: University of California Press, 1977), pp. 163–65.

15. Cf. Evans, *CJ* 74 (1978): 34–40. J. Cargill, "The Nabonidus Chronicle and the fall of Lydia," *AJAH* 2 (1977): 97–116, argues for a less precise date.

16. Hdt. 1. 87. 3. For Croesus's transformation, see Hans-Peter Stahl, "Learning through Suffering? Croesus' conversations in the history of Herodotus," *YCS* 24 (1975): 1–36.

17. Pind., *Pyth.* 1. 94.

18. D. D. Luckenbill, *Ancient Records of Assyria and Babylonia* (Chicago: University of Chicago Press, 1927), 2: 56 (display inscription from Khorsabad); R. Dyson, "Problems of protohistoric Iran as seen from Hasanlu," *JNES* 24 (1965): 193–217.

19. Dyson, p. 203.

20. R. N. Frye, *The Heritage of Persia* (London: Weidenfield and Nicolson, 1962), pp. 70–72; R. Ghirshman, *Iran from the Earliest Times to the Islamic Conquest* (Harmondsworth: Penguin, 1954), pp. 96–112; William Culican, *The Medes and the Persians* (London: Thames and Hudson, 1965), pp. 31–47.

21. 1. 130. 3; cf. Henry R. Immerwahr, *Form and Thought in Herodotus* (Cleveland: 1966), pp. 52–53.

22. On Herodotus's concept of *nomoi*: M. Ostwald, *Nomos and the Beginnings of Athenian Democracy* (Oxford: Clarendon Press, 1969), pp. 20–54; M. Gigante, *Nomos Basileus* (Naples: Glaux, 1956), p. 111; J. A. S. Evans, "Despotes Nomos," *Athenaeum* 43 (1965): 142–53.

23. *HW*, 1:115.

24. J. P. Barron, "Religious Propaganda of the Delian League," *JHS* 84 (1964): 35–48.

25. *ANET,* 2d ed., 315–16.

26. *ANET,* 2d ed., p. 317; cf. J. Duchesne-Guillemin, "Réligion et politique de Cyrus à Xerxes," *Persica* 3 (1967–8): 1–9, esp. 7–9.

27. 1.181.5; cf. O. E. Ravn, p. 93; G. Roux, *Ancient Iraq* (London, 1964), pp. 34–50.

28. T. Jacobsen, *Iraq* 22 (1960): 176–77; R. D. Barnett, *JHS* 83 (1963): 11.

29. We cannot, however, exclude the possibility that Herodotus has reported what he saw, for canals ran between the palace and the *Etemenanki:*

Giovanni Bergamini, "Levels of Babylon Reconsidered," *Mesopotamia* 12 (1977): 111–52, esp. pp. 132–35; cf. O. E. Ravn, pp. 61–66.

30. *ANET,* 2d ed., p. 306 (Nabonidus Chron.); p. 315 (Cyrus Cyl.)

31. M. Mallowan, *Iran* 10 (1972): 4.

Chapter Three

1. *FGrHist.* F. 1a; cf. Lloyd, 2: 9–12.

2. John Ball, *Egypt in the Classical Geographers* (Cairo, 1942), p. 13; Lloyd, 2: 42.

3. H. Frankel, *Early Greek Poetry and Philosophy* (Oxford; Blackwell, 1975), p. 519; Ingrid Beck, *Die Ringkomposition bei Herodot und ihre Bedeutung für die Beweistechnik* (Hildesheim: G. Olms, 1971), pp. 18–20; Immerwahr, *Form and Thought,* pp. 54–58.

4. H. Lyons, in K. Baedeker, *Egypt and the Sudan,* 8th ed. (Leipzig, 1929), pp. lxvi–lxvii.

5. J. A. S. Evans, *YCS* 17 (1961): 190–91; Lloyd, 1: 112–13.

6. W. Spiegelberg, *The Credibility of Herodotus' Account of Egypt,* trans. A. M. Blackman (Oxford: Blackwell, 1929), pp. 17–18; G. A. Wainwright, "Herodotus II, 28, on the Sources of the Nile," *JHS* 73 (1953): 104–7.

7. Rhys Carpenter, *Beyond the Pillars of Heracles* (New York: Delacorte Press, 1966), pp. 126–28; Lloyd, 2: 137–38.

8. Lloyd, 2: 168; Legrand, vol. 3.

9. Hdt. 2.178–79; R. M. Cook, "Amasis and the Greeks in Egypt," *JHS* 57 (1937): 227–37; J. Boardman, *The Greeks Overseas* (Harmondsworth; Penguin, 1964), pp. 115–31; D. Mallet, *Les Rapports des Grecs avec Egypte* (De la Conquête de Cambyse, 525, à celle d'Alexandre, 331) (Cairo; Memoires de l'Institute français d'Archéologie orientale du Caire, 48, 1922), pp. 19–21.

10. E. Meyer, *Forschungen zur älten Geschichte,* vol. 1 (Halle: M. Niemeyer, 1892), p. 194; R. Lattimore, *CP* 34 (1939): 357–65.

11. J. Cerny, *Ancient Egyptian Religion* (London; Hutchinson, 1952), p. 25; G. A. Wainwright, "The Ram-Headed God of Hermopolis," *JEA* 19 (1933): 160–61; Lloyd, 2: 191–92.

12. *ANET,* 2d ed., pp. 4–6; Cerny, pp. 43–50.

13. Cerny, p. 27.

14. *HW,* 1: 187–88; Lloyd, 2: 201–2.

15. J. Gwyn Griffiths, "The Order of Gods in Greece and Egypt," *JHS* 75 (1955): 21–23; Cerny, p. 44.

16. Lloyd, 2: 205–11.

17. Cf. John A. Wilson, *Herodotus in Egypt*, (Leiden: Nederlands Instituut voor Het Nabije Oosten, 1970).

18. I. E. S. Edwards, *CAH*, 3d ed., vol. 1 (1971), pp. 11–15.

19. Spiegelberg, p. 24.

20. Stith Thompson, pp. 171–72.

21. Cf. Lloyd, 1: 188–89.

22. Cf. Manetho, Frg. 21(a), (W. C. Waddell, *LCL*, pp. 54–55); W. Stevenson Smith, *CAH*, 3d ed., vol. 1 (1971), pp. 178–79; Christiane Coche-Zivie, *BIFAO* 72 (1972): 115–37.

23. 2 Kings 19.

24. Spiegelberg, p. 26; *HW*, 1: 236.

25. K. Michalowski, "The Labyrinth Enigma: Archaeological Suggestions," *JEA* 54 (1968): 219–22; A. B. Lloyd, "The Egyptian Labyrinth," *JEA* 56 (1970): 51–100.

26. J. A. S. Evans, "Herodotus and the Problem of Lake Moeris," *CW* 56 (1962–1963): 275–77.

Chapter Four

1. Culican, pp. 59–62. The legends surrounding Cambyses' birth have a parallel in the later Persian legend about Alexander the Great's birth: he was the son of the Persian king by Philip of Macedon's daughter whom the king divorced and returned to her father.

2. Hdt. 2.29.6; 3.17–18; cf. P. L. Shinnie, *Meroe, A Civilization of Sudan* (London; Thames and Hudson, 1967), pp. 13–16.

3. Baedeker, p. 448.

4. M. M. Austin, *Greece and Egypt in the Archaic Age*, in *PCPhS*, supp. 2 (1970), pp. 13–14.

5. Diod. Sic., 20.14; Quint. Curt. Ruf., 4.2.10.

6. Bezabel Porten, *Archives from Elephantine: The Life of an Ancient Jewish Military Colony* (Berkeley: University of California Press, 1968), p. 26.

7. G. Posener, *La Première Domination Perse en Egypte: Recueil d' Inscriptions Hieroglyphiques* (Cairo, 1936), no. 1; cf. A. T. Olmstead, *History of the Persian Empire* (Chicago: University of Chicago Press, 1948), pp. 90–91; Mary Francis Gyles, *Pharaonic Policies and Administration, 663 to 323 B.C.* (Chapel Hill: University of North Carolina Press, 1959), pp. 39–40.

8. Posener, nos. 3, 4.

9. John Boardman, *AntJ* 39 (1959): 199–203; J. P. Barron, *The Silver Coins of Samos* (London: Athlone Press, 1966), p. 34; Barron, *CQ* 14 (1964): 213–14; Oscar Reuther, *Der Heratempel von Samos: Der Bau Seit der Zeit des Polykrates* (Berlin: Gerb. Mann Verlag, 1957), p. 63. The Rhoecus-temple may have been burned in a Persian raid in the 540s though Hdt. 1.169.2 indicates that submisson to Persia at the time was peaceful, and seems to have thought that the temple stood intact in Polycrates' day. For its impressive ruins: Paus. 7.5.4.

10. Plut., *Mot.* 303E–304C; Mary White, "The Duration of the Samian Tyranny," *JHS* 74 (1954): 36–43, argued that Polycrates' father, Aiakes, preceded him as tyrant, but her key evidence, a dedication by Aiakes (Meiggs-Lewis, no. 16), cannot be connected with Polycrates' father. Barron, *CQ* 14 (1964): 210–29, argues for an earlier tyrant also called Polycrates.

11. Stith Thompson, *Motif-Index of Folk Literature* (Bloomington: Indiana University Press, 1955–1958), N211.1.

12. For a contrary view, B. M. Mitchell, *JHS* 95 (1975): 70; Anne Burton, *Diodorus Siculus, Book I: A Commentary* (Leiden: Brill, 1972), p. 274.

13. Barron, *Silver Coins*, pp. 17–18.

14. Cf. M. Dandamaev, "Achaemenid Babylonia," in *Ancient Mesopotamia*, ed. I. M. Diakonoff (Moscow: Nauka Publishing House, 1969), p. 307.

15. Cf. M. A. Dandamaev, *Persien unter den ersten Achaemeniden* (6 Jahrhundert v. Chr.), trans. H-D Pöhl (Wiesbaden: L. Reichert Verlag, 1976), pp. 157–58; *HW*, 1: 175–76. For the inscription, see R. G. Kent, *Old Persian, Grammar, Texts, Lexicon* (New Haven: Yale University Press, 1953), pp. 116–34; G. C. Cameron, "The Monument of King Darius at Bisitun," *Archaeology* 13 (1960): 162–71.

16. Richard T. Hallock, "The 'One Year' of Darius I," *JNES* 19 (1960): 36–39.

17. The name Patizeithes probably derives from the Persian for "grand chamberlain": J. Marquart, *Untersuchungen zur Geschichte von Eran* (Leipzig: Teubner, 1905), 2: 145. Bardiya is "Mardos" in Aeschylus (*Pers.* 774) and becomes "Smerdis" in Hdt., a name common in Asia Minor: D. Hegyi, "Historical Authenticity of Herodotus in the Persian 'Logoi,'" *ActaAntiqAcadScient Hungaricae* 21 (1973): 73–87. On folktale elements, see E. J. Bickerman and J. Tadmor, "Darius I, Pseudo-Smerdis, and the Magi," *Athenaeum* 56 (1978): 239–61.

18. Bickerman-Tadmor, p. 256. J. Duchesne-Guillemin (*Historia Einzelschr* 18 [1972]: 72) suggests that Darius slew a number of Gaumata's

magian followers, and this was commemorated in the *magophonia;* cf. W. B. Henning, *JRAS,* (1944), 133–44.

19. Dandamaev, pp. 163–65; P. T. Brannan, "Herodotus and History," *Traditio* 19 (1963): 427–38. Darius's father and grandfather were both still alive: Kent, pp. 149–50 (XPf).

20. Pindar, *Pyth.* 2: 86–88, assumes such a division.

21. Cf. J. S. Morrison, "The place of Protagoras in Athenian Public Life," *CQ* 35 (1941): 1–16; F. Lasserre, "Hérodote et Protagoras: Le débat sur les constitutions," *MusHelv* 33 (1976): 65–84.

22. An idea perhaps borrowed from Heracleitus by way of Protagoras: Plato, *Theat.* 160C ff.

23. G. C. Cameron, "The Persian Satrapies and Related Matters," *JNES* 32 (1973): 47–56. For the satrapies, see E. Herzfeld, *The Persian Empire: Studies in Geography and Ethnography of the Ancient Near East* (Weisbaden: Franz Steiner Verlag, 1969), pp. 298–340.

24. It was also a royal residence for a part of the year: A. Shapur Shahbazi, *Gymnasium* 85 (1978): 487–500.

25. W. M. Calder, III, *GRBS* 9 (1968): 389–407; L. Woodbury, *Phoenix* 24 (1970): 209–24, dates it to 442. On the folktale, see Wolf Aly, *Volkmärchen, Sage und Novelle bei Herodot und seinen Zeitgenossen* (1921; reprint ed., Gottingen: Vandenhoeck and Ruprecht, 1969), p. 109.

26. Strabo, 14.1.17; Zenobius 3.90; cf. V. LaBua, *Quarta Miscellanea Greca e Romana* (Rome: Istituto Italiano Per la Storia Antica, 1975), pp. 50–51.

27. Richard A. Parker and W. H. Dubberstein, *Babylonian Chronology, 626 B.C.–A.D. 75* (Providence, R.I.: Brown University Press, 1956), pp. 15–16.

28. Aly, pp. 111–12.

Chapter Five

1. *IG,* xiv, 1297; cf. G. C. Cameron, *JNES* 2 (1943): 313. M. Miller, *Klio* 37 (1959): 34, followed by J. M. Balcer, *HSCP* 76 (1972): 99–132, prefers 519 B.C.

2. E. H. Minns, *Scythians and Greeks* (Cambridge: Cambridge University Press, 1913), pp. 152–54; E. D. Phillips, *The Royal Hordes, Nomad Peoples of the Steppes* (London: Thames and Hudson, 1963), pp. 66–78.

3. T. Sulimirski, "The Cimmerian Problem," *Bull. of the Inst. of Archaeology, Univ. of London* 2 (1959): 45–64.

4. J. P. D. Bolton, pp. 207–14, prints them but is dubious of their authenticity.

5. E.g., Olen of Lycia: 4.35.5; Bakis: 8.20.2; perhaps Onomakritos: 7.6.3.

6. E. D. Phillips, "The Legend of Aristeas: Fact and Fancy in Early Greek Notions of East Russia, Siberia and Inner Asia," *Artibus Asiae* 18 (1955): 161–77; Phillips, "A Further Note on Aristeas," *Artibus Asiae* 20, (1957): 159–62.

7. Bolton, pp. 115–16.

8. *HW*, 1: 34–35; cf. C. W. Beck, G. C. Southard, and A. B. Adams, *GRBS* 9 (1968): 5–19. J. Harmatta, *ActaAntiqAcadScientHungaricae* 3 (1955): 57–64, dates the origin of the legend to the second millenium B.C.

9. John L. Myres, "An Attempt to Reconstruct the Maps Used by Herodotus," *Geographical Journal* 8 (1896): 605–31.

10. Cf. R. Mauney, *Archéologie* 96 (1976): 44–45.

11. Minns, pp. 28–29, cf. H. Kothe, *Klio* 51 (1969): 33.

12. O. K. Armayor, *HSCP* 82 (1978): 52-57, estimates 6244 gallons.

13. Phillips, *Artibus Asiae* 18 (1955): 165.

14. It is rejected by H. Berve, *Miltiades, Hermes Einzelschr* 2 (1937): 41–43; H. Berve, *Die Tyrannis, bei den Griechen* (Munich: 1969) 2: 567.

15. Pindar, *Pyth.* 4.

16. Cf. Arnold Toynbee, *Some Problems of Greek History* (London: Oxford University Press, 1969), pp. 174–78; G. L. Huxley, *Early Sparta* (London: Faber, 1962), p. 316.

17. L. H. Jeffery, *The Local Scripts of Archaic Greece* (Oxford: Clarendon Press, 1961), p. 316.

18. Meiggs-Lewis, no. 5; cf. A. J. Graham, *Colony and Mother City in Ancient Greece* (Manchester: University of Manchester Press, 1964), pp. 224–26.

19. B. M. Mitchell, *JHS* 86 (1966): 101–2. F. Chamoux, *Cyrène sous la Monarchie des Battiades* (Paris: E. de Boccard, 1953), pp. 144–50, dates it earlier, while Polycrates was tyrant of Samos.

20. Aly, p. 136.

21. Cf. Zoltán Kadar, "Some Problems Concerning the Scientific Authority of Classical Authors on Libyan Fauna," *Acta Classica Universitatis Scientiarum Debreceniensis* 8 (1972): 11–16.

22. C. B. M. McBurney, *The Stone Age of Northern Africa* (Harmonds-

worth: Penguin, 1960), p. 267; M. Cary and E. H. Warmington, *The Ancient Explorers* (Harmondsworth: Penguin, 1963), pp. 218–19.

23. U. Paradisi, *PP* 17 (1962): 201–5.

24. The land of Kinyps (4.198.1) seems to be Tripolitana, which has greater water resources than the Cyrenaean plateau, though its annual rainfall is less: cf. Claudio Vita-Fenzi, *The Mediterranean Valleys: Geological Change in Historical Times* (Cambridge: Cambridge University Press, 1969), pp. 12–26; R. G. Goodchild, "Mapping Roman Libya," *Geographical Journal* 18 (1952): 142–52.

25. John Boardman, J. G. Pedley, and D. White, *Libya Antiqua* 3–4 (1966–1967): 179–98.

Chapter Six

1. *Iliad*, 5.62; 11.604.

2. Cf. J. A. S. Evans, *AJP* 84 (1963): 117.

3. R. Ross Holloway, "The Crown of Naxos," *ANSMN* 10 (1962): 1–8.

4. Cf. P. B. Manville, "Aristagoras and Histiaios: The Leadership Struggle in the Ionian Revolt," *CQ* 27 (1977): 80–91.

5. Cf. H. W. Pleket, "Isonomia and Cleisthenes: A Note," *Talanta* 4 (1972): 63–81.

6. Cf. J. K. Davies, *Athenian Properties Families, 600–300 B.C. (Oxford: Clarendon Press, 1971), p. 296;* D. M. Lewis, *Historia* 12 (1963): 25–26. D. J. McCargar (*Phoenix* 38 [1974]: 275–81), argues that Isagoras the archon, and Isagoras, Cleisthenes' rival, were not identical, but this is unlikely.

7. Cf. B. Jordan, "Herodotus 5.71.2, and the Naukraroi of Athens," *CSCA* 3 (1970): 153–75.

8. Alternatively, it may have been Solon's Council of 400 (Arist. *AP*, 8.4; Plut., *Solon*, 19.1) but if so, this is the only recorded action of this council.

9. Dated generally ca. 658–ca. 585 B.C.; cf. R. Sealey, *A History of the Greek City States, ca. 700–338 B.C. (Berkeley: University of California Press, 1976), pp. 53–55;* D. E. W. Wormell, *"Studies in Greek Tyranny, I—The Cypselids," Hermathena* 66 (1954): 1–24.

10. Mabel Lang, "Herodotus and the Ionian Revolt," *Historia* 17 (1968): 24–36; R. Meiggs, *The Athenian Empire* (Oxford: Clarendon Press, 1972), p. 24.

11. *HW*, 2:71; J. M. Bigwood, *Phoenix* 32 (1978): 36–39.

Chapter Seven

1. Possibly Miltiades' departure took place during Pisistratus's first tyranny: cf. T. J. Cadoux, *JHS* 68 (1948): 110, n. 217, but it was too insecure and brief to provide a motive, except in retrospect.

2. A. R. Burn, *Persia and the Greeks: The Defense of the West, 546–478 B.C.* (London, 1962), pp. 218–20; J. A. S. Evans, "Notes on Miltiades' Capture of Lemnos," *CP* 58 (1963): 168–70; Arnold Toynbee, p. 129, n. 3; cf. F. Prontera, "Per l'interpretazione di Erodoto VI, 40," *PP* 27 (1972): 111–23.

3. J. A. S. Evans, "The Settlement of Artaphrenes," *CP* 71 (1976): 344–48.

4. E.g., Theomester at Samos (8.85.3).

5. Burn, p. 233.

6. Philostr. *VA*, 1.24.1; cf. J. R. Green and R. K. Sinclair, "Athens in Eretria," *Historia* 19 (1970): 515–27, esp. pp. 517–18.

7. Cf. W. K. Pritchett, *Ancient Greek Military Practices*, (Berkeley: University of California Press, 1971), 1:116–26.

8. Cf. Peter Frisch, *Die Traüme bei Herodot* (Meisenheim am Glan: Verlag Anton Hain, 1968), pp. 26–27.

9. The deadlock meant no action, and thus Hdt. (6.109.2) can say, "The worse policy was winning out." But cf. C. Hignett, *Xerxes' Invasion of Greece* (Oxford, 1963), p. 57.

10. Cf. Walter Donlan, and James Thompson, "The Charge at Marathon: Herodotus 6.112," *CJ* 71 (1976): 339–43.

11. For this view, see F. Jacoby, *Atthis* (Oxford: Clarendon Press, 1949), p. 223; D. Gillis, *GRBS* 18 (1969): 133–45. For the opposite view, see Hans-Friedrich Bornitz, *Herodot-Studien, Beitrage zum Verständnis der Einheit des Geschichtswerkes* (Berlin: de Gruyter, 1968), pp. 94–105.

12. Meiggs-Lewis, no. 6; cf. Mary White, in *Polis and Imperium*, ed. J. A. S. Evans, pp. 86–87.

13. H. Berve, *Die Tyrannis*, pp. 27–33.

14. Probably this is a case of attraction: a famous name was included in a famous folktale. But T. Kelly, *A History of Argos to 500 B.C.* (Minneapolis: University of Minnesota Press, 1976), pp. 109–11, defends Hdt.'s date.

Chapter Eight

1. Ca. 498 B.C.: Henrik Samuel Nyberg, *Historia Mundi*, vol. 3 (Munich, 1954), p. 98; Culican, pp. 80–100; cf. Kent., pp. 149–50, 163.

2. David Grene, "Herodotus: The Historian as Dramatist," *Journal of Philosophy* 58 (1961): 477–88.

3. Cf. Max Pohlenz, *Herodot, der erste Geschichtsschreiber des Abendlandes* (Darmstadt: Wissenschaftliche Buchgesellschaft, 1961), p. 125.

4. Cf. J. A. S. Evans, "The Dream of Xerxes and the 'Nomoi' of the Persians," *CJ* 57 (1961): 109–11.

5. P. Amandry, *BCH* 70 (1949): 1–8; A. Walker, *Delphi* (Athens: Lycabettus Press, 1977), p. 56.

6. Cf. Dietram Müller, "Von Doriscus nach Therma," *Chiron* 5 (1975): 1–11.

7. Ch. Chrysanthaki, "Ek tön Thasion Ipeiro," *AAA* 6 (1973): 230–40.

8. *HW*, 2:173; Müller, pp. 10–11.

9. However, there is some doubt if the *tageia* ("elective kingship") of Thessaly existed at this time, though Hdt. 7.6.2 refers to the Aleuads as "kings": cf. N. Robertson *JHS* 96 (1976): 102–8.

10. Cf. J. A. R. Munro, *CAH*, 4:282.

11. Cf. W. K. Pritchett, "Xerxes' Route over Mt. Olympus," *AJA* 65 (1961): 369–75.

12. This differs from the view of P. A. Brunt, "The Hellenic League against Persia," *Historia* 2 (1953–1954): 135–63, esp. 136–37, who dates the oath to the first meeting of the "league" in 481. However, Herodotus implies that the oath was a reaction to the surrender.

13. I find it hard to believe that Themistocles engineered the "Wooden Wall" oracle, as argued by J. Labarbe, *La Loi Navale de Thémistocle* (Paris: Société d'Editions "Les Belles Lettres," 1957), pp. 109–19. Its tone is pessimistic, and the reference to Salamis would fit a Greek defeat there as well as a victory. Cf. J. Fontenrose, *The Delphic Oracle* (Berkeley: University of California Press, 1978), pp. 124–28 who argues that the oracle was part of the Salamis legend, and not historical.

14. The general view is that Herodotus is here belittling Themistocles: Frank J. Frost: "Themistocles' Place in Athenian Politics," *CSCA* 1 (1968): 105–24, esp. 119; G. L. Cawkwell, "The Fall of Themistocles," in *Auckland Classical Essays presented to E. M. Blaiklock*, ed. B. F. Harris (Auckland: Auckland University Press, 1970), pp. 39–58; A. J. Podlecki, *The Life of Themistocles* (Montreal: McGill-Queen's University Press, 1975), pp. 68–69; *contra:* R. W. Macan, *Herodotus, VII–IX* (Oxford, 1908); C. W. Fornara, *Herodotus, An Interpretative Essay* (Oxford, 1971), pp. 67–69.

15. Dion. Hal., *Ant. Rom.* 6.43.1.

16. Cf. J. A. R. Munro, *CAH*, 4:265–67. It must have been possible for

a politician to organize a campaign to ostracize a rival: cf. D. M. Lewis, *ZPE* 14 (1974): 3–4.

17. Labarbe, pp. 42–51; Podlecki, pp. 201–4.

18. *HW*, 2:198.

19. Plato, *Laws*, 707 bc; cf. Glen R. Morrow, *The Cretan City* (Princeton: Princeton University Press, 1966), pp. 25–26.

20. Pritchett, *AJA* 65 (1961): 369–75, argues for the latter route; N. Robertson, *JHS* 96 (1976): 100–120, less convincingly for the former. Cf. Pritchett, *Studies in Ancient Greek Topography*, Pt. III, (*Roads*), University of California Classical Studies, Vol. 22 (Berkeley, 1980), pp. 347–69.

21. Cf. Pritchett, *The Greek State at War*, 1:127–33.

22. Cf. Hdt. 7.184–87; Burn, pp. 326–32.

23. F. Maurice, *JHS* 50 (1930): 277, estimates that supplies of water, forage, etc., would support a combatant force of only 175,000, but this is highly speculative.

24. See A. Dascalakis, *Problèmes autour de la Bataille de Thermopyla* (Paris: E. de Boccard, 1962), pp. 122–28.

25. Cf. W. Kendrick Pritchett, *AJA* 67 (1963): 1–6, esp. 3; H. Horhager, *Chiron* 3 (1973): 48–49.

26. A voyage of some fifteen hours: cf. J. F. Lazenby, *Hermes* 92 (1964): 272, n. 3.

27. For this path, see W. Kendrick Pritchett, "New Light on Thermopylae," *AJA* 62 (1958): 203–13; A. R. Burn, in *Greece and the Eastern Mediterranean in Ancient History*, ed. K. H. Kinzl (Berlin: de Gruyter, 1977), pp. 98–103; cf. also P. W. Wallace, *AJA* 84 (1980): 15–23.

28. I have argued (*Historia* 18 [1969]: 389–406) that the Greek strategy was to hold the Persians at Thermopylae until lack of supplies and autumn storms would halt the invasion for the year. The date of the battle is uncertain: see J. Labarbe, *BCH* 78 (1954): 1–21 (end of July); K. R. Sacks, *CQ* 26 (1976): 232–48 (mid-September). Herodotus (8.12.1) says only "midsummer."

29. Plut. *Mor.* 864E; 866D–867B (*de Mal. Her.* 31; 33), cf. J. A. S. Evans, *GBRS* 5 (1964): 236, n. 24; R. Hope Simpson, *Phoenix* 26 (1972): 8–9; cf. R. J. Buck, *A History of Boeotia* (Edmonton: University of Alberta Press, 1979), p. 132.

30. Hugh J. Mason and M. B. Wallace, *Hesperia* 41 (1972): 136–40; H. Horhager, *Chiron* 3 (1973): 57.

31. Xerxes' Thessalian guides probably used the route that they had used in the past to invade Phocia (7.215). Cf. Pierre A. MacKay, *AJA* 67

(1963): 253–54; Hignett, p. 139; Peter Green, *Xerxes at Salamis* (New York, 1970), p. 114.

32. R. Demangel, *Fouilles de Delphes,* vol. 2, pt. 1 (Paris, 1923), p. 25.

33. Cf. Diod. Sic., 11.4.3–5; cf. Hignett, pp. 371–78.

34. Meiggs-Lewis, no. 23; cf. Podlecki, pp. 147–67; Robert J. Lenardon, *The Saga of Themistocles* (London: Thames and Hudson, 1978), pp. 69–72.

35. The ostracized seem to have already returned to Athens: *Arist. Ath. Pol.* 22.8; Stanley M. Burstein, *CSCA* 4 (1971): 98–104.

36. Cf. J. B. Bury, "Aristides at Salamis," *CR* 10 (1896): 414–18; R. Sealey, "Again the Siege of the Acropolis," *CSCA* 5 (1972): 183–94.

37. Plut., *Them.* 2.4; cf. Frank J. Frost, "Themistocles and Mnesiphilus," *Historia* 20 (1971): 20–25.

38. Cf. Podlecki, pp. 69–70; D. W. Knight, *Historia Einzelschr* 13 (1970): 33–44.

39. For the role of godfather among the Sarakatsani in modern Greece, see J. K. Campbell, *Honour, Family and Patronage* (Oxford: Clarendon, 1964), pp. 217–24. Mnesiphilus's relation to Themistocles was probably analogous.

40. W. Kendrick Pritchett, *AJA* 63 (1959): 251–52; Paul W. Wallace, *AJA* 73 (1969): 293–303; *contra:* N. G. L. Hammond, *JHS* 76 (1956): 32–54, who makes Psyttaleia modern Ayios Georgios, wrongly, in my opinion.

41. Cf. Meiggs-Lewis, no. 24.

42. Shrewdness was a virtue: cf. J. C. Lawson, *Modern Greek Folklore and Ancient Greek Religion: A Study in Survivals* (1909; reprint ed., New York: University Books, 1964), p. 31.

Chapter Nine

1. *HW,* 2:276–77: E. Herzfeld, *The Persian Empire: Studies in Geography and Ethnography of the Ancient Near East* (Wiesbaden, 1968), pp. 298–349.

2. Xen. *Hell.,* 4.5.11.

3. J. A. R. Munro, *CAH,* 4:321.

4. Paus. 1.44.1.

5. For Skolos, see W. K. Pritchett, *AJA* 61 (1957): 13; also *Studies in Ancient Greek Topography,* Pt. III, pp. 289–94.

6. On sacrifices before battle: W. Kendrick Pritchett, *The Greek State at War,* 1:109–13.

7. For the pass, see Pritchett, *AJA* 61 (1957): 18–21.

8. Evans *CJ* 57 (1961): 109–11; Immerwahr, *Form and Thought,* pp. 321–22.

9. Cf. G. B. Grundy, *The Great Persian War and its Preliminaries,* (London: John Murray, 1901), pp. 480–87. Pritchett, *AJA* 61 (1957): 26, is in partial agreement with Grundy.

10. *HW,* 2:310; Myres, *Herodotus, Father of History,* p. 291.

11. Cf. Hdt. 7.229–32.

12. Burn, p. 549.

Chapter Ten

1. Dion, Hal. *Thuc.,* 5; cf. W. K. Pritchett, *Dionysius of Halicarnassus: On Thucydides* (Berkeley: University of California Press, 1975), pp. 50–57; A. Momigliano, "Greek Historiography," *History and Theory* 17 (1978): 1–28.

2. *Pace* Legrand, 1: 22; Sourdille, p. 205.

3. *FGrHist.* F. 324a; cf. L. Pearson, *Early Ionian Historians* (Oxford: Clarendon Press, 1939), pp. 81–90; Saara Lilja, "Indebtedness to Hecataeus in Herodotus II, 70–73," *Arctos* 5 (1967): 85–96.

4. *FGrHist.* F. 305.

5. Cf. Herzfeld, *The Persian Empire,* p. 288.

6. Cf. V. Ehrenberg, "Zu Herodot," *Klio* 16 (1920): 318–33 (= *Polis und Imperium,* pp. 345–58, esp. pp. 355–58.

7. Hdt. 2.23; 4.36; 4.40–42; 4.45; cf. *HW,* 1: 170; Myres, *Geographical Journal* 8 (1896): 625–29.

8. Such as claimed by W. A. Heidel, "Hecataeus and the Egyptian Priests in Herodotus, Book II," *American Academy of Arts and Sciences, Memoirs* 18, no. 2, (1935): 53–134.

9. F. Jacoby, *Atthis* (Oxford, 1949), p. 59; cf. *GG,* 1:519–20; Pearson, pp. 139–51; W. den Boer, *Laconian Studies* (Amsterdam: North Holland Publishing Co., 1954): pp. 33–35.

10. *HW,* 1:22–23; J. G. Pedley, pp. 30–37; T. S. Brown, *The Greek Historians* (Lexington, Mass: D. C. Heath, 1973), pp. 12–14; Legrand, 1:235.

11. *GG,* 1:415; J. B. Bury, *The Ancient Greek Historians* (New York: Dover Books, 1958), p. 22.

12. C. Masetti, "Le Fonti di Erodoto per la Storia dell'Antico Oriente," *Helikon* 11–12 (1971–1972): 279–88.

13. P. Oxy. 1611; cf. J. T. Kakridis, "Caeneus," *CR* 61 (1947): 77–80.

14. Jacoby, *Atthis,* pp. 176–85; Pearson, pp. 203–8.

15. F. Jacoby, "The First Athenian Prose Writer," *Mnemosyne* 3 (1947): 13–64.

16. Immerwahr, *Form and Thought,* pp. 6–7.

17. For a list, see Jacoby, *RE,* supp. 2, pp. 398–99.

18. Hdt. 3.55.2; 4.76.6; 8.65; 9.16.1.

19. Cf. Detlev Fehling, *Die Quellenangaben bei Herodot: Studien zur Erzählkunst Herodots* (Berlin: de Gruyter, 1971), pp. 112–18.

20. Cf. Jack Goody and Ian Watt, "The Consequences of Literacy," in *Literacy in Traditional Societies,* ed. J. Goody, (Cambridge: Cambridge University Press, 1968), pp. 27–68; J. A. Davison, "Literature and Literacy in Ancient Greece, I," *Phoenix* 16 (1962): 141–56.

21. D. H. Jones, "Problems in African Chronology," *Journal of African History* 11 (1970): 161–76.

22. David P. Henige, *The Chronology of the Oral Tradition* (Oxford: Clarendon Press, 1974), pp. 42–46.

23. Jan Vansina, *Oral Tradition: A Study in Historical Methodology* (Chicago: Aldine Publishing Co., 1965), pp. 36–39.

24. Goody and Watts, p. 32.

25. Henige, pp. 123–24.

26. Pl. *Hp. Ma.* 285 B.

27. Fordyce Mitchel, "Herodotus' Use of Genealogical Chronology," *Phoenix* 10 (1956): 48–69; W. den Boer, "Herodot und die Systeme der Chronologie," *Mnemosyne* 20 (1967): 30–60.

28. Vansina, pp. 39–49.

29. Cf. H. Verdin,"Notes sur l'attitude des historiens grecs à l'égard de la tradition locale," *Ancient Society* 1 (1970): 183–200.

30. E.g., Hdt. 6.84; 6.52–54.

31. Hdt. 4.195.2; 7.152.3.

32. *Pol.* 1321 b 39; cf. E. Weiss, "Mnemones," *RE,* 15, Pt. 2, cols. 2261–64.

33. Lilian H. Jeffery and Anna Morpurgo-Davies, *Kadmos* 9 (1970): 118–54.

34. R. Crahay, *La Littérature Oraculaire chez Hérodote* (Paris: Société d'Edition "Les Belles Lettres," 1956), argues against such an archive. But oracles were kept by the recipients and were reused.

35. Hdt. 2.28; cf. Evans, *YCS* 17 (1961): 190–91.

36. Hdt. 6.35; 6.123; cf. Meiggs-Lewis, pp. 9–12.

37. Xen., *Hell.* 3.1.6.

38. A. Cowley, *Aramaic Papyri of the Fifth Century B.C.* (Oxford: Clarendon Press, 1923), pp. 248–71.

39. Joseph. *Ap.* 1. 21; cf. R. S. Stroud, *Drakon's Law on Homicide,* (Berkeley: University of California Press, 1968), pp. 28–29; N. Lewis, *Papyrus in Classical Antiquity* (New York: Oxford University Press, 1974), p. 88; E. Posner, *Archives in the Ancient World* (Cambridge, Mass.: Harvard University Press, 1972), pp. 101–4.

40. Cf. *SIG,* 608, Posner, pp. 115–17.

Chapter Eleven

1. Cf. Legrand, 1:97–100.

2. The Greek *men-de* construction here cannot denote opposition.

3. Plut. *Mor.* 869 F (de Mal. Her. 38) notes that Themistocles was nicknamed "Odysseus."

4. Cf. J. A. S. Evans, "Herodotus and Athens: The Evidence of the Encomium," *AC* 48 (1979): 112–18.

5. Thuc. 3.62.3–4; cf. R. J. Buck, pp. 133–35.

Chapter Twelve

1. On Herodotus's reputation, see Amédée Hauvette, *Hérodote, Historien des Guerres Mediques* (Paris: Thorin, 1894), pp 65–180; A. Momigliano, "The place of Herodotus in the history of Historiography," *History* 43 (1958): 1–13; J. A. S. Evans, "The Reputation of Herodotus," *CJ* 64 (1968): 11–17.

2. Cf. Daniel Allan Penick, *Herodotus in the Greek Renascence* (Baltimore: Murphy, 1902), pp. 4–7.

3. Cf. Averil Cameron, *BZ* 57 (1964): 51.

4. Cf. A. E. Wardman, "Myth in Greek Historiography," *Historia* 9 (1960): 401–13, esp. 401–5.

5. Marcello Gigante, "Lettera alla regina o dello stile di Ctesia," *RFIC* 40 (1962): 249–72; Joan M. Bigwood, "Ctesias as Historian of the Persian Wars," *Phoenix* 32 (1978): 19–41; K. A. Riemann, pp. 27–29.

6. Diod. Sic. 2.32.

7. R. Henry, *Ctésias, La Perse, L'Inde; Les Sommaires de Photius* (Brussels, 1947), 23–26 (pp. 28–32).

8. Hauvette, pp. 92–93.

9. Peter Burke, "A Survey of the popularity of ancient historians," *History and Theory* 5 (1966): 135–52, esp. 136.

Selected Bibliography

The student of Herodotus may find excellent bibliographies by Paul MacKendrick in *Classical World* 47 (1953–1954): 145–52; 56 (1962–1963): 269–75; 63 (1969): 37–44; and by Leif Bergson, "Herodot, 1937–60," *Lustrum* 11 (1966): 71–138. The following bibliography is restricted to a small number of books in English.

Benardete, Seth. *Herodotean Inquiries*. The Hague: Nijhoff, 1969. Interpretative essays on Herodotus that are sometimes penetrating.

Burn, A. R. *Persia and the Greeks: The Defence of the West, 546–478* B.C. London: Edward Arnold, 1962. This work is the best comprehensive study thus far of Persian-Greek relations up to and including the Persian War.

Fornara, Charles W. *Herodotus. An Interpretative Essay*. Oxford: Clarendon Press, 1971. Five essays, in fact, on Herodotus that place him in his historical setting.

Hignett, C. *Xerxes' Invasion of Greece*. Oxford: Clarendon Press, 1963. A study of Persian strategy, best for its criticism of earlier authors.

How, W. W. and Wells, J. *A Commentary on Herodotus*. 2 vols. Oxford: Oxford University Press, 1928. "How and Wells" in its first edition appeared in 1912 and has been the standard student's commentary ever since. It does not entirely replace the work of R. W. Macan: *Herodotus, The Fourth, Fifth and Sixth Books* (London: Macmillan, 1895), and *Herodotus, The Seventh, Eighth and Ninth Books* (London: Macmillan, 1908).

Immerwahr, H. H. *Form and Thought in Herodotus*. Philological Monographs, no. 23. Cleveland: American Philological Association, 1966. A seminal work that deals with form in the *History* and with Herodotus's historical concepts.

Myres, J. L. *Herodotus, Father of History*. Oxford: Clarendon Press, 1953. A study of the architecture of the *History*.

Wells, J. *Studies in Herodotus*. Oxford: Blackwell, 1923. A group of essays on Herodotus.

Index

Abydos, 103
Achaeans, 106
Achaemenes, son of Darius, 8, 116
Acusilaus of Argos, 142, 144
Acharnians, 17
Adeimantos, Corinthian admiral, 117, 123–24, 125–26, 158
Aegina, 85, 92, 109, 120, 124–25, 129–30; Aeginetan expulsion, 16; Medism quelled, 92–94
Aeneid, 64
Aeschylus, Athenian dramatist, 14, 126; his *Persians,* 126
Agamemnon, 72, 101
Agariste, marriage of, 97–98
Agathias, 162
Agathyrsi, 72
Aglauros, shrine of, 122
Aias, Homeric hero, 90
Aigeidae, clan in Sparta and Thera, 74
Ahura-Mazda, 105, 156
Akanthos, 105
Aleuads, 99, 106, 137
Alexander I of Macedon, 78
Alexander the Great, 164
Alexandria, 8, 16
Alexandroupolis, 104
Aliakman River, 105
Alkmaeon, 97
Alkmaeonid family, 83, 84, 96, 97, 98, 150, 151

Alyattes, King of Lydia, 22
Amasis, pharaoh of Egypt, 41, 49, 59
Amalesagoras of Chalcedon, 142
Ammon, oracle of, 38
Amompharetos, 136
Amphiareus, 23
Amun, 41, 44, 47
Amyklae, 130, 131
Amyntas, king of Macedon, 78
Amyrtaeus, 9, 46
Amytis, 32
Anacharsis, one of the Seven Sages, 70
Anaxagoras, 16, 38
Anaxandridas, father of Cleomenes of Sparta, 81
Anchimolius, 83
Androkrates, 133
Andros, 127
Anopaea path, 113, 114, 115
Antigone, 13–14; *see also* Sophocles
Anysis, 46
Aphetae, 116, 117
Aphrodite, 34, 42
Apis bull, 41, 51, 52
Apollo, 3, 23, 25, 41, 42, 105, 112, 121, 155; Hyakinthos, 131; Ismenian, 150
Apries, pharaoh, 48, 49
Araxes (Volga), 66, 72
Arcadia, 118